THE CRUEL
AND THE MEEK

SADISM, MASOCHISM AND
FLAGELLATION

WALTER BRAUN

Translation and additional material by
N. Meyer

SENATE

The Cruel and the Meek

First published in 1967 by Luxor Press, London.

This edition published in 1996 by Senate,
an imprint of Random House UK Ltd,
Random House, 20 Vauxhall Bridge Road,
London SW1V 2SA.

Copyright © Walter Braun 1967

ISBN 1 85170 554 6

Printed and bound in Great Britain by
Cox & Wyman, Reading, Berkshire

CONTENTS

MASOCHISM IN THE MALE:
Equus eroticus, a manifestation
of submission to the female

(Drawing by Hata Delhi)

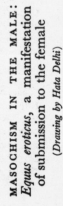

SADISM IN THE FEMALE: The
"Domina" and her female slave
in a lesbian relationship

*('Flagellation in the Boudoir', a water-colour by
Z. Phegor)*

1

INTRODUCTION

Sadism, masochism, and sado-masochism[1] are generally loosely called perversions. But what, precisely, is a perversion? Clearly opinions differ.

In most areas of our Western society actions like *cunnilinctus* and *fellatio*, although widely practised in secret, are commonly regarded as perversions, or at least as aberrations (which is almost the same thing), whereas elsewhere these practices are considered not only as quite unexceptionable variations of normal love-play but as pleasurable preliminaries or accompaniments of heterosexual erotic relations.

Nor will ordinary dictionary definitions help us very much. The *Concise Oxford Dictionary*, for instance, explains 'perversion' as derived from the adjective 'perverse', meaning '... different from what is reasonable or required; wayward; perverted; wicked;' etc. (An 'aberration', by the way, in the same dictionary, is defined as 'a straying from the path, lit. and fig.; breaking of rules; moral slip', etc.) Such definitions get us nowhere, of course, unless we are all agreed on what constitutes wickedness, what is the straight and narrow path we are supposed to follow.

Hence it seems we may have to fall back upon generalisation and diagrammatic representation. Someone may intervene at this stage to suggest: surely, by a perversion we mean whatever practice lies beyond or outside the activities of normal sexual intercourse. But this, too, I am afraid, is a glib oversimplification, since it presupposes that there is no room for doubt as to what normal sexual intercourse means.

Now if we represent the human *libido sexualis* as we know

---

[1] Sado-masochism implies a spontaneous interaction of both conditions, whether in the same individual or in partners of either or opposite sex or in group manifestations.

7

it in the form of a straight line (figure A) going from man to woman, this will give us a convenient starting-point.

(A) Man ———————————————▶ Woman

Seen from a strictly biological point of view, man goes direct and unhampered to his goal, coital orgasm. Thus it is with the lower animals, and most probably was with the earliest ancestors of man.

The sex act is basically an act of violence by the male. Our remote ancestors—for it seems safe to presume that this animalistic trait was dominant in our original forebears—pursued the female they wanted; the female offered resistance, or pretended to do so ; she was overcome and taken by force. Let us represent this show of resistance by a thin vertical line (figure B). In so far as it was easily penetrated by a resourceful male—and it is demonstrable that in imposing this resistance the female merely intends it to be demolished—then our direct line from man to woman need suffer no deviation in its directness or diminution in its impetus. It is probable that the female's reluctance is simply a device to intensify man's aggressiveness and thereby enhance the ardour of his wooing. It may well be that Nature invested human kind with this challenge and this aggressiveness for the purpose of ensuring only the procreation of the strongest specimens.

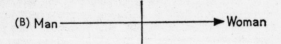

(B) Man ———————————┼————————▶ Woman

Though we may not like the thought, this primitive feature still clings to heterosexual behaviour in our own day. (Our language bears traces of it: we speak of the *conquest* of a woman.) It is not difficult to see, however, that in advanced and highly organised societies such a way of mating is infeasible. Chaos would result. We can witness the sort of thing that would happen whenever wars or revolutions cause the jettisoning of habitual restraints. Many individuals make use of such an occasion to give free rein to their secret desires under cover of impunity. Rape, as often as not accompanied by grievous bodily harm or fatal injury, as well as serious psychological effects, is the result.

8

So society attaches sanctions, prohibitions and restraints to the satisfaction of sexual desire, erecting as it were a wall of resistance that reinforces and largely supersedes the flimsy barrier of woman's natural coyness. In figure C the dividing line has been thickened, to demonstrate this more formidable barrier. Although Christianity has provided the most diligent bricklayers, even the most primitive societies have their sex barriers. Indeed it must be so, for, as we observed just now, without some such control there would be no protection for the female, and ultimately for the society itself. In modern times sex regulations have often become tantamount to sex strangulations.

So long as the wall of resistance is not inordinately or unnaturally strong (such as, for example, when it is reinforced by the admixture of some pathological aversion or some overstringent moral sanction), the *libido sexualis* will find its way through with sufficient diminution of impetus and velocity to render it socially respectable. But if the wall is too strong and the sex urge too weak, a stoppage may occur, through lack of interest, causing insufficiency (impotency). See figure C.

Where the wall is too formidable for the sex urge (normal strength) to pass through in pursuit of the natural goal, there may be a striking back (figure D), resulting in inversions (masturbation, homosexuality, narcissism, auto-eroticism).

In figure E the *libido sexualis* makes a détour round the wall. The goal (coital orgasm) is reached ultimately, but to achieve it deviations are resorted to (sadism, masochism, sadomasochism, flagellation, fetishism, etc.).

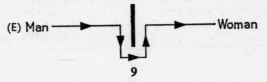

9

In the final figure (F) the *libido sexualis* sees no way to break through or go round the barrier. Parental control and youthful experiences have been too strong, or some pathological cause has supervened to bring about a distortion or misdirection of the libido. Coital orgasm is no longer the goal sought. The aberration or perversion (sadism, masochism, sado-masochism, flagellomania, fetishism, scopophilia, the urge to procure, necrophilia, etc.) is itself the end sought.[1]

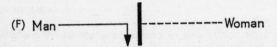

We see now that the sadistic, masochistic, or sado-masochistic complex is a deviation when it is a means for the attainment of coital orgasm ; it is an aberration or a perversion when it is an end in itself.

Another point may seem to have become clear from figures D, E and F. The sex urge loses nothing of its original vigour. At first sight this appears to be in accordance with the place the deviation or aberration occupies in the life of the deviate or pervert. Such people are constantly preoccupied and tormented by the demands of their strange and difficult passions. But we must also take into account that their most stringent desires seldom find full and total gratification. The sadist, especially, suffers from this problem. The sadist's bizarre wishes range from childish acts and imaginings to urges of a distinctly violent and lethal nature.

The sadistic pervert who is inclined to violent deeds (rather than fancies) has to choose between gratifying his wishes, which will bring him into conflict with the law, and suppressing them, confining them to imaginary situations, which will lead with no less inexorability to neuroses and psychoses.

This, as we are about to see, was precisely the dilemma that beset the Marquis de Sade himself and led him through a chequered course to end his days in the lunatic asylum at Charenton.

[1] These figures, I need hardly point out, are intended only as an aid to make my point clear. They have no significance in themselves apart from that; nor do I pretend that they cover all possibilities.

PART ONE
SADISM

VISUAL SADISM: A young woman is flogged
in public (about the year 1800)

(*Drawing by an anonymous artist*)

CHAPTER ONE

Sadism in the Male

On 3rd April 1768 a deposition was recorded against the Marquis de Sade concerning offences allegedly committed by him against the person of Rose Keller, aged thirty-six.

The plaintiff declared that on the previous Easter Sunday she had been visited by an individual wearing a grey frock-coat, with a hunting-knife at his side, and holding a cane and a whitish muff, and that this person, whom she now identified as the said marquis, had offered her a certain sum of money if she would consent to accompany him to his quarters for the purpose of cleaning his room. The plaintiff agreed to the proposal and followed the visitor to a building in which he showed her into a room on the second floor.

He told her to be seated and then asked her whether she would be willing to go into the country with him, to which she replied that she did not mind where she went to earn her living. The accused left her, explaining that he had to pay a number of visits but would return for her in about an hour's time. In fact about an hour later he did return, with a cab, and invited the plaintiff to get into it.

He caused the carriage to stop near the village of Arcueil and ordered the plaintiff to follow him: the gentleman then passed through a house doorway and led her to an upper room overlooking the garden. In the room there were two beds and some straw-seated chairs. She was told to remain in the room while he went to look for bread and something to drink and not to make herself weary in his absence. He then left her, securing the door with double locks.

About an hour later he came back, opened the door and told her to come downstairs, which she did. He conducted her across a small garden into a closet, the door of which he

13

fastened, and then ordered her to undress. She asked him why he demanded such a thing, and he replied that it was "for enjoyment". She reminded him that that was not what he had asked her to come for. He said that if she did not undress he would kill her and bury her himself. He then left her again.

After he had gone and she was once more alone she began to undress. She was not completely nude when he returned and, finding her still in her shift, he said that must also come off. She told him she would rather die, and at this he himself pulled the shift over her head denuding her entirely. Then he took her into another room adjoining, in the centre of which there was a divan covered with white-spotted red chintz. He flung her face downward on to this divan, bound her to it hand and foot with hempen cord, and placed a bolster at her neck. The plaintiff observed that when he came to fetch her from the closet he had taken off his coat and shirt and had put on a sleeveless vest and tied a white kerchief round his head, and that when she entered the room in which she was tied to the divan the curtains were drawn.

The plaintiff went on to assert that while she lay thus attached to the divan the man took up a birch and with this he beat her severely. He then made a number of incisions in her flesh with a small knife or a penknife, and poured large quantities of sealing-wax into the wounds. After that he began beating her again, made further incisions and poured in more wax, all of which ill-treatment he repeated up to seven or eight times. As the plaintiff had been weeping and shouting from the time that this ill-treatment began, he then showed her a knife and threatened that if she continued screaming he would kill her and bury her himself as he had said before. She then ceased to cry out.

The plaintiff declared that at each birching he also gave her blows with a cane. She added that in the midst of this torture she made various protests to him and also implored him not to let her die as she had not taken the Easter Sacrament; to this he replied that he would confess her himself. After she told him she could never confess herself to him and having made further vehement protests, she was at last released. He set about uttering very loud and frightening cries, then cut the cords that bound her and took her back to the closet to dress again.

14

He brought her a jug of water and a large bowl to wash in ;
by that time she had already covered herself again with her
shift and skirt. She washed and dried herself, using a towel
that he had brought her, and when he saw that this towel was
covered with blood he made her wash it. He then brought her
a small phial in which there was a liquid the colour of *eau de
vie* and told her to rub herself with it, assuring her that in an
hour or so the marks would disappear. She rubbed herself
with it on all the cicatrised parts, and this caused her very
sharp pain.

Now that she was completely clothed again, he brought her
a small piece of bread, a small quantity of beef, about half a
litre of wine in a bottle, and took her back to the room upstairs. He shut her up in this same room, telling her to stay
away from the window and be careful not to show herself
or make any noise, and that he would let her leave towards
evening. On hearing this she begged him to release her earlier
as she had no idea where she was and had no money and did
not want to have to sleep in the street. He told her she had no
need to worry.

After that he went away, having shut her in the room. The
plaintiff secured the door on the inside by means of a hook.
Then she seized two bed-covers which were on the two beds,
and with her knife picked the lock of the casement window
overlooking the garden, and then, having attached the bed-
covers (now joined together) by means of two large pins to
an oak crossbar in the centre of the window, she slid down
them into the garden. From there she succeeded in reaching a
wall, which she scaled with the help of trellises beside a sum-
mer-house. She fell into a close and hurt her arm and her left
hand in falling. From this close she managed to reach the
street.

A servant from the house ran after her, telling her to come
back and that his master wished to reach an agreement with
her. She refused to obey ; on this the said servant drew out a
purse and said he was going to give her some money, which
she refused in like manner.

Asked how she could tell that the man had poured red wax
on to her wounds, the plaintiff answered that she had found a
way of loosening the bonds with her left hand, and having
moved her hand behind her she had drawn it back to find red

15

wax on it; also, when washing after the attack she found a considerable amount of wax in the basin.[1]

She met some women from the village who assisted her and took her to the *château*, where she stayed for five days. She claimed to remember nothing more.

The deposition was read to her and the plaintiff duly affirmed that it contained nothing but the truth; she stated, however, that she was unable to write and could not sign the summons that was issued for the apprehension of the marquis.

De Sade was arrested and charged. But he was released six weeks afterwards on the intercession of his wife. The Court of Lyons ordered him to pay two hundred gold francs *pour le pain des pauvres prisonniers* (i.e. to assist in the feeding of impoverished prisoners).

I have begun this chapter about masculine sadism with a factual reference to the so-called 'Rose Keller affair', in which the infamous Marquis Donatien A. F. de Sade (1740–1814) was accused and found guilty of cruelly misusing a defenceless woman, because it contains several characteristics of a certain aberration—the infliction of pain on others as a sex-replacing factor—which almost one hundred and twenty years later was to be named after him 'sadism' by the pioneer of sexology, R. von Krafft-Ebing (1840–1902), in his work *Psychopathia Sexualis* (1886).

Firstly, de Sade's reply to Rose Keller's pleading not to let her die because she had not taken the Easter Sacrament— "Well, you confess to *me* then"—is no merely facetiously blasphemous remark. To de Sade life is one long chain of sexuality: everything man does originates in sexual impulses; consequently, man's acts, whatever they may be, are basically sex-acts and as such can only lead to new sex-stimulations which inevitably will result in further actions that are basically sexual. To de Sade life is a continuous chain of sexually regulated and interrelated events. In short, not God but sex rules the world. Mankind as a whole de Sade conceives as a coward not daring to face this new truth: de Sade himself does accept it and believes himself to be the incarnate representative of

---

[1] At his trial de Sade nonchalantly claimed that the substance he had applied was in fact an entirely new unguent he had perfected, which immediately healed the minor wounds he had inflicted, and that he was therefore doing society a favour.

16

sexuality, a (sex-) god-like being. What, then, is more logical in his peculiar reasoning than to tell this woman: "Confess to me"? It is not an intentionally blasphemous remark because the speaker denies the divinity of God: *he* is God. Nor is it intended to be cynical or derisory: it is the bald expression of supreme complacency on the part of a man who feels immeasurably superior to the toy he is playing with. This mixture of crudeness and indifference, this ineffable pomposity, above all, *this absolute lack of compassion towards his fellowmen*, are fundamental characteristics of the sadist.

Secondly, de Sade conducts his victim to an isolated place, because, as he states, it is an absolute certainty that "to be alone in the world, to have no contact whatever with human beings, enhances lust. All inhibitions disappear, and the favourable circumstance of knowing one will not be punished intensifies one's voluptuousness in such unlimited ways that God and conscience have no place in life any more".

The preference for being alone which de Sade expresses is shared by the mystic. But in the mystic's mind this preference originates in his single-minded devotion to God. His need to avoid man is not born of hate, it is born of love; it is an ultimate necessity in order to attain to God, i.e. Love; consequently, it involves understanding of and compassion for one's fellow-men who are still bound up in day-to-day striving.

In de Sade's mind this choice of aloofness resolves itself merely into the determination to have no contact whatever with human beings. Whereas the mystic forswears men, de Sade ignores them; whereas the mystic endeavours to submerge his individuality, de Sade clings to it with the desperate tenacity of a little child who, conceiving only his ego as the entire world, lives in continual fear of having to give something away, for everything given means a loss, a diminution of his ego. De Sade is as avaricious with his predilections as a child with its toys and sweets. And *this avariciousness with his affections is one of the many forms of infantilism on which sadism is based*.

Besides, de Sade's preference for isolating himself from mankind is false: he needs mankind because only in his fellowman can his hatred express itself and take shape. Apart from that, his craving for solitude, as he himself states, is fundamentally an expression of fear. As long as he is alone nothing can happen to him: his crimes remain undiscovered and un-

17

punished. Whereas the mystic expects to encounter dangers when he is alone, de Sade hopes to evade them. Both are, in their preference for solitude, outsiders ; but whereas the mystic has become one on principle, de Sade has placed himself outside the pale through opportunism. His pretence of being an outsider is only a pose: he is in reality a bourgeois. *This bourgeois wish for personal security while inflicting unlimited harm upon others is another characteristic of sadism.*

Thirdly, it should be noted that de Sade does not perform sexual intercourse with Rose Keller after having maltreated her. To many researchers this lack of sexual interest in the woman proves his homosexuality. Charles Nodier seems to hint at this when he writes in his *Souvenirs, Épisodes et Portraits pour servir à l'Histoire de la Révolution et de l'Empire* (1831): "The Marquis was so courteous that he became almost submissive. His manner of speech was flowery, sometimes unctuous, and always full of respect . . ." Octave Uzanne takes the description a stage further in his *Idée sur les Romans par D. A. F. de Sade* by describing him as "an extremely good-looking youth with a pale, almost femininely handsome face with large and shining eyes", and as "a man with a voice soft and gently caressing, his gait graceful as a woman's".

Presumably de Sade must have had the usual share of homosexual experiences that fall to the lot of most boys during their student days. He attended the *Collège Louis le Grand,* which was famous for the excellent education it provided and its strict disciplinary methods, from his tenth to his fifteenth year. It may be assumed that he practised homosexuality to some extent in after-life as well, for to the aristocracy of those days it was just another way of satisfying lust, and because to de Sade, being an unprincipled roué, it did not in the least matter how he managed to obtain sexual satisfaction as long as he did so.

Nevertheless, I do not believe that de Sade was, in the true sense, a homosexual. His marriage to Renée de Montreuil (in 1763) ; the fits of jealousy he threw in prison when he allowed himself to dwell on the loose way he imagined his wife to be living; his liaison with Renée's sister Louise; his many intimate relationships with women from 1790 (the year he left the mental hospital of Charenton after his removal from the Bastille) until 1801 (the year Napoleon had him arrested be-

18

cause of his *Zoloé*, in which he exposed the sexual debaucheries of Napoleon's wife, Joséphine de Beauharnais, and her
friend, Madame Tallien); his outspoken preference for female
prostitutes (as exemplified in the Marseilles affair)—all these
facts prove to me that de Sade was a heterosexual. The fact
that he did not commit sexual intercourse with Rose Keller
only indicates his sadistic disposition: coition was superseded
by the aberration: the aberration had become a sex-replacing
factor, at that particular moment anyhow.

Though de Sade definitely was a sex maniac he was not
exclusively what we now understand as a sadist. If he had been
one, he could not (or at least would not) have had all the normal relations with women just mentioned, and he undoubtedly
would have practised all his horrible theories and fancies
during the short period (1790–1795) of the Terror, when revolution convulsed the whole of France. One may say, perhaps,
that he had to behave carefully during those days because,
despite the fact that he had been a victim of the *ancien régime*,
he still by birth belonged to the class of the suspected. But
even during the seven-year war with Prussia—he served, by
the way, from his fifteenth to his twenty-second year as an
officer in a regiment that was all but wiped out during that
war—his behaviour was not in any way exceptionable. The
reports concerning his military career contain no special mention of his being a cruel or immoral soldier.

Taking all these facts into consideration, one is more or less
forced to the conclusion that de Sade was a '*salon*-terrorist'
who indulged his passions mainly in his writings, while on
almost the only occasion when he really *practised* sadism he
did not even then destroy his victim.

Even so, this lack of sexual interest in Rose Keller after
having tortured her reveals how at that moment his natural
impulses had been replaced by his need for cruelty. In short,
as I have said above, *the aberration had become a sex-replacing factor, an independent entity, and it is precisely this
situation that is one of the elementary characteristics of any
aberration—in this case, sadism.*

De Sade's lack of tenderness and compassion predisposes
him to inflict cruelty; his fear of being discovered and punished prevents him from overtly giving vent to his cruel impulses. In this respect he does not differ from many neurotics.
The combination of his neurotic character and the mediocrity

19

of his literary talent produce only sick and tedious writings. In this respect he does not differ from most authors of pornography.

What makes de Sade outstanding and lends interest to his work even today is his psychological insight into man's mind and emotions. In particular, his *120 Days of Sodom, or the School of Libertinism* (1785) and his *Bedroom Philosophy* (1795) demonstrate, despite their erotic monomania and philosophical sophisms, de Sade's insight into the motives behind man's behaviour. He probes sentiments and rationalisations; the egoistic animalism he discovers at the bottom of man's soul, however, does not inspire him to create a new and effective sexology but only serves him as the final proof of what he presupposes from the start: that life is ruled by sexual impulse and sexual aggressiveness. He who understands this law will conquer; he who ignores it will suffer.

120 Days of Sodom is in a way the first *psychopathia sexualis*, but whereas Krafft-Ebing seeks to classify, because he wants to explain, phenomena, de Sade classifies because arranging perversions fits in with his personal fancies and theories. Still, as he draws attention in this book to forms of sexual behaviour never described or explained before, one may up to a point regard him as a sexologist *avant la lettre*.

I have said his artistic talents were mediocre: he is only able, in fact, to give his characters a superficial schematic stature while most of his attention is focused on the action of the story; and even the action itself often remains so static that de Sade, apparently instinctively, tries to intensify it by dramatic exaggeration. (In his *Juliette* three dozen hospitals in Rome are burnt down and twenty thousand persons killed, just for fun. In the same book the voluptuous monk Claude has three testicles, and the ogre Minski drinks sixty bottles of wine at a single meal. In the 'Theatre of Cruelty' in Naples one thousand one hundred and seventy-six persons are killed during one performance so that the scene shall look more 'life-like').

Naturally, his books reveal the most complex intrigues. Dr Iwan Bloch, who discovered the manuscript of *120 Days of Sodom* in 1904, needed more than thirty pages to give an outline of de Sade's *Juliette*. De Sade himself, with astonishing ease it seems, finds his way in this labyrinth of happenings. But not always. Now and then even he loses himself in the chaos of debaucheries and atrocities: at the end of *120 Days of Sodom* (a book for the most part no more than a schematic outline, as de Sade could not finish it because he had to abandon the manuscript in the Bastille when he left the prison) he wonders what has happened to two of his characters whom he introduced at the beginning of the text but lost somewhere in the course of the story.

To facilitate the writing of this work de Sade prepared a kind of 'ground-plan'. When at the end of *120 Days of Sodom* most of the characters are murdered, the deaths have occurred strictly in accordance with the following scheme, which the author drafted for the sake of convenience when he began work on the book:

On March 1st Fanchon; on March 2nd Louison; on March 3rd Thérèse; on March 4th Marie; on March 5th Fanni; on March 6th and 7th the two lovers Sophie and Seladon. They die, as decided, impaled one on top of the other. On March 8th one of the minor lovers; on March 9th Hébé; on March 10th another of the minor lovers; on March 11th Colombe; on March 12th the last of the minor lovers; on March 13th Zélamir; on March 14th Cupido; on March 15th Zéphir; on March 16th Adonis; on March 17th Hyacinthe; on March 18th the three taken prisoner. They are killed on March 18th, 19th and 20th. Total number of victims: 20.

Besides these 20 another 10 were killed in the orgies of March 1st, so that of the total of 46 inhabitants of the castle, only 16 actually return to Paris.

120 Days of Sodom was produced by de Sade in prison, and it is clearly the creation of a mind interested only in erotic subjects of a perverted nature and denied any possibility of ventilation. Yet it is also a representative product of the age in which de Sade was living. In this connexion Iwan Bloch shows how closely de Sade describes facts well known in his time and depicts characters that really existed.

Many of the horrible torments described in *Juliette*, and comparable outbursts of unspeakable fiendishness, actually were perpetrated in the troubled times in which de Sade lived; and the monsters in human form of the kind he presents did exist in the persons of some of the powerful nobles of that epoch. Even some of the theories his books contain were either directly inspired by, or closely correspond to, the concepts of

21

contemporary philosophers like Holbach, Malthus, Mirabeau, and others.

As one example to indicate how clearly de Sade recognised the power of sensory stimulation in man as a means of intensifying emotional response and augmenting sexual gratification, let me refer again to *120 Days of Sodom*. There, catering, as always, for the appetites of the utterly depraved, he stresses the importance of exploiting, not only the obvious sense of touch, but the other four senses as well, as a means of enhancing erotic pleasure. During the debaucheries, terms of blasphemy and foul language are to be used, as this will stimulate the sense of hearing. He advises his characters to watch avidly everything that happens in the orgies, as this will titillate their scopophil[1] tendencies. Olfactory sensations are cloyed by the lavish use of perfumes as well as whiffs of urine and excreta, while the sense of taste is catered for by the drinking of blood, semen and urine and the consumption of faeces.

As I have said above, *120 Days of Sodom* (though of course not even remotely comparable with Krafft-Ebing's famous work) is in its way the first *psychopathia sexualis*, in that it provides a fairly complete panorama of human sexual perversions and aberrations.

I should like to conclude my remarks on de Sade with a few references to his *Juliette*, one of the most horrible books ever produced. It embraces the whole gamut of perversions, anomalies and sexual enormities, from multiplex performances of simultaneous *fellatio, cunnilinctus, coitus,* and sodomy, to patricide, infanticide and mass murder. De Sade regales the reader with his usual absurd exaggerations of sexual prowess and gastronomic gluttony. Here, too, we see reflected the utter lack of all affection and compassion, the rejoicing at the sufferings of others, the monstrous egoism, the infantile selfishness, the fanatical obsession with unassailability through total immunity from discovery and punishment.

Juliette, who narrates the story, is travelling with her evil companions in Italy. They come to the domain of an ogre, named Minski, who invites them to his castle. They accept the invitation and there Minski tells them of his way of life.

He keeps two harems, one comprising two hundred girls

See footnote on p. 32.

aged from 5 to 20. These he consumes for food when they succumb to the fantastic sexual demands made of them or are of no further use in exciting his lust. (All the meat eaten at the castle, Minski explains, is human flesh, and very tasty morsels he finds the young boys and girls when "done to a turn"). The second harem is made up of two hundred older women (20–30 years of age). Fifty servants of either sex are employed in the service of the giant's bizarre establishment, and new blood is constantly recruited by a hundred roving female agents distributed throughout the principal cities of the world.

Up to this point we might be reading the prelude to a fairy tale by Grimm or some improbable adventure of Baron Munchausen. But next comes the premonitory reference to aloofness and unassailability, and we may be sure that the most incredible excesses are about to be related...

" 'Not, mark you, that I have the slightest reason for worrying; we are here inside the territories of the Duke of Tuscany; the whole extent of my irregular doings is known in those circles, and the *pourboires* I scatter about protect it from undue publicity as well as from interference...' "

When Juliette asks him if he is not afraid of justice he replies: " 'Non-existent in this country! That is why I chose it for my domicile in the first place: with money you do anything you like here, and I spend a lot' ". In a curiously revelatory footnote de Sade quite unashamedly makes the claim that the sadistic libertine should be by law permitted to pay in cash for indulgence in his caprices: "The far less inconvenient way would be for the State to allow *persons of condition* to do all they wished in return for money, and *to buy absolution for every crime*; better this, surely, than to have them die on the scaffold. The latter measure is of no profit to the government, whilst the former could easily become an important source of revenue, yielding funds to cover all sorts of unforeseen expenses which are met today by levying countless taxes: these are onerous to innocent and guilty alike, whereas what I propose distributes the burden equitably, the heavier share of it falling where it fairly belongs". (The italics are mine.)

There follow some of the author's customary wild exaggerations. Minski boasts: " 'I am 45, and at this age my lubrickal (*sic*) faculties are such that I never retire for the night without

23

having discharged ten times... Since it is my hope that we shall discharge together, it is essential that you be forewarned of the appalling symptoms which distinguish my crisis: dreadful outbursts herald and accompany it, and the jets of sperm thereupon released mount to the ceiling, often in the number of fifteen or twenty; the repetition of pleasures has never left me dry so far; my tenth ejaculation is just as tumultuous, just as abundant, as the first; nor have I ever found myself tired and out of sorts today because of last night's efforts. As regards the member whence all that comes, here it is...'" and he hauled forth a *membrum virile* eighteen inches in length and sixteen in circumference, surmounted by a crimson glans "the size of a military helmet".[1]

Later Juliette, in another episode, admits that she is "at last obliged to beg quarter": she has been copulated with frontally and rectally continuously one hundred and ninety times! Even so, her friend Olympia (who apparently has more than Olympian appetites) is disgruntled: she does not want the orgy to end so soon. She claims that she usually organises these playful festivities seven or eight times a month, and they always go on for twenty-four hours at a stretch.

Apart from such nonsense concerning sexual prowess, male and female, we find all manner of other exaggerations—of food and drink consumed; of cruelties which although largely inconceivable in their enormity, reveal that characteristic already referred to—complete lack of compassion, coupled with positive enjoyment deriving from the sufferings of others. In Minski's castle the dining-table, chairs and side-tables are composed of live nude girls. "Twelve naked girls of between twenty and twenty-five brought the dishes; and as they were massive silver and very hot, by scorching the breasts and buttocks of the elements composing the table, there was a pleasant convulsive stir produced: it resembled the rippling of waves at sea. Above twenty *entrées* or roast platters decked the table and upon side-tables, built of four grouped girls each and which also ambled up at the snap of a finger, were ranged wines of every kind..."

Minski "drank the way he ate; he had tossed off his thirtieth bottle of burgundy by the time the second course came on; this he washed down with champagne; and Aleatico, Falern-

---

[1] The length of a male organ in erection seldom exceeds seven inches.

ian and other rare Italian vintages were swallowed at dessert.

"Yet another good thirty bottles of wine were in our cannibal's guts when, his senses sufficiently enlivened by all these physical and moral excesses, the rogue declared that he was now in a discharging mood". His enormous organ kills a little girl of 7 whom Juliette has asked him to violate, front and back, before her eyes just for her amusement; he is delighted with the result. " 'Never mind!' he says, eyeing the child; 'no need to tie her this time, she'll lie still'. And flopping her over stone dead as she is, the libertine sodomises her, the while strangling one of the girls who had been serving at table and whom he has summoned into reach."

Juliette asks him: " 'Do you then never taste this pleasure without it costing some individual his life?' " and Minski replies: " 'It often costs the lives of several ... For it is death's sighs answering my lubricity's that fetch forth my ejaculation, d'ye see, and were it not for the death my discharge occasions I don't know how I'd be able to discharge at all' ".

Again the reader will observe the utter contempt for the lives of fellow-creatures.

Yet, as has already been remarked, de Sade himself did not commit crimes in any way commensurate with the hideous things he wrote about and which therefore must have taken place in his imagination. Certainly he was no murderer. Was it, perhaps, that he lacked the courage of his convictions, or was it rather that his diseased fancies were hardly convictions at all?

Was de Sade in the grip of a pleasure-lust heightened by imagined cruelties which he himself, perhaps in moments of relative sanity, despised and disapproved? Those cruelties which he did actually put into practice in his life-time were, it might be argued, *experimental* (as though he were not absolutely sure of himself at all)—aimed at finding out what degree of pleasure really was attainable from extremes of conduct such as he was ordinarily content to envisage only in phantasy. The victims (like Rose Keller) were women of low class, creatures that to a man of his background and upbringing were 'expendable'.

His contemptuous rejection of God, his intense hatred towards the Church, may have been brought about in the first place, or at least encouraged, by reflecting upon the endless catalogue of ferocious atrocities perpetrated in the name of religion.[1] It might be thought that there is irony and a touch of apologetic bitterness discernible in such comments as the following, also quoted from *Juliette*:

" 'At the time of the Dragonnades, girls who were loath to embrace the True Faith were seized and, in order to bring about a change in their minds, their anus and womb were funnelled full of gunpowder. Next, they were exploded like bombs. You have simply no idea how this gave them a taste for the Host and for auricular confession. And how can one help but love a God in whose name such wondrous fine deeds are wrought!

" 'Coming back again to classical tortures, we see Saint Catherine bound to a nail-studded cylinder and rolled down a mountain-side. Now there, Juliette, is a pleasant way of getting to heaven, don't you agree?' "

.　　　.　　　.　　　.　　　.　　　.

SADISM AND CRUELTY

As I have already mentioned, it was Krafft-Ebing who gave the name of sadism to the particular perversion we are at present examining. He did more than that. He was the first psychologist to make a classification of perversions in general. He was also the first, but not the last, psychologist who was plainly bewildered by the sado-masochistic complex. The phenomenon is still the subject of much speculation. Research workers, in their endeavour to explain the origin of sadism, clutch at every straw. Very easily they are misled by a confusion of ideas, e.g. between cruelty and sadism. The element of cruelty is always present in sadism, but the reverse is not true.

This is the familiar philosophical fallacy of irreversibility: from the statement 'A rabbit is a four-footed animal' we cannot conclude that therefore every four-footed animal is a rabbit. It is equally fallacious that sadism is innate because children are cruel by nature. That children are cruel by nature is assumed from the fact that many children are fascinated by the mutilation of insects. It is my opinion that a much more

[1] Referring to God and Christianity de Sade writes in *Juliette*: "My blood boils at his very name. I think I see around me all the trembling shadows of the poor wretches whom this horrible superstition has sacrificed.'

feasible explanation of this tendency is to be found in children's insatiable curiosity. Children are constantly discovering new things in their world. When they pull off the leg of an insect, they are absorbingly interested in the way the insect reacts to this treatment, without being fully aware that they are performing a cruel act. They do not identify themselves with the insect, and if they wonder about the creature's capacity to feel pain at all they do not suppose that it must feel as they would feel if they were subjected to similar treatment. They may do the same with a clock, with an equally clear conscience, to discover what makes it tick, and end up by taking the entire mechanism to pieces. It seems to me somewhat far-fetched to suppose that children experience sexual excitement when dissecting insects and small animals. This may be of some comfort to anxious parents who see their child already showing signs of growing up into a sadist because it has at some time taken pleasure in tearing out the wings of a fly or cutting worms in two.

In the same way we must make a distinction between cruelty (mental and physical) that springs from revenge for some real or imagined grievance in the field of social relations and cruelty as revenge for some slight in the field of sexual relations. The man who has no authority at home bullies his subordinates at the office; the man who feels neglected or unfairly treated at the office terrorises his wife and children. Men who have no authority, either at home or at the office, take it out on the dog. Forms of cruelty can exist, then, without sexual emotions supervening at all.

SADISM AND CANNIBALISM

Only when cruelty and sexuality merge can sadism, properly so called, arise, for sadism is an essentially sexual abnormality. Since, as already explained in the Introduction, the male sex act is basically an act of violence, this link may always be (latently) present. From the fact that in the sex act the male is active and the female passive (though there is reason to believe that the female's passivity is only so in appearance), Krafft-Ebing draws the conclusion that sadism is predominantly a male perversion. This makes his suggestion untenable that an atavistic trait of cannibalism must be the origin of sadism. Nature's ultimate goal, the continuation of the species, is not served by the killing and disposal of the female during or after

27

the sex act. In the world of inferior creatures the only such evidence we find of a cannibalistic nature is of the *male* being disposed of after the act of procreation. It is when the male spider has fecundated the female that he can serve no more useful purpose than to provide her with a meal.

Cannibalism might possibly serve as an explanation of the female sadist's motives, but I shall have more to say about that point later. According to Krafft-Ebing, the male is the active partner in sex; aggression is exaggerated activity; cruelty is exaggerated aggression. But how can we explain that coition is not the sadist's first aim and may not be part of his intention at all? Freud believed that sadism is to be explained as an aggressive component of the sexual instinct which has become independent and exaggerated and has been brought to the foreground by displacement. This, at least, leads us a little further forward. But I should like now to try approaching the problem from another angle.

ORGIASTIC SENSUALISM

As soon as man began living in communities he must have felt the need to communicate with his fellow-man. Miming led on to dance and language, so that there were then three methods of communication. But these were not altogether satisfying. The participants in such communion still remained their own isolated individual selves. Man longed for more: a more complete togetherness, the doing away with limitations that make individuals captives of their own selves. What he wanted was to be welded together, to become one indivisible unit, experiencing common and reciprocal emotions. He had already discovered that in sexual intercourse (originally only a means of relieving an unpleasant sense of tension) such an ideal communication was possible, through the synchronised emotion of simultaneous mutual orgasm.

Man sought feverishly in all directions to extend this direct communication. Art was born: the artist expressed his emotion in pictures, and then in sounds, ever striving to evoke the same emotions in others. But only a state of frenzy could produce this result. Soon man discovered how to bring about this state of synchronised ecstasy. Rhythmic chanting and beating of drums, alcoholic and narcotic concoctions, were the surest expedients. Infliction of pain, whether self-inflicted

28

or with the help of others, was also found to be a means of arousing a high-strung emotional response.

THE SADIST'S QUEST FOR FULFILMENT

The need for direct communication is still a basic feature in the make-up of mankind. It is easy to see that sex, being so integral a part of man's essential being, is inseparable both from this need and its fulfilment.

The sadist is a defeatist, someone who has been disillusioned in his early youth, obsessed with the awareness of inadequacy. He is disappointed with his parents. If I cannot reach my parents, who are my own flesh and blood, he seems to think, how then can I possibly reach anybody else? From this disappointment, this acceptance of failure, stems his hatred of mankind in general. He scorns other people who do not think as he does. He is the perfect prototype of Colin Wilson's 'Outsider'. His distorted or exaggerated feeling of isolation creates an exaggerated wish for communication. In a desperate attempt to reach the other he falls back upon the old medium —frenzy. Cruelty, a frenzied offshoot of aggression, is the means by which he hopes to break through the wall that separates him from the other. Through aggression he makes his existence known, expressing himself by coercion upon the partner. He does not seek in a partner a component for his ego: he looks for an opponent. He sees in the partner only an instrument and a tool, an intermediary for the attainment of his goal. Tormenting the partner is not the sadist's one and only aim. Breaking the partner's will is the object he pursues.

It will be appreciated, then, that I do not agree with Jean-Paul Sartre when he says that the sadist is not trying to suppress the freedom of the one he is tormenting: his only aim is to force this freedom to identify itself with the tormented flesh. The one thing, according to Sartre, that the sadist demands, is a "reaction to the situation" from the partner. He claims that the sadist "sees himself as an individual who has all the time in the world. He is resigned; he is in no hurry; his actions are those of a technician with his instruments. He tries them one after another, as a locksmith tries several keys in a lock. He enjoys his ambiguous and contradictory situation. On the one hand he plays the part of a person resolutely and patiently employing every manner of means to achieve his purpose, a purpose that will be achieved as automatically

29

as the lock gives way as soon as the right key is produced; on the other hand he can only achieve this preconceived purpose through the voluntarily-given full consent of the partner."

If Sartre's view were correct then the masochist who enjoys being tormented would be the ideal partner for the tormentor's zealous ingenuity. But this is by no means invariably the case, as we shall see in the following chapter.

CHAPTER TWO

From the General to the Specific

THE INCIDENCE OF SADISM

In the previous chapter I have been attempting to convey a very general impression of the male sadist's psychic attitude. Up to this point generalisations have been useful aids to obtaining an insight into the subject; but the time has now come to turn our attention to more specific considerations.

Sadists are found among all classes, among the rich and the poor, the high-born and the low. Their mental capacities range from highly intellectual to downright cretinous; their sadistic preferences from harmless imaginings to monstrous cruelties and murder. The desire to kill may lurk in any individual, but the more intelligent he is the more he is likely to recognise the consequences, moral and social. Thus, in most cases the intellectual will try to curb his passion, limiting it to phantasies (often relieved by masturbation), or to relatively innocuous activities such as flagellating a willing victim or other forms of minor ill-treatment. But the imbecile who is possessed by the urge to maim or kill does not clearly foresee all the consequences. He may be devoid of moral scruples altogether and in that case will sooner or later give way to his morbid desire. In sadism possibilities literally proliferate: every imaginable (and unimaginable) aberration may be encountered, and frequently sadistic conduct is of such a kind as to suggest a combination of anomalies.

Single-minded, obsessionistic, genuine sadists do exist but they are rare. In most cases the sadist's perversity springs, as I have just implied, from a combination of anomalous inclinations. To be able to analyse all the possible combinations we should need the help of a computer. As that lies far beyond the scope of this book, we must limit ourselves to the most significant ones.

31

GENUINE AND PSEUDO-SADISM

We must be careful to distinguish between genuine sadism and what may be termed pseudo-sadism. The former is sometimes called 'pure' sadism, though clearly the word 'pure' is liable to misinterpretation; the latter is alternatively known as 'minor' sadism.

Fortunately for society, of all individuals with sadistic tastes (and their name is legion) the vast majority confine the indulgence of their predilection to imaginary situations. Large numbers, too, are content to witness sadistic scenes without being an active participant. For this reason the interest displayed on such occasions by those who do not actually take part in the act of violence themselves is sometimes erroneously called by the contradictory name of 'passive' sadism. Properly speaking, however, this is visual sadism—a mingling of sadism with scopophilia.[1]

VISUAL SADISM

In the category of visual sadists must be included all those who experience intense sensual pleasure from witnessing public boxing and wrestling contests, bullfights, bear-baiting, cockfighting and indeed any violent spectacle. Many people become sexually stimulated simply by being spectators at some exhibition in which blood is deliberately shed or life taken, whether human or animal. In former times judicial executions were staged in the open like public entertainments, and in fact quite recently, in one of the newly-independent African territories, a number of prominent political figures who had been found guilty of plotting to overthrow the government were publicly hanged. In the same month a British television programme reporting on the march of events in oil-rich Saudi Arabia showed a crowd of many hundreds that had assembled to watch the public mutilation of a thief. Although the cameras were confiscated by the Saudi authorities to prevent them from filming the actual amputation of the culprit's right hand, the apparatus was returned to the reporters immediately afterwards, while many of the spectators were still gazing

---

[1] Scopophilia is one of the commonest and relatively most innocuous of all anomalies. Literally the term means 'love of seeing' and in its widest connotation it implies deriving sexual pleasure from viewing or observing something. (When what is viewed or observed lasciviously is other people performing sexual intercourse or engaging in love-play, another term, which is perhaps more accurate, is mixoscopia, or mixoscopy.)

reflectively at the blood-stained spot where the severed hand had fallen. After the amputation the crowd watched in fascination while the hand was ceremonially burnt.

As recently as the second half of the nineteenth century, certainly, widespread interest in the spectacle of a public execution was still a commonplace in England, for Schlesinger records the reply of "a highly-cultured English lady" to a question of his as follows: " 'Well, sir, our people celebrate at Newgate, whenever there is a hanging, or in Horsemonger Lane, or at any similar nice place outside a county jail. At such times there is a great deal of life and movement at the place of execution from early dawn till the moment when the executioner has carried out his gruesome task. The windows of neighbouring houses are let at high prices, platforms are erected, stalls and booths for the sale of food and drink spring up quite close to the scaffold, and there is a ready sale for beer and gin at good prices. People travel great distances, on foot, by horse, and by coach, in order to witness the shameful show. And the front row is occupied by women, my countrywomen, not only the women of the poorer classes, but also gently nurtured ladies. It is disgraceful, but true. And after the event it is the duty of our newspapers, a duty of which no genuine Englishman would be prepared to relieve them, to describe with hair-raising minuteness the last writhings and twitchings of the unfortunate criminal.' "[1]

Holtzendorff in his book emphasising the futility of capital punishment says: " 'An otherwise good-natured and respectable crowd of country folk revealed its worst side at an execution which took place in a small town, and one is therefore justified in arguing that the execution of death sentences not only brings out the evil side of bad people but also affects the better elements. Dymond reports in connection with an execution at the small town of Chelmsford that the country folk who attended in large numbers "indulged in a veritable carnival of licence". On the eve of the execution a banquet was given in honour of the hangman at a local inn, in order to make him talk about his professional experiences. People came from a radius of twenty miles and young men and women made up parties for the excursion'.

"This latter fact provides the clearest possible evidence of

[1] Iwan Bloch: *History of English Sexual Morals.*

33

the connection between the gruesome pleasure in witnessing executions and the sexual factor, so that the appetite for such 'shows' may be characterised as specifically sadistic. Under the influence of these shows and their frequent repetition certain individuals developed into execution 'fans'—and some of them were persons of 'quality' "[1]

Such public exhibitions as those I have been referring to are sometimes regarded as safety-valves for the release of the pent-up sadistic impulses of the masses. That there is a hidden morbid sexual factor present is, I am afraid, unquestionably true. Iwan Bloch, in *History of English Sexual Morals*, gives the following instance: "Colonel Turner, having witnessed the quartering of the law expert John Coke, gave certain instructions, as a result of which another condemned man, Hugh Peters, was brought forward by the executioner's assistants and asked by the executioner, who rubbed his bloody hands together as he spoke, whether he—Hugh Peters—was satisfied with their method of work. Characteristically enough, these cruel nobles hastened straight from the scene of the executions to the most abandoned orgies—which proves in the most striking manner the sexual basis of their cruelty."

In most countries floggings of persons of either sex as a punishment were frequently administered in public. It can readily be imagined what a stimulating spectacle it must have been to many observers when women and girls were undressed and whipped for some (usually trivial) misdemeanour. Men and women in all walks of life gathered to enjoy such spectacles, and indeed ladies and gentlemen of quality were among the most eager onlookers when prostitutes or girls arrested for petty pilfering were savagely beaten: it was natural that members of the upper classes should, in general, be those with most leisure to attend these exhibitions.

When women were admitted to the bridewells (women's prisons) they were given a thrashing known familiarly as the 'Welcome', and when they were released at the expiration of their sentence they were given another, called the 'Farewell'. In a well-known book, *Lenchen im Zuchthause*, the author W. Reinhard furnished a description of the system of corporal punishment in the female prisons of South Germany up to the year 1848. The book has been translated into English[2] under

---

[1] *Op. cit.*   [2] *Nell in Bridewell*, Luxor Press, 9/6.

the title of *Nell in Bridewell,* and to give the reader some idea
of the shocking treatment the inmates were subjected to, I
append some excerpts in continuous narrative form, though
the text is too long to quote in its entirety.

Nell, or Lenchen, who has been committed to prison for a
small theft she perpetrated to shield her fiancé, is about to be
released. Her sentence has been completed, but she is to be
subjected to the infamous 'Farewell' (twenty strokes of the
bull's pizzle) before she may leave . . .

"I was now called upon; the moment had come. I shud-
dered, my limbs trembled, for a moment my sense of hearing
was obliterated . . . I called upon God . . . and prayed for that
strength . . . which lifts one above all that is physical and common, and cares nothing for even the most fashionable mob . . .

"All this sustained me and, proud and determined, I stepped
forward . . .

"My appearance and the history of what had brought me
here set all tongues in motion . . .

" 'Oh, how handsome, how very handsome, but at the same
time how proud! Well, she will have her pride rather brought
down when she is on the bench!'

" 'But look, what a splendid figure she has; how beautifully
the drawers will fit her!' . . . I was already laid upon the bench.
I was fastened down by the neck and the heels, my frock was
forcibly thrown up, nearly to the shoulders so that it could
hardly hold together, and a considerable portion of my naked
skin was exposed . . . I closed my eyes, a warm flood of blood
rose to my cheeks and a boiling heat invaded my heart. In
this shameful position, exposed to the gaze of so many eyes,
how did I differ from a common criminal? . . .

"Oh! my revered good parents, could you ever have imagined to yourselves your daughter in such a terrible situation?
Was it for this you educated me, my teachers? . . .

"The Overseer now placed himself at my head and, stooping
down, seized my drawers with both hands at the loins and the
hips and pulled them down on both sides so as to stretch them
to the utmost, which he did with such force as to cause the
groove between the legs to hurt me . . . He now passed his
coarse vulgar hands along my person, in order fully and properly to convince himself that between the very light whip-
ping-drawers and my skin nothing had been smuggled in for
the strokes . . . No doubt he also wanted to take note of the

firmness of my flesh and of its resonant power. Shame and dread vied with hellish distress. This was worse than the guillotine ...

"The spectators, nearly all of them of the female sex, ... now crowded closely round, almost all of them manifesting the utmost delight at being able to assist at such a pleasant spectacle, their eyes fixed upon my face to observe the least signs of anguish and of fear, and still more upon the threatened parts, accompanied by experienced prognostics of the effects of the strokes and of the pain caused thereby, so soon to be visible ...

"The Governor now slowly read out in a loud voice my sentence ...

"I lie shivering in a deathly sweat in fear of the first bodily pain. From one second to another the deadly bolt may fall.

" 'Ah! the girl has indeed a fine bottom!' said an aristocratic old lady. 'I've really never seen quite such a fine one before, so admirably built and rounded for whipping ... it is indeed an indestructible mass and every agitation ... must cause a sympathetic chord to vibrate among the men, ay, and among the women too ...'

"The first stroke fell ... I felt the flesh quiver and swell up, a glowing heat spread itself quickly over the part which had been struck ... And there are nineteen more to come, thought I; Oh, God in Heaven, what will become of me? ... I had left the vestibule of hell and entered hell itself ...

" 'Ha! ha! Now she's had a taste what it'll be like!' said a female voice ...

" 'Well', said another dame, 'I do call this a fullness of the flesh! It is for all the world as if the strokes fell upon a high cushion tightly stuffed with horsehair'."

Other strokes followed each other in quick succession.

" 'Merciful God!' I screamed, 'behold a victim of love! Oh, Heaven, my poor limbs! Poor, unhappy, defenceless Nell!'

" 'Oh! the poor, poor girl', I heard somebody say, sobbing. 'Could they not stop; surely she has suffered enough? She will not be able to stand many more such blows'.

"So there is even here a commiserating soul, I said to myself.

" 'Oh!' said another voice, 'such a part, particularly when so richly developed, can stand a great deal!' ...

" 'But how the flesh already works! and how full of life are her limbs!' ...

36

"At the eighth blow I cried out loud in my despair ...

" 'Ah!' said another. 'How I do pity her. She's indeed no common vulgar creature; you can see that in a moment, and hear it too' ...

"The tenth and eleventh strokes now fell at short intervals ...

"My whole frame was twisting, struggling and contracting, in a sort of unnatural turmoil ...

"A cry of despair escaped me, and another, and then the words:

" 'Oh! God, oh! merciful Father, give me strength for the torture that I may be able to endure it!'

"A young girl wept aloud, but her mother reproved her, saying:

" 'You silly thing, what are you crying for? It's all nothing but acting; they all do it; only this girl is cleverer at her trade than the others'....

"The Overseer now laid the bull's pizzle along the line which he felt with his hand was most swelled up, and, pressing it down, drew it backwards and forwards several times (this is called ... sawing or filing), causing me a really hellish pain ...

" 'Oh! sir Governor,' I called out ... 'I die, my girlish body can stand no more'....

"My limbs ... were now racked by continual cramps, and in perpetual violent motion ... the portion of my body that was attacked seemed ... to have its own separate life of pain, sending the stream of its feelings to the brain. I trembled in every limb ...

"And now the sixteenth stroke fell, exactly upon a swollen, very sore place. It cracked and burst open, and blood flowed freely ...

" 'I suppose it's quite hot all over now?' said the aristocratic old lady ...

" 'Only two more stripes', said a young lady. 'But oh, what *must* her posterior now look like? ... Oh! how the flesh must burn! May one not touch it?'

" 'No!' said the Overseer, 'the Governor and the acting Overseer alone have the right to touch the body of a delinquent on the bench of punishment ... But now all is glowing with heat; you might cook little birds over it or roast chestnuts'....

37

"My strength was nearly exhausted. I could, however, still hear the following unfeeling remarks:

" 'Ah! here comes the last stroke. Oh! but I could go on a long while yet enjoying the sight, and drinking in her cries'....

"But a serious-looking person, who had hitherto always remained silent, said:

" 'Why is this poor girl so fearfully, so exceptionally punished? ... Blows have never yet been inflicted with such force with such an arm, and almost uninterruptedly, on one and the same place!' "

I fully realise that this type of fiction can hardly be called good literature. Nevertheless, books of this kind must be mentioned, for they have flooded across Europe (in a surreptitious stream) since the beginning of the nineteenth century. Undoubtedly such books are calculatedly sensational, but then so were the novels of Charles Dickens and other social reformers who made it their mission to expose abuses. Public indignation *was* aroused at last, and the infamous practices described in this book were brought to an end within a single generation after the disclosures became general knowledge. The fact remains, however, that such books themselves provided a particular kind of sexual stimulation for those avid to read about what they could not themselves witness.

COLLECTIVE VISUAL SADISM

Ceremonies such as the slaughtering of a sacred animal (e.g. a totem animal) in a ritualistic way, the elaborate rites leading to an ever-increasing frenzy and concluding with a sexual free-for-all, may be classified under the above heading. Certain orgies of later ages and the sado-masochistic orgies of today must be regarded as degenerated descendants of ancient tribal ceremonies. In fact, I am firmly of the opinion that human reactions to fundamental sensual urges, whether viewed 'horizontally' or 'vertically', invariably conform to a remarkably unchanging pattern. (By 'horizontally' I refer to the diasporic spread of human beings over the earth; by 'vertically' I wish to imply the relation of man's existence to time). Whether we consider the Neanderthaler, the African pygmy, or the civilised Westerner, they all instinctively choose the same means of gratifying those urges. Even the rituals of today's sado-masochistic orgies bear a close resemblance to those that took place in ancient days.

That sexual orgies are celebrated in practically all the countries of the Western hemisphere I have known for a long time. The publication of Leigh's *Velvet Underground* failed to shock me in this respect. Sado-masochistic parties comprise participants who are sadistically or masochistically inclined.

THE MODERN SADO-MASOCHISTIC ORGY

One of my clients who used to participate in sado-masochistic parties supplied me with a description of such an event. As I have a tape recording of that particular interview, I will give the substance of it in his own words. The questions which I interpolated here and there are omitted: from the answers one can readily surmise what the questions were.

I arrived there at nine. After greeting the hostess I went upstairs to change. There were two bedrooms reserved for this purpose, one for the men, one for the women.

—Why two rooms? Well, that's quite obvious I should think. One changing-room for men *and* women would be rather indecent, wouldn't it?

Three or four men were already busy undressing. I disrobed too, keeping only my trunks on. Then I put on a silk shirt and went down again.

—No, there is no uniformity in the men's attire. Some have gaudy-coloured underpants, some leave their torso bare, others appear completely dressed, getting rid of their garments in the course of the evening.

—The ladies, yes. Generally they wear a tight-fitting tunic-thing that leaves their arms and legs bare. The colours they favour are mainly black and red. On this occasion there was one woman who was dressed in blue satin. But that's an exception. The materials used are satin, silk, soft leather, suède. Some have breasts and buttocks exposed. Long gloves and black silk or nylon stockings are worn—and shoes with spindly high heels. Some women wear riding-boots.

When everybody was present, the hostess (who also acted as MC) opened the evening's proceedings with words of greeting, and thanks to those who had brought certain articles.

—Drinks . . . films . . . whips . . . things like that.

Next she announced that a complaint had been brought against Mrs X.

(I have not yet given you a description of the room we were

occupying. It was a very large room with a platform at one end.)

Mrs X was summoned to the platform. The MC addressed her in a stern voice:

'You are accused of having broken your partner's favourite ash-tray. Is that so?'

Mrs X bowed her head and answered, 'Yes, that is right.'

'Have you anything to say, to defend yourself?'

Mrs X shook her head. 'No, madam.'

'You must receive a sound whipping for your carelessness.'

Two strongly-built young men ascended the platform. They were naked, except for black diving-caps and wrist-protectors of black leather. They stripped Mrs X, bound her hands together and tied them to a ring that was let down from the ceiling on a thick rope. Her arms were then hoisted by this rope until she was obliged to stand on tiptoe. Then the lights in the room were dimmed and spotlights switched on.

The two assistants began beating the woman with slow, steady strokes. One of them worked on her buttocks with a supple reed, the other struck her thighs with a dog-whip.

There was tense silence in the room, all eyes focused on the stage. The only sounds audible were the swishing of the whip, the dull thwack of the reed, the sighing and gasping of the victim, and the heavy breathing of the audience watching the scene intently and without stirring a finger. Presently the victim began making moaning sounds. Faint noises of rustling and fumbling then arose in the room; here and there a sigh was heard.

The MC all the time was keeping an observant eye on the stage and on the audience. As the audience became restive her voice rang out sharply: 'Stop!'

Lights flashed on in the room, the spotlights went out. Mrs X was untied, dressed again and brought back into the body of the room. Tension disappeared. Drinks were served, records played. Some started dancing; more drinks were served. Except for the rather unusual clothing, it might have been any ordinary party.

—The tension *had* to be relieved; if not, the party would have been all over in an hour. A Master of Ceremonies is therefore necessary. He (or she) regulates the mounting and subsiding of emotional tension.

After a while the MC announced the showing of a film,

brought by one of the guests. I don't remember what it was about, but it proved to be a very mediocre affair and we all agreed we had seen better. It failed to arouse any enthusiasm among the audience. After that the MC made known to the assembled company that complaints had been brought jointly by Mr and Mrs M, each accusing the other. They were thereupon summoned to the stage and interrogated by the MC in arrogant tones, rather in the way I have related in the case of Mrs X.

—I don't suppose so. I imagine the accusations are just made up to provide enjoyment for all concerned.

After some cross-examination the MC announced her verdict. As they were both guilty they should both be punished publicly, and in this special case the punishment would be combined.

The assistants set up a bench on the stage, about five feet long, two feet wide and one foot six inches high. It was lacquered bright red. They both had to undress completely. Mr M was laid face upward on this bench, his hands and feet tied to the legs of it. Mrs M was now invited to administer the thrashing. For this she was given a sort of broom made of thin flexible nerves of palm leaves bound together, with which she alternately flogged and prodded with the sharp points of the nerves' ends the tenderer parts of the man's body.

When, after some time, the reaction of the culprit became visible, it was Mrs M's turn to be punished. She had to stand, with her legs spread, over the bench on which her husband was lying. The ring was lowered from the ceiling and her hands tied to it; then she was ordered to sit on her husband's erect organ. The MC herself made the connexion; the length of rope was so adjusted that she had to sit up straight but with slightly concave back. Then one of the assistants started whipping Mrs M with an instrument made of six soft chamois leather thongs tied to a handle. With this he struck her on the breasts, belly, back and flanks. It was clear that the thongs stung but did not hurt her much. The tingling made her squirm and sway about on her pivot, attempting to stand up and falling back again, all the while uttering sighs and low moaning sounds.

After some minutes Mr M on the bench began jerking convulsively, groaning and grunting at the same time. The tension among the audience was palpable. Their uneven breathing and sighing mingled with the now unsuppressed cries and writhings of the couple on the stage. The whipping-master went on mercilessly to wield slow, well-aimed strokes, Mrs M more and more desperately trying to stand up and falling back with more abandon, until she at last uttered high-pitched cries of ecstasy and wriggled like mad. Mr M roared. Abruptly the rope was lowered and Mrs M collapsed in a heap upon her husband's torso. The audience was no longer watching the stage; they were all moving apart in pairs, each pair attending to their own business.

In the ceremonies of the peoples of olden times and among primitive tribes even today, the orgy is generally preceded by an elaborately-staged blood offering. Usually the sacrificed creature is an animal, though the Aztecs, for example, sacrificed human beings for this purpose. But we must not forget that this offering was meant to appease the gods. Even in the Judao-Christian Bible there are references to live human offerings sacrificed to God. In pagan societies the orgy that followed was in reality an act of communion with each other and with the gods. It was, incidentally, also a safety-valve for the pent-up emotions of the participants.

In the sado-masochistic orgy the offering is replaced by a public punishment of a (usually voluntary) victim. In the example described above the castigation administered was, in each case, of a mild sort. No blood flowed. But I have heard of parties where the lashings and tortures are carried on until the victims are bleeding and unconscious. The mass frenzy aroused is of the same order as in ancient tribal ceremonies. Perhaps equally it serves as a safety-valve. But here the similarity ends. In sado-masochistic orgies no communication is sought with the deities, nor with the community. Lust is the spur; sensual pleasure the only goal. The means have become confused with the end.

My patient's prudish reaction to the question, 'Why two dressing-rooms?' may seem rather ironical in the light of what followed. But I think we must see this as a wish to establish that the orgy was only incidental and could not influence the normal everyday life with all its implicated codes and rules.

It goes without saying that the participants in sado-masochistic parties or orgies are generally carefully selected and 'screened'. Even so, the organisers of such activities (who naturally are anxious not to be exposed to the police or the outside world by anyone who 'does not belong') do occasionally slip up. Here is an adventure as related to me by one of my patients, a 21-year-old girl whom we will call Ann. The country in which this happened—on the Continent by the way —does not seem to me to be of material importance. The realm of sado-masochism differs from circumstances usually encountered in novels, for it is a sphere in which truth is generally stranger than fiction. This is the story that Ann told me.

Some weeks before, her boy-friend Peter, who worked as a photographer, had mentioned to her that he had become acquainted with a female colleague named Astrid who had come to live in the town a few months previously. Peter found her a peculiarly interesting person, but both he and Ann knew that although Astrid had been living in the locality such a short time there were already strange rumours in circulation about mysterious goings-on at her apartment. When Astrid invited Peter to come to one of her 'parties' Peter begged Ann to go with him. But let Ann continue the story in her own way.

"I wasn't very interested as I had a suspicion about the kind of thing we might get mixed up in. Besides, the impression I had formed of Astrid was not encouraging.

"However, Peter is the sort of fellow that can't take 'no' for an answer, and as with me it's anything for a quiet life I gave in. Astrid seemed delighted to know that I was coming too, and assured Peter that she knew just the right friend to invite to make up a perfect foursome. So the so-called 'party' was going to be a very small and intimate affair. Just how intimate I was to find out later.

"On the appointed evening I felt nervous, and a little scared I believe. I told Peter I wished we were going to the movies, but he wouldn't hear of a last-minute cancellation.

"Astrid lived alone in a flat of her own. She was a heavily-built woman of about 34, rather mannish in appearance. She was wearing slacks and a sweater. The fourth guest was already there when we arrived. She introduced him as Joe, but I'm pretty sure that wasn't his real name at all. He was a quiet middle-aged man of the managerial type.

"As soon as we were all sitting down Astrid started serving drinks. She put some records on the radiogram and asked Joe to dance with her. Peter and I danced together. I had the

43

feeling that there was a strange, uncanny atmosphere about the whole set-up, and I suggested to Peter while we were dancing that we ought to slip away on some pretext or other, but he wouldn't hear of it.

"Astrid served more drinks and I began to feel just a little bit light-headed, as though I didn't care much what happened anyway. Most of the lights were put out; the music became more seductive, the dancing more intimate, more amorous. Then Astrid suddenly peeled off her sweater: she had only a skimpy bra underneath.

"She went into another room and when she came back she was wearing a leather strap on her right wrist and carrying a whip. Joe didn't show any surprise, but I could see that Peter was clearly shocked. Not to mention myself!

" 'Come on,' Astrid said to me. 'You have to undress too, my dear.'

"I told her I had no wish to follow her example. 'Oh, but you're not going to follow my example,' she said, smiling. '*You're* going to undress completely!'

"I looked at Peter. He shrugged his shoulders, and I could see I wasn't going to get any moral support from him. He had lost any grip on the situation he might once have had, and just didn't know how to handle Astrid.

" 'Aw, come on,' Joe said. 'Undress! We're your friends!'

"I shook my head and made for the door. Suddenly I heard the whistle of a whiplash and felt a stinging blow on my shoulders. Astrid said quietly: 'That's just a warning. I'm the one here who gives the orders and I expect to be obeyed.'

"I could see there was no use hoping for any help from the two men and so perfunctorily I began taking my clothes off.

" 'Faster!' Astrid said sharply. Again the whip struck me and in a sort of daze I went on taking my things off; as I did so I heard Astrid telling the men she was showing them a 'whiptease' act.

"When I was quite naked Astrid served drinks again. She was very friendly now and we all talked. Then Peter, who was evidently feeling reckless (the effect of the drinks I expect), started to make love to me. He did so in the way we were accustomed to and didn't seem to mind in the least having spectators looking on. Strangely enough, neither did I. In fact I was feeling quite ready to be seduced.

"But Astrid stopped us. She told Peter she didn't want 'any

44

of that business' in her house, and when he ignored her and tried to get on with it she picked up the whip and struck him severely.

" 'Now I'll tell you what is going to happen next,' she said.

"Joe had to undress. She fastened his hands behind his back and forced him to kneel down in front of me. Then she tied me up. Peter made rather a lame protest but she took no notice.

" 'Joe, you're going to honour Ann in a very special way,' she said.

"As Joe started to kiss my thighs right the way up from my knees to my groin, slowly and tantalisingly, she whipped him from behind. Joe clearly showed his excitement at being humiliated and whipped and as his passion increased I could feel his lips and his breath get hotter. Then Astrid wanted Joe to perform *cunnilinctus* on me, but this time he didn't get far, as Peter, though he seemed to be in a strange, apathetic mood, protested vigorously. So Astrid, to humour him I suppose, let him caress my breasts and stroke my back and bottom. Then she picked up her whip and began to strike all three of us. As for me, I felt as if it was all happening in a gigantic nightmare.

"That night Astrid untiringly thought up new arrangements in which the four of us took part. No one protested any more. She directed the actions but none of us was permitted to have any sexual contact with her or even touch her. All night she never bared more than the upper part of her body though we other three were entirely nude. And although *cunnilinctus* and *fellatio* were performed repeatedly, together with a few other sexual acts, no normal copulation was permitted. Time and again Peter, Joe and I varied our rôles. At one moment I was being whipped by Peter and the next I had to play the part of the severe mistress and chastise the two men. Astrid never relinquished her rôle of directress and none of us dared even to suggest what we should do next or hesitate to obey her. We clearly recognised her as 'the boss'."

After this amazing confession Ann told me:

"Now I cannot understand why I ever went to Astrid's flat. Of course, after that horrible night Peter and I parted. I would have nothing more to do with him . . . I obeyed and did all the things Astrid made me do because I didn't want to be a spoil-sport or let the others think I was afraid. But I *was* afraid—of

45

Astrid. Secretly, though, I was excited, I suppose because up to then sex had been a big mystery to me. I had thought of it as over-rated and I hoped that that evening I would learn a few things. Nevertheless, if I had known—or even vaguely surmised—what was going to happen, wild horses would not have dragged me there: I would have fled, Peter or no Peter."

After a few sessions with me Ann talked again about this experience with Astrid and blushingly confessed:

"You know, there's one thing about that night I shall never forget. At one moment the four of us were in a real frenzy—ecstasy I suppose you could call it—and at that moment I was able to forget my own personality completely... That was a wonderful feeling and I shall always remember it. It was nice for a few minutes not to be able to recall what and who I was... It was glorious to feel, for a short time, my own personality recede completely and fade away... That experience was so unforgettable that I sometimes find myself longing for it to happen again. But I know that it never will and never can happen again, because I feel that if it did I wouldn't be able to get back to normality afterwards."

It is this 'ecstasy beyond words' that one reads about in sado-masochistic novels that makes the experience unique. This loss of the ego, or rather the surrender of it, is something some people want to experience over and over again, and at this point the sado-masochist resembles very closely those people who become addicted to drugs like opium, heroin, marijuana and LSD. They too are seeking an escape from the normality of everyday life.

THE SADIST AND THE MASOCHIST AS PARTNERS

This is perhaps as good a point as any to enquire what exactly the sadist's and the masochist's ideal partner should be. Superficially, no doubt, one would think that masochist and sadist, respectively, are their natural complements. (This is the mistake which Sartre makes, in my opinion, and to which I referred in the previous chapter). Research and experience present objections to this thesis. I think it is true that the sadist is often the masochist's ideal counterpart; but the masochist can never be the ideal of the true sadist. If we recall that the sadist wants to destroy the personality of his victim and humiliate the victim to breaking-point, he has no use for someone who is by nature prone to submissiveness. There is but little resistance to be expected from such an object. The only way for the sadist to derive pleasure from a masochist is to administer such severe tortures that even the masochist can no longer enjoy the treatment. So, even though the masochist may dream of the sadist as an ideal partner, I doubt whether he would enjoy the experience in practice. In *The Story of O,* to which I shall refer in more detail later, we find a clear illustration of this point. When O's personality has been completely destroyed and her submissiveness established for ever, her master is no longer interested in his 'creation'. He sells her like a dog to a friend.

SADISM AND MINOR FORMS OF EXHIBITIONISM

Krafft-Ebing, Freud, and others, have observed with apparent surprise that male homosexuals sometimes choose a virile profession such as that of pugilist, wrestler, footballer, bull-fighter, etc. In my opinion the probable explanation is that their homosexuality is tinged with sadism. In so far as they are not consciously or inordinately sadistic, their sadistic inclination being masked even from their own consciousness, we may call this minor sadism. And because their especial pleasure derives from pursuing acts of aggressiveness or potential aggressiveness before assembled spectators, there is an added element of exhibitionism in their attitude. Most of us have witnessed, I dare say, the fierce grimaces, the grunts and snarls of vengeful violence (often indeed simulated for the benefit of the spectators) used by these public performers while engaged in combat. It is equally illuminating to observe the spectators at these displays and to listen to their blood-thirsty yells ("Kill him!"; "Tear his arms off!"; "Murder the bastard!"—and so on). There are always people present who all but swoon with pleasurable excitement, identifying themselves either with the winner or the loser, giving indications of an apparent erection or clitoridean stimulation, and even orgasm. When a person makes evident in public his or her lustful inclinations, making it clear to the discerning observer that physiologically, as well as mentally, sexual tension is mounting, we may be justified in referring to it as pseudo-exhibitionism. It is not true exhibitionism, of course, which consists in deliberately exposing intimate parts of the body (most commonly the genitals) in the presence of one or more persons on whom the subject desires to make an erotic impression. In the pseudo-exhibitionism to which we are referring there is no actual uncovering of the genitals, and probably even the deliberateness is absent.

It is understandable that many people with sadistic inclinations feel attracted to professions and occupations that enable them to exercise a dominant rôle vis-à-vis the persons under their control, particularly when those persons are young or helpless and in a situation of subordination that precludes all possibility of resistance. We have all heard, or read about, sadistic sergeants in the Armed Forces, guards and warders in concentration camps and penal establishments, overseers, masters and mistresses in workhouses, mental hospitals, reformatories and schools. There are still educational institutions in some places which offer an opportunity to those with a sadistic urge to practise their hobby of corporal punishment. I have heard many eye-witness accounts of teachers who become sexually elated when they administer canings or birchings, especially in front of the other pupils. These witnesses have sometimes expressed surprise at the fact that teachers who plainly evince exultation when thrashing a helpless student are so noticeably dull and apathetic at other times. Here again it is evident that pseudo-exhibitionism is present. Such sadists are, generally, affected by the need to have other people witness their triumph over their victims. The pleasure they derive from their victorious dominance is redoubled by the thought that it is being observed and appreciated by an audience.

Both in fact and fiction there are many records of scholastic flagellation. Certainly numerous famous men went through the mill in this respect in former days, and though the writer of the following letter, dating from 1859, was not himself celebrated, still his note is remarkably interesting.

"In my boyish days it was customary in preparatory schools to have boys and girls together under a woman, and where the rod was used on all occasions with the utmost severity. We used to be birched in the presence of each other, the girls across the knee, or held under the arm, the boys on the back of a maid-servant. This latter used often to come to our rooms, and play the school-mistress, so did most of the girls. I have a vivid recollection of some extraordinary scenes in this line which have given me the perfect conviction of numerous women possessing the taste in question. In the school which was concerned, the female who always assisted the mistress was evidently most fond of seeing the operation, though she liked us all, and was herself a great favourite with the boys; but it was always with a giggle and a joke that she told several boys almost every morning that they were not to get up until *Missus* had 'paid them a visit,' or after seeing them in bed, telling them they were to keep awake until *Missus* should have had 'a little conversation with them,' that moreover she might be expected every moment with a couple of tremendous rods. This girl put us up to a great deal, and I fear developed our puberty far too precociously; she had a very large breast, and she arranged her dress so that, while being horsed, we had our hands completely slipped into, and feeling her bubbies; and the rocking and plunging used repeatedly to bring on emission. Many of the boys used to try to get whipped, merely to experience this sensation. Although 40 years have elapsed since all this, yet the remembrance is as vivid as if it had occurred only yesterday." (*Slightly adapted*).

Even a rather worthless erotic tale of the period could furnish factual information, as is shown in this excerpt from *Venus School-mistress, or Birchen Sports:*

"There was a man she [the headmistress] employed in bringing every Monday a regular supply of birch brooms for the use of the school, which he cut fresh from the trees. Sometimes she whipped the bigger scholars, particularly the boys, for we had several great boys on account of the English, behind a large folding screen, which was at the bottom of the schoolroom, and concealed the closet door, where she usually deposited her store of birch, and from which a back staircase led to another part of the house; sometimes in her bedroom, but more frequently in the school. I once saw her flogging a great girl, about fifteen years of age, who had taken some money privately out of one of her school-fellows' pockets; she gave it her for near half an hour; and wore out two large birchen rods, well steeped in vinegar, over her thighs and buttocks. She had that day more the appearance of a fury than a rational being; passion, lust, etc., by turns discovered themselves in her countenance. She used also a kind of cat-o'-nine tails, or rather o' sixty tails, for it had about sixty lashes to it, of the length of the arm. It was made of thin slips of parchment, which had been first moistened, and closely twisted, with five knots at the end, but she only made use of it when she flogged the bigger boys or girls, and even then but rarely, preferring the birch upon most occasions; and it was but once during my residence with her, that I saw her apply it to a girl who had been detected in frequent acts of pilfering."

Flagellation fiction, however, excels more in descriptions of the following kind, typical of such works:

"Dossy hesitated and looked shyly at the teacher who, with rod in her hand, was waiting impatiently.

" 'Come on! Hurry up!' the teacher cried. 'Are you ready?' The rod whizzed through the air.

"With a heavy sigh Dossy unfastened her slip and pushed it down her legs. Then she bent over the chair so that her backside, which was turned to the class, was covered only by a chemise.

"I held my breath in expectation of the things to come. The class was as still as a mouse and none of the girls dared to make a movement. All eyes were fastened on the white portion of chemise that covered her thighs. The legs were covered by black stockings. Underneath her thin batiste chemise one could clearly see the curved shapes of the two rosy globes.

"Unceasing sobbing shook the body of the girl. Ashamed and frightened, Dossy buried her head in her arms.

" 'You know how to receive your punishment,' the teacher said ruthlessly. 'You have to feel humiliated and ashamed, that is the most important purpose of this punishment. Lift up your chemise!'

" 'Miss . . . Please! I have already undressed! Please . . . ! I . . .'

" 'Do I have to give you a helping hand?' the teacher interrupted. She approached the unhappy girl who quickly put her hands behind her back, grasped her chemise and pulled it down taut.

" 'If you want to cause trouble, I've got a few surprises for you! First you are lazy and careless and now you want to slow down the course of events! Come on! Hurry up!' the teacher cried. 'I'll count three and after that I'll make short work of it! One . . . two . . .'

" 'Huuuuuuuu, ohhhhhh!' the girl sobbed with a tearful voice, 'huhuhuhuhu . . . nnnnnnn . . . ,' but her fingers pulled the edge of the chemise higher and higher. The crack that divided the two rounded cheeks became more and more visible and at last the uncovered buttocks shone in all their glory.

50

" 'You may count yourself lucky!' the teacher whispered. We were shaking like leaves and looked on with glowing cheeks, totally fascinated by the uncovered protruding behind of Dossy that cast an increasingly powerful spell over us.

"Though my face glowed, cold shivers ran down my back. My hands were ice cold and it seemed as if my lungs were bursting. Feverishly I looked up and down, from her feet to the pulled-up chemise and back. I fixed my eyes upon the two naked and fleshy globes and saw how they contracted with fright. I no longer thought of Dossy whom I liked very much. I had only eyes for those naked buttocks and could only think of the rod that now ... now ... would whizz down upon this intimate, helplessly bared part of the body.

"However the teacher did not make ready to start the chastisement. She pulled up Dossy's chemise a little more, pushed with her foot the girl's legs apart, stroked the rod lightly with her hand, went to her desk and addressed the class:

" 'Now you can see for yourselves the painful consequences of carelessness. Humiliation, pain and shame are the punishment of the sinner who dares defy the regulations. Never forget what you are going to witness now and be on guard!'

"Having spoken these words she left her desk, approached Dossy and struck the first blows.

"With a loud and painful cry Dossy clenched her legs, contracted her buttocks, threw them into the air and down again, lurched to the right and then to the left, threw up her head and rasped the floor with her toes.

"Her shrieks sounded more and more inhuman and then turned into an inarticulate groaning that was horrible to hear.

"I could hardly bear the sound and it set my teeth on edge, but nevertheless I was spellbound. My ears drank in these gargling sounds and my eyes would not miss the least movement of the jerking muscles. Though I am ashamed of my feelings I must confess it seemed as if I bathed in a stream of insane lust and mad passions. I felt as if I soared free and at a tearing pace through endless spaces; as if everything that burdened me now finally disappeared and as if I was lifted until I reached spheres that are situated far above our earth and where a wild and yet indescribably blessed fire blazed. I didn't feel myself any more. It seemed as if I had disintegrated.

"Dossy tried to bring her hands to her back to protect her

scarlet glowing bottom but the teacher grasped her wrists and the buttocks were now more helplessly at the mercy of the rod than before.

"Finally the last blow was struck. For a few moments Dossy didn't move. Then she slipped backwards, fell on her knees, rubbed her heels with her buttocks and stroked her thighs with her hands.

"I had reached the height of ecstasy. A convulsive pain seared through my body, from my legs to my breast and then to my head, which seemed to enlarge suddenly as if it was going to burst. I felt as if I were going to swoon, bent my body backwards and let my arms and legs fall back limply.

"Slowly I woke up. Indistinctly and as if behind a veil I saw the people around me. I saw how Dossy quickly and yet laboriously put her slip back in place, fastened her skirt, combed her hair with her fingers and then, bathed in tears, returned to her place.

'All that day I had a strange, shaky feeling in my arms and legs. I felt terrified, and a mysterious power forced me time and time again to review in my mind every detail of the spectacle—a spectacle full of a dark and terrifying bliss I shall not forget as long as I live."

In this fragment is demonstrated very clearly the inner change of the girl narrating the story—an inner change that turns her classmate Dossy into a superhuman fetish. The narrator enters another world, the gates of heaven seem to open. A gruesome "ritual" is started and Dossy is the "sacrifice". In the class the girls are as silent as during a religious ceremony. The bared buttocks have a demoniacal power and everybody is spellbound. Dossy herself does not exist any more. Her 'personality' is no longer important. The female narrator states she liked her classmate in daily life, but at this moment all she could see was this "intimate, helplessly bared part of the body".

The ties between fetish and audience lead to their being wholly engrossed in each other as soon as the chastisement starts. At this moment the female narrator experiences a growing feeling of ecstasy that turns into a complete orgasm.

In this fragment from Dorothy Rodshake's novel *Girls under the Rod* the loss of consciousness and the immersion in a bliss-giving stream from the unconscious are clearly illustrated.

The part of the body that started this uncanny chain of emotions has turned into a fetish—into a magical object that is in no way different from the strange objects and often frightening images primitive man used as fetishes in remote times. This phenomenon is not only encountered in novels. In the sex-life of modern man the fetish often plays an important part.

But now, before I go on to consider specifically some of the commoner of tangled sadistic complexes, I wish to refer to a peculiar case that came to my knowledge through a woman patient of mine. During treatment the woman revealed that her husband had strong sadistic inclinations, actually the main cause of her sufferings. She told me the following astonishing story.

One evening she suggested to her husband that it might be wise to tell their son that he ought to wash his genitals more frequently. "I'll see to it at once!" replied the husband with unexpected eagerness. He rushed upstairs two at a time. When he came down again his face was flushed and there was a strange light in his eyes. He related explicitly to his wife what he had done. When he got upstairs, the boy and his sister were in the bathroom brushing their teeth, both already in their pyjamas. He roughly drew the boy aside, abruptly pulled down his pyjama trousers, took the member in his hands and gave it a thorough cleansing with soap and water. During this treatment the boy got an erection and cried with shame and pain. All this while the girl looked on with prurient interest. When the woman asked her husband why he had not sent the girl away first, he answered: "It adds to his humiliation. It's good for him. That will teach him a lesson."

This repulsive instance is complicated by other aberrations besides sadism, both active and visual. The father's unnatural behaviour shows that he intensified the pleasure he derived from cruelty by pandering to the urge to procure: he deliberately prostituted his own daughter's sense of decorum by an act of vicarious exhibitionism.

SADISM AND HOMOSEXUALITY

In the summer of 1938 I was called to give testimony as an expert in the case of Johann T., accused of the attempted murder of his friend S. Examination disclosed the following facts. (Excerpt from my report):

53

"His build is distinctly puerile, in comparison with his habitus. His penis is strongly developed; the right testicle is atrophied. Mental development below average.

"In his seventh year he underwent an operation for a strangulated scrotal hernia. His mother took him to the hospital. Since his operation he has had a growing dislike and distrust of his mother.

"At the age of 20 he experienced his first erection. Soon after, he started masturbating at long intervals. He first experienced orgasm when dreaming that he was strangling a woman, the orgasm occurring without friction. After that he learned to produce orgasm by masturbation while imagining the strangling of a woman. For some time he toyed with the idea of realising his fancy but abandoned this because it would involve close acquaintance with a woman, which he found extremely repulsive.

"He obtained work as a bottle-cleaner in a distillery where he met S., who lived alone in a flat. S. invited J.T. to come and live with him. Because J.T. disliked his whole family, he consented. They started a homosexual relationship. On the fatal evening, he tried to throttle S., acting on impulse. Strong orgasm and ejaculation followed. After the act, J.T. fled in panic, leaving the door open. On seeing the prostrate naked body of S. lying on the floor, one of the neighbours called a doctor, who succeeded in bringing S. to his senses." The case was reported to the police.

Lange and others have tried to find a relation between corporal build and sadistic impulses, reasoning that disturbed mental development influences the development of the body. Krafft-Ebing suggests that the genitals of sadists are underdeveloped, orgasm weak or insufficient, impotency frequent. Though practice has since proved that these ideas cannot serve as general indications, in this case they were both present (except that the penis was overdeveloped in size rather than otherwise). The hatred and distrust towards the mother were clearly caused by the operation, identified as a castration at the mother's instigation. (It was she who took him to the hospital.) This hatred became directed against all women. Inquiries disclosed that S., a homosexual of the feminine type, had a fancy for transvestitism. This brought about the link with J.T.'s dream-wishes.

54

The combination of homosexuality with sadism is not strange, if we take the following theories into account:

Freud states that the mother is the child's first sex object selection. Over-veneration of the mother and imprinted taboos make the sex object unattainable. This is later extended to all women, resulting in a quest for other sex objects. They may be animals (zoöphilia), other men (homosexuality), or the subject's own body (auto-eroticism, narcissism).

Sadism originating from hatred of the mother also causes a turning away from the first sex object, resulting in a quest for other sex objects, but combined with hatred of women in general.

SADISM AND FETISHISM

In my opinion sadism and fetishism are always related. To be able to reach orgasm, the sadist always makes use of the same kind of phantasy. This phantasy becomes the *fetish*.

SADISM AND BESTIALITY

The case of the insane "chicken rapist" came to my attention when, some time during 1935, the police brought a young man to me for observation and examination. He was suspected of having sexually assaulted chickens on various occasions. The young man, a student named Georg V., denied having committed these acts. At first his denial was not taken seriously because he had written two letters to butchers, both of which contained a remarkable yet frightening message. The first had been sent some months before and was addressed to an elderly butcher who lived in a small village near Dresden. The letter was handwritten and read:

"Dear Mr. D.,

"Please forgive me for writing you this letter. I suffer from a mental illness that cannot be cured by doctors. As life is getting more and more unbearable to me, the only thing that is left for me to do is to ask you to kill me. You could do it with the instrument you use for killing pigs. We could arrange it in a way that would make it look like suicide and this wouldn't be very difficult as we're total strangers and people wouldn't think of a connexion between the two of us. I wouldn't like to kill myself as I prefer to have somebody around me during my last minutes on earth.

"My father never loved me. If you would be so kind as to kill me, I would have the illusion that you are my father. If you're willing to use your lethal instrument on me, we could first go for a little walk. I could tell you then more about myself. After that I'd be very grateful if you'd be so kind as to embrace me and press me to your heart—as if I were a little boy and you were my father.

"I can't find happiness in life any more. Now I hope to find it in death. I don't know how to live any more. Somebody promised me this morning I could come to him to have a talk. When I arrived there was nobody at home and I felt disappointed again. I can't be a burden to other people all my life. I haven't much money, but I would give everything to you if you would kill me. Please don't say no! Please answer me! I hope you're not going to disappoint me too!

Hans Schneider."

The butcher did not believe in this 'appeal for suicide'. He thought it was a threatening letter and went to the police to bring an action. He was sure all the sender of the letter wanted was to lure him into lonely surroundings and kill him with his own weapon.

The police studied the letter and then remembered another letter written in 1934 by "Hans Schneider." This letter was also addressed to a butcher and read:

"Dear Mr. B.,

"For the last few weeks I have been in such a depressed mood that I just had to write you this letter, though we don't know each other. I'm suffering from a mental illness—the doctors call it arrested development—which I think is incurable. I've thought and thought how I could help myself till suddenly I got the idea that maybe you could help me.

"I have the remarkable habit of buying a chicken or a rabbit from a farmer and having it killed in my presence. During the killing I experience a strange emotion of utter happiness, probably caused by the fact that I am spared and that nothing painful happens to me. I know it sounds ridiculous but I'm quite sure this must be the cause of that strange happiness. Of course the person in question doesn't suspect anything of my emotions.

"Soon after the killing I get very depressed and while in this

56

mood I often consider suicide. This happens so often it's almost unbearable and I'm afraid one of these days I'll have to be admitted to a lunatic asylum. I'm a student and I'd like to finish my studies. Now I thought maybe you could help me by killing an animal before my eyes now and then. Through the fact that you know now what happens to me during the killing maybe I shall not have to suffer any more from these depressions. Maybe you could do it a few times with ever longer intervals between the killings. In the end I wouldn't be interested in them any more, I think.

"In this way you could help me to get rid of this illness and of course I would be very grateful to you. Please think it over and let me know what you think of this proposition. If you haven't understood clearly what I mean we can talk it over. Of course I expect you to treat this matter confidentially. Please help me. I hope you're not angry about my writing to you. It was the only thing left to me.

Hans Schneider."

Inquiries made by the police led to Georg V., a student of biology who confessed having written both letters.

Now at this time poultry-owners in the surroundings of Dresden were making some gruesome discoveries. When a chicken-farmer early one morning went to the chicken-house to feed his poultry he saw nine of his chickens had been monstrously killed. The hindquarters of the chickens had been ripped open and the heads had been torn off. There were clear indications that the wretched creatures had been sexually abused. In the neighbourhood of the chicken-house footprints were found. One chicken had disappeared completely. The farmer went to the police to lodge a complaint.

The investigation had hardly begun when a second and a third chicken-farmer made similar discoveries. Newspapers began publishing articles about "The Mad Chicken Rapist" and at that moment a policeman remembered the letters written by Georg V., alias Hans Schneider. He was arrested but denied having anything to do with the "Chicken-house Murder Mystery". While he continued to deny everything I was asked to meet the suspect and have a few talks with him.

A few sessions with Georg V. revealed to me that he was a very intelligent and very shy young man. He convinced me that he himself had never killed or tortured an animal. Women played no part in his life.

Quite soon it became clear that Georg V. was a very lonely young man who knew absolutely no normal sex-life. His seemingly sadistic actions arose from a death-wish, a purely masochistic impulse. In wishing to witness the killing of rabbits or chickens he was, out of self-preservation, transmitting this death-wish to another object. In this case the connexion that exists between a death-wish and sexual passion is revealed by the choice of the victims. Rabbits, perhaps because of their proverbial fertility, are sex symbols. So are chickens and other poultry.

During Georg V.'s detention more chickens were massacred and it was at once clear that the student could not possibly be the culprit. The police warned all poultry-farmers to keep close watch and within a few weeks the true offender was apprehended. It turned out that he was a labourer. I had the opportunity to meet this man also, and I soon discovered that he lacked something very significant that Georg V. possessed: all notion of moral right and wrong. It was also found that the man showed marked sadistic tendencies, and his bestial-sadistic propensities were only one aspect of his disordered sex-life, which included assaults on women and children.

The labourer told me he had had his first heterosexual contact at the age of eighteen; he was an alcoholic and had never had a lasting relationship with any woman. He admitted, with apparent indifference, that he had first sodomised the chickens and then destroyed them by biting off their heads. He was convicted and sent to prison. Georg V. asked for psycho-analytical treatment, and only after a number of years did the first satisfactory results become noticeable.

As for bestial inclinations in general, it may be remarked that sexual relations with animals figure in the dream-wishes of many otherwise normal persons and may be due, or closely related, to zoöphilia. Many obscene jokes are bandied about that presuppose unnatural sexual relations between animals and humans and their popularity suggests that in many people they find a prurient sympathy. Another joke takes the form of a riddle: Which is the only virgin in Arabia? The answer is: the she-goat because she can run faster than any Arab. Arabs and others in the Middle and Far East are commonly believed to copulate with nanny-goats. The notorious side-shows in

Aden, Port Said, Cairo and Alexandria, specially staged for passengers off the mail boats, offer exhibitions in which animals play an important part: a mule copulating with a woman, a man with a goose, and so on. Magnus Hirschfeld records an incident in which "a man was denounced to the authorities for making a large dog perform the sexual act on his own wife. He seized the struggling woman and, by threats of punishment, succeeded in stripping her. Then he introduced the dog's penis into her vagina. The dog understood what was required of him and performed the act, while the man stood by. The defendant had committed this crime repeatedly. He was sentenced for 'Sodomy and indecent assault'." The relations some elderly women and sex-starved spinsters have with their pet dogs are well known. Leigh reports a case of a woman defiantly admitting that she preferred a dog's attentions to a man's. This last case may also be explainable as a strong masochistic inclination, the urge to look for the greatest possible humiliation.

SADISM AND PAEDOPHILIA

Just as some genuine sadists prefer to practise their cruelties upon animals, others choose children, of either or both sexes, as the victims of their unnatural passion.

Bretschneider relates a case that dates back to the end of the nineteenth century. "The teacher Franja M., of Pozega, was in the habit of flogging five or six of his pupils at a time on their naked bodies. After these floggings, which lasted for hours, he would hurry to a local brothel. The cries and lamentations of the children made him smile with delight and his blue eyes sparkled with lust."

Sadistic paedophilia—I am here using the term somewhat loosely to imply the preference on the part of a genuine sadist for children, up to and even beyond the age of puberty, as the objects of his or her sadistic attentions—is a well-known and rather widespread perversion. It seems to be a fairly common characteristic of sadists of both sexes. In fact, one of the most remarkable cases on record will be mentioned in the following chapter, in which I propose to deal with sadism in the female: in that case, cited by Magnus Hirschfeld, it will be seen once more how involved, sometimes, these complexes are, for the woman in question evinced symptoms of feminine

59

sadism, masochism, visual sadism, and the impulse to procure.

SADISM AND GERONTOPHILIA

Other genuine (i.e. active) sadists choose old or elderly men or women as victims in the satisfying of their bizarre appetites. I am suggesting that a convenient term for this particular aberration is sadistic gerontophilia.

If we recall the case of Johann T., recorded under the heading *Sadism and Homosexuality*, we may remember that the reason why this man hated women originated in his dislike and distrust of his mother. In this case it led to a quest for other sex objects, viz. men. Obviously he had a fear of women: they might 'castrate' him.

Whether or not this dread of castration is present it might happen that a sadist may wish to revenge himself on an older woman, who is then clearly a mother-substitute. That this inclination is by no means rare we can see from the newspapers. Assaults on middle-aged and elderly women would be better kept out of the papers. After the publication of one such crime it often happens that other crimes of the same type are committed by persons who have been encouraged by the example. But more often sadists with this specific leaning content themselves with humiliating and mentally crushing their objects. These cases very seldom come to light, the victims generally being too ashamed to lodge a complaint.

One very peculiar case is that of Klaus W. He enlisted as a young man in the Dutch colonial Army. After a period of training he was sent to the Far East. Up to that time he believed he was simply a homosexual; he had many girl friends but never felt sexually attracted to them. He had had some homosexual experiences but they did not satisfy him either. When he was in the former Dutch East Indies he accidentally found out what his real inclination was.

One Saturday night, while on a 'pub crawl', he found himself in a state of semi-drunkenness in the Chinese quarter of Sourabaya. A fat old Chinaman who was sitting in his front porch invited him inside and treated him to some beer. After a time this man offered him money if he would go to bed with him. Klaus did not mind. But it all turned out otherwise than the old Chinaman had hoped. For as soon as they had undressed in the bedroom Klaus took the initiative and in a most unexpected manner. He wrestled with the Chinaman, slapped him in the face, bit and insulted him, and when the man at last no longer resisted Klaus had a complete orgasm for the first time in his life. He never went back to this man, but thought that he now knew what he wanted.

Later he found opportunities for satisfying his bizarre wishes with old Chinamen who were willing to submit to being knocked about and insulted for money. Thus he became addicted to the fixation that only fat old Chinamen could give him satisfaction.

During the Japanese occupation he was in Siam (Thailand) as a prisoner of war. After the liberation he was sent back to Europe and later demobilised. He returned to his birth-place in Germany. He found a job, but was always restless. There were no fat old Chinamen in his village; in fact there were no Chinese at all. He applied for a post in the Far East, but having no other qualifications than that he had been a sergeant in the Army, he was unsuccessful. It was because of a mental breakdown that he came to see me.

During the treatment I learned the following facts about his youth. His father was an ill-tempered, jealous man who demanded strict obedience from his wife and child. (Klaus had no brothers or sisters). For the merest trifle the boy would be given a severe thrashing. He came to hate his father, to whom he always referred as "that fat old pig". He adored his mother in a very exaggerated way. As I have said earlier, homosexuality in the male can be caused by over-veneration of the mother. The old Chinaman was a substitute for the father, whom he wanted to debase.

CAUSATION OF SADISTIC COMPLEXES

For the fact that some sadists choose animals, or children, or old men or women, as the objects of their peculiar cravings, Krafft-Ebing and others have offered the explanation that these victims are easy to master. This is undoubtedly true in some cases, but as a general rule the cause of the sadist's special preference is much deeper rooted. The strange predilections we have been considering are almost certain to have some pathological causation, and frequently the services of the psycho-analyst prove effective in leading the patient back to normality.

In particular, paedophil and gerontophil yearnings are often traceable to experiences in the youth or early childhood of the individual affected. Let us examine, by way of example, a specific case with which I personally have been concerned. The patient, Hans T., might very well, as a result of his experiences, have developed a deep-rooted dislike of children, perhaps girl children especially. The sexual humiliations he underwent led, incidentally, to a hatred (and dread) of women, of the female sex in general.

Hans T. came to me because he was deeply troubled: he was desperately anxious to find out the cause of the profound disgust he felt whenever he was in the presence of a woman.

"The only thing that interests me is torturing women," he confessed. "But don't be afraid. Only when I was a child have I hurt people. Since my first experience of intercourse taught me how unimportant sexual union was to me and that sexual ecstasy only inspired the most sadistic phantasies, I have given it up completely. Besides, I soon observed that the presence of women disgusted me. Fortunately I'm an engineer and in my job I only meet men. As a bachelor I've rented a room. I take care to meet my landlady as little as possible. When I'm in a shop and a girl serves me I try to get away as soon as the occasion permits.

"In my room I have—of course under lock and key!—an extensive collection of books on torture, which is enlarged almost week by week. I've got scientific studies like Helbing-Bauer's *The Story of Torture in the History of Man,* books *The Hammer of the Witches,* and a book by Hans Rau on sexual sadism. Of course I own a number of historical novels, but the main part of my collection consists of pornographic novels. Among them are the wonderful books of the 'divine' marquis, as well as cheap obscene novels in which, among chapters filled with the different positions of *coitus,* oral sex-play and boring scenes of flagellation, a few pages are of interest to me.

"Every month I pay an awful lot of money for sadistic comic-strips I receive from the United States. Out of a high stack of these magazines there are only a few drawings I can use. Out of these drawings I cut the most interesting parts, so that my attention won't be diverted. What I like about these American publications are the really amazing contraptions the executioners make use of. I don't like the fact that in these

stories the bullies are also females and I try to overlook it—
a thing that isn't as easy as it sounds.

"The pictures I choose are pasted in my album, together
with a handwritten story that explains the actions."

I asked Hans T. to show me his album and saw an un-
equalled collection of sadistic illustrations. One of the stories
concerned a girl named Wanda and read:

"Now Wanda hears her sentence. As she knows escape is
impossible she submits to her fate. First her head is covered
by a leather hood so that she can't hear the orders her executioners receive and is ignorant of the things that are going to
happen to her. Leather straps are fastened around her jaws,
making it impossible for her to utter a sound. In this way I
shan't hear her cries for mercy. Now she's undressed, her feet
are strapped together and she has to kneel on a triangular piece
of wood, her knees being cut by the sharp edge. A chain is
fastened to her hood, passed over a pulley and fitted with a
heavy weight, keeping the body of the kneeling girl erect. The
arms are fastened at her back and fixed to this chain. Her
hands are also tied up and fastened to a cord that is conducted
to a pulley that is fastened to the floor and to another triangular piece of wood that is cutting the fronts of her thighs. A
third piece of wood with very sharp edges is placed between
her calves and thighs and then fastened to a pair of heavy
springs in the floor.

"The weight that keeps the body erect is changed after a
few minutes for a much heavier weight. Again after a few
minutes more weight is applied to the chain. Then the assistant
of the executioner approaches the tortured girl and asks: 'Isn't
this an interesting apparatus? Or do you want to be still more
stretched, bent, tightened and cut?' The next moment she takes
the weight from the chain. The body of the girl collapses."

Male sadism is very often caused by disgust for women.
This is illustrated very clearly in the case of Hans T. The origin
of his hostile attitude towards women was brought to light
when he told me about his youth and about an incident that
must have made a much deeper impression unconsciously than
he suspected.

"My father was a very religious man. I was about six years
old when my mother died and the only thing I remember of
this period is that my father was very cold. He never showed
any love for me and maintained iron discipline in the house.

63

I can't tell you anything more, I'm afraid. My memories of these years are like pieces of a dream one can't put together. After my eighth birthday I was brought up mainly by my stepmother. She married my father and brought three daughters with her. The three girls bullied me from the beginning. My stepmother always took their part and my father told me I had to be masculine enough to dominate them.

"On the few occasions when I resisted their bantering, my stepmother lectured me. Besides, the three girls were older and stronger than I. Everything they did to me they did, as they said, 'just in fun', but most of the time it was deliberate torture.

"One day they went as far as to make me undergo a 'sexual examination'. I think I was thirteen or fourteen years old when they took me to a wood in front of our house where, as they knew, no witnesses would be present. The eldest girl, who was seventeen and had probably more sexual knowledge than my father, suggested this examination.

"I was tied to a tree, and I thought they were going to play their usual cowboys and Indians, in which it was always my fate to be tortured, when suddenly they pulled down my trousers. They made obscene remarks about my member and manipulated it till I had an erection. That result didn't satisfy them. One of them took a tin she found on the ground and went to a brooklet to get some water. She poured it over my erect member 'to cool it down'. Then their little game started all over again, all the time accompanied by shouting and obscene remarks. I ejaculated, much to the merriment of the three girls, and they couldn't stop laughing . . ."

I think it understandable that after experiences of this kind, Hans T. hated women and wouldn't think of marrying one. The tortures he dreams of inflicting on women are a revenge for the tortures he had to endure.

MENTAL SADISM

Hans T., despite the reality and intensity of his obsessive hatred, had not actually inflicted cruelties upon women. He was satisfied with *imagining* what he would like to do to them. His aversion to the notion of women being tortured by others of their own sex is an indication that his phantasy had to demonstrate his superiority as a male. He had been disgrace-

fully humiliated in his boyhood—by girls of all creatures!
(which to a boy is far worse than being bullied by other boys)
—and he was constantly impelled by the urge to humiliate in
return, but the humiliation *must* involve the re-establishment
of his impaired masculine dignity.

As I have remarked already, the majority of sadists (or of
those whom in the circumstances we may call 'pseudo'-sadists)
are mental sadists only. That is to say, they construct in day-
dreams circumstances propitious to the indulgence of their
whims, and proceed to imagine themselves uninhibitedly performing feats of cruelty that in the cold light of reality they
could never carry out—and very probably would not if they
could. This sadistic day-dreaming is what we may call mental
sadism.

Frequently, of course, such phantasies are accompanied by
the relief afforded by masturbation. It has been said that masturbation may fulfil, in a paradoxical way, a social mission—
in protecting society from extreme forms of conduct that
otherwise might demand—and find—an outlet.

THE SADIST AND HIS DAY-DREAM

Certain it is that few sadists are able to attain to complete
fulfilment of their desires. Some resort to reading sado-masochistic novels; others fall back on the ingenuity of their own
fancy. They have to find what gratification they may in some
substitute for the real thing.

Some years ago I had a patient whom we will call Henri D.,
who was possessed of a truly extraordinary imagination, certainly among the most vivid I have ever encountered. He was
capable of creating not just mental images but sounds, tastes,
colours, and even smells, with his peculiar mental inventive-
ness, and in this way he built up a world of his own into which
he could withdraw whenever it suited him to do so.

He had one special favourite among his repertoire of day-
dreams, which returned with tremendous frequency and never
failed to give him complete satisfaction. When I asked him to
write down for me the details of this phantasy he hesitated,
as if he were afraid he would be parting with something intimate and sacred. Then one day he gave me a closely-written
account on a piece of paper, the text of which, translated into
English, is as follows:

"I picture myself at the steering-wheel of a big, flashy car. In reality I don't own a car and as a matter of fact I can't even drive. In my day-dream I'm a very competent driver, and while driving I nonchalantly take my hands off the wheel to light a cigarette. I leave town and enter a main highway that leads into the unknown. I drive faster, and at that moment a strange feeling of eager expectation invades me: I am soon in the grip of a mounting excitement.

"Now I approach a crossroads from which one road leads away to a small town. There is a petrol station and I can see a few hitch-hikers standing about. I pull up and my eyes light on two girls. One is wearing sports clothes and has a rucksack on her back; the other is more smartly dressed and carries a small suitcase. Both are very good-looking. One has a rather introvert face and fair hair; the other girl is a redhead with a permanent mischievous smile on her face. The blonde has a firm, robust, healthy figure. The redhead is much slimmer and looks rather like a doll. Then I notice their hands. The fair girl has broad, powerful fingers and short, squarish finger-nails. I don't know exactly myself how I can possibly notice all these things in the short time it takes me to halt the car in front of them.

"I ask them where they are making for and they tell me they are going to some far-away city. They say they're on holiday and, being students, they haven't much money. I tell them I happen to be heading that way myself and they can come with me if they like. Driving alone gets very boring, I assure them. They get into the car and both sit beside me in the front seat.

"The next moment I'm driving along again at high speed. We talk freely and I ask questions about modern youth and their ways of making love. The blonde gives very short answers, rather non-committal, as though she thinks the subject beneath her. Unconsciously she gives the impression that she is secretly longing for the 'right' man. The redhead acts differently. She hints at her sexual conquests and makes it sound as if she thinks it would be a very easy matter indeed for her to seduce me. Both attitudes irritate me and I say to myself: 'I'll teach these girls a lesson they'll never forget!'

"Suddenly I remember that about two hours' journey from this spot I own a small secluded castle. (Of course, this doesn't

66

exist in reality either!) On previous occasions I have brought women and girls to this secret domain when I have given them a lift. Now they are kept prisoner there.

"I make up my mind to suggest to these two girls—as I did to the other girls on those respective occasions—that they accompany me to the house of an acquaintance of mine where we can have some refreshments. Afterwards I will drive them on to their destination, I add. The strange thing about this decision is that I seem to think it up on the spur of the moment: it does not seem, at the time when it comes into my mind, to have occurred to me before.

"As in a film, the scene changes, and we are now on the road that leads to my castle. The two girls are not so cheerful as they were before; they seem uneasy. The redhead is visibly frightened, and the blonde, though she tries to bluff, talks too much and too loudly to be feeling really at ease. We reach my castle, an overgrown, half-ruined building situated in the midst of a dense wood that conceals it completely. We go in, and at the same moment I wonder—like a director planning a scene in a movie—whether to summon my strapping servant-girl to take the blonde and the redhead prisoner straight away or leave that till later. I decide to postpone it. It gives me more fun, more mischievous satisfaction to prolong the show and keep them in suspense a bit longer. I take them into the draw-ing-room, where, catching a glimpse of myself in a mirror hanging on a wall, I notice the expression of satanical expect-ancy on my face. My feeling of sexual excitement is intense.

"The girls are bewildered and helpless. I explain to them that I am the owner of the castle. I mention with ostensible indifference that coffee will be ready in a minute. Then I press a bell.

"Everything now happens very quickly. I know that any second after this the servant-girl will come in. She will be stark naked and there will be livid weals and scars all over her lovely body, the effects of a severe whipping one of the other ser-vants has given her on my orders. At once the two girls will understand what is going to happen to them, why I have brought them here. They will realise that they are about to be seized and stripped and flogged for my pleasure into a state of absolute submission. But at this point I can't think clearly any more. I am intensely excited, on the point of orgasm, and

67

suddenly all the details of my day-dream become blurred and disappear as I experience sexual satisfaction."

THE SIGNIFICANCE OF THE SADIST'S DAY-DREAMING

Henri D.'s day-dream is clearly a masturbation-phantasy, and in the various stages of the reverie one can distinguish the processes of normal love-play: first, arousal—the excitement of tantalisation; then, the deliberate prolonging and intensification of that excitement; finally, the satisfaction of a complete orgasm.

It is obvious that the image of the ostentatious automobile has its source in an inferiority complex that Henri D. suffers from. As a matter of fact, a woman he was once in love with, but who did not love him, told him that to her the ultimate symbol of masculinity was a man at the wheel of a powerful car, especially if he smoked as he drove. (Henri D. does not smoke).

A few talks with my patient revealed the origins of other aspects of his day-dream. Years ago, during a visit to another town, he lost his train ticket and his money and was obliged to find his way home by hitch-hiking. During the journey he met a robust blonde prostitute, who was also hitch-hiking, and she left a deep impression on his mind. The other dream-girl, the redhead, had the appearance of a girl he met only once, when he was a boy, and with whom he fell in love. Henri D. is a middle-aged man. He works in an office and it hurts him to know that the girls in the office refer to him as "the Old Man". More than once he has wished he could "teach them a lesson".

As soon as Henri D. reaches his imaginary castle, the story of the dream—feasible up to that moment—turns into a fairy tale. No longer do we find a theme we can relate back to occurrences in everyday life. The secluded castle is a favourite scene of operations in the books of the Marquis de Sade. (Note again how this feature emphasises the element of immunity from detection and punishment). Henri D. probably 'borrows' the castle from one of de Sade's books he has read.

One peculiarity of this day-dream is that it consists almost solely of preparations for an impressive sadistic scene that never occurs. Even the end of the phantasy has no more to it than the *crescendo* of triumphant eagerness concerning how the two girls must feel when it dawns on them, as the naked,

68

whipped servant-girl comes in, what is in store for them. This build-up of excitement and expectation means more to Henri D. than a carefully imagined scene of lust and passion.

Such masturbation-phantasies are safety-valves. Masturbation, in these cases, may be compared to a lightning-conductor that diverts the potential explosive danger of perverted fancy away from society and buries it in the hidden depths of the masturbator's soul.

OTHER AIDS TO RELEASE

Not all sadistically-minded people are endowed with a vivid imagination, however. Many of them, although willing to forgo full physical satisfaction of their urge, are unable to provide a satisfying compromise entirely by means of their own fanciful ingenuity. They need help in the form of artificial stimulus. For such individuals the collections of reading-matter and illustrations that sado-masochists are so fond of seem to provide an acceptable substitute. Such collections, for example comprising pictures showing situations dear to the owner's libido, are known as 'Satan's bibles'.[1] The illustrations are very seldom made to order. They are usually clippings from magazines, accumulated with infinite patience and pasted into an album, a sort of scrap-book. Sometimes the pictures are cunningly altered to render them better suited to the collector's taste: even a fashion-plate, for instance, can be made into a sado-masochistic scene. Illustrations, adapted in this way to the owner's requirements, are pasted into the album in a certain order so as to form a connected sequence.

The phantasies depicted in these sado-masochistic sequences can reveal a great deal about the peculiar sexual appetites of the collectors. The renowned German sexologist Dr. Wilhelm Stekel, in his book *Sexual Aberrations,* cites an interesting case. He once knew a policeman who showed him a very elegantly-bound album of magazine clippings that the man had altered by drawing obscene figures on them and adding grotesque sexual organs. In a handwritten story accompanying the illustrations the 36-year-old policeman described how he tortured and raped these phantasy-women. Scenes of sexual assault and torments occurred time and again, in a way that

[1] Or 'satanic bibles. See also my book, *Lesbian Love Old and New,* Luxor Press, 9/6.

69

clearly showed how the man's imagination worked. Stekel refers to this sort of painstaking composition as "the bible" of the sado-masochist. The amazing thing is that in real life this sexually obsessed guardian of public morality was a shy, weak, even impotent human being, who in all his life—even after he married—had never successfully engaged in sexual intercourse. Nor had he ever molested anybody. Giving written and pictorial form to his phantasies in his 'bible' was his only way of approximating to sexual satisfaction.

Some years ago I myself met a young Army officer who had been afflicted by a nervous breakdown. A.M., as I shall call him, complained of disquieting disturbances in his nervous system. After a few sessions in my consulting-room he told me of his sado-masochistic interests. He was fascinated by phantasies of corseted women, who were bound, raped, flogged and tortured. At the same time these phantasies disgusted him, and he told me tearfully that he would never think of actually doing horrible things like that to women. He was a small, somewhat reticent young man, who was in reality afraid of women, and had ultimately come to me because he dreaded that one day he would forget himself and commit one of these sex-crimes he so often dreamed of. I told him that merely repressing his phantasies would not solve anything.

"But I'm so ashamed of all these disgraceful ideas!" he said.

At a subsequent session he revealed to me that, some months before, he had taken what was to him a very drastic decision. Until then he had kept his own 'Satan's bible': in that book he had amassed pictures of corseted women that he found in women's magazines, fashion catalogues and so on. With pen and ink he used to adapt those illustrations to his requirements. He was very pleased with his collection and would pore over it for hours in rapture.

"What happened to it?" I asked.

He shrugged his shoulders. "I destroyed it ... I destroyed all trace of it ... Sometimes I am sorry I took that decision, but on soberer reflection I know it was a wise thing to do ..."

"But what made you do that?"

Again he shrugged his shoulders and looked a little embarrassed. "I started to think about myself and about what I was doing in compiling that collection. It struck me as a very childish thing indeed—imagine! a grown-up man carefully

70

cutting out pictures and touching them up in ink and sticking them in a book! I mean to say ... I *had* to put a stop to it, didn't I?"

"Why?"

"Well, because ... because it couldn't go on. It doesn't make sense. I'm twenty-eight now, I'm no longer a child ... I don't need a collection like that any more to keep me happy ..."

"Are you quite sure about that?"

He didn't answer.

I told A.M. that he probably did need that album and that it represented to him a harmless compensation for all those things he would like to do but which could never happen in reality. I warned him that he might only succeed in turning himself into a very unsettled, neurotic and morose person, and the long-term effects of that might be unpredictable but scarcely encouraging.

"But common sense ...", he began.

I told him that in cases like his it wasn't wise to follow the dictates of common sense if these imposed inhibitions that could bring worse consequences in their train. In dealing with people's imaginations it is not easy to say what is childish and what is sensible and so on. I wonder how many sexual offenders have committed their crimes after having tried to do what common sense demanded. It may well be that A.M. still sometimes feels childish, or ashamed of himself, but I am quite sure he is not going to give vent to any act of sadism, for he has his safety-valve once more.

SADISM AND PORNOGRAPHY

There are extraordinary quantities of sadistic literature available, more or less on the open market, to the mental sadist nowadays. Even in television programmes, especially in Britain and the United States, there have been many evidences of sadism, real or implied; and American 'comic'-strips literally abound with representations of whippings, torturings and sex crimes of all descriptions. As I have said, the mental sadist seldom takes these as they stand, for his taste is peculiarly original, and he does not care to be spoon-fed: hence the adaptations I have mentioned. The real danger involved in the dissemination of sadistic 'propaganda' is that it is eagerly sought after and devoured by young people who have not pre-

71

viously been aware of sadistic leanings and the direction of whose libido has not yet been firmly orientated. In other words, these influences may *create* trends besides pandering to those that already exist.

It would, incidentally, be wrong to suppose that this kind of propaganda is of recent origin. As a matter of fact, I have seen American magazines, published in the middle 'thirties—at the time of the Italian campaign in Abyssinia—which are a great deal more outspoken as examples of undiluted pornography than anything I have been shown lately from similar sources. One carries a story called *The White Witch of Addis Ababa*, which deals with two rival newspaper correspondents, a man and a young woman, who suspect each other of double-crossing on a scoop. The male overpowers the female at her apartment in the Ethiopian capital, strips her and binds her, to conduct a search for the secret document he needs and which he has convinced himself she has concealed in her person. "She permitted him to move her limbs freely", the text relates, and as his fumbling arouses sexual desire in them both she asks him to untie her wrists so that they can make love more unrestrictedly. This turns out to be his undoing, for while they are locked in a seemingly ardent embrace she cunningly presses a blood vessel in the back of his neck and causes him to lose consciousness. She manages to slip away from under him and to escape from the building. But her journalist rival has all his weight on her shed clothes and she has to leave without them!

As for sheer sadism, it is difficult to beat a story in one of these magazines, printed, be it noted, mainly for the entertainment of members of the American Armed Forces, in which a woman, still in her early thirties, and her teen-age daughter are captured by a band of a dozen ruffians, who turn out to be lepers. (From the sadist's point of view, the more hideous the oppressor the better!) The poor woman pleads with the gang to spare her virgin daughter. "Do what you like to me, but please," she begs, "have mercy on my little girl!" The men are delighted with this suggestion and force the woman to strip and submit to them each in turn. The daughter is obliged to look on, from a place of concealment, while her mother is used in this way, and ironically caused to think that her mother is giving herself voluntarily in intercourse. This shatters her faith in her mother, so that she no longer cares what happens to them. The culminating indignity comes when the lepers, callously ignoring their promise, strip and deflower the girl and then proceed to submit her to every imaginable humiliation before the eyes of her exhausted mother.

THE APPEAL OF MENTAL SADISM IS TO MEN

In my consulting-rooms I have met many patients who have been ardent collectors of erotic pictures and texts. Countless patients have told me how they hunt day after day for the erotic pictures, pornographic stories, and obscene drawings, that suit their purpose. None of these patients was a woman.

Kinsey has shown that males feel sexually stimulated by looking at certain photographs and drawings or reading obscene literature. Only very few women react in a comparable manner. Women, by and large, are stimulated by different means: by the sound of a voice, perhaps, or while reading a romantic novel.[1]

As a psychiatrist I have questioned hundreds of women and I have learnt that they also have their secret longings, their hidden interests, and sometimes a wild imagination, which may cause them shame or embarrassment. In women's hearts, however, there is more room for romantic feelings and therefore they dream more of idyllic love than men do, and less of lust. That presumably is the reason why so many women fall in love with some unattainable ideal—with film stars, with 'pop singers', with their doctor—or with their psychiatrist.

SYMBOLIC SADISM

The concept of a woman tightly confined in a corset, which we saw was a feature in the case of A.M. cited above, is typical of the imagery of what is called symbolic sadism. The paraphernalia of this symbolism embrace a whole gamut of restrictive devices like cords, chains, handcuffs, corsets, chastity belts, gags, blindfolds, etc.

The symbolic sadist does not actually commit acts of severe cruelty or violence: it is enough for him to render a woman helpless by binding her in such a way that she is completely at his mercy. The mere knowledge that he can do with her what-

[1] This point is more fully dealt with in Dr Vyvyan Howarth's excellent book *Secret Techniques of Erotic Delight*, Luxor Press, 9/6.

ever he likes without the possibility of physical resistance on her part gives him the satisfaction he craves. Astrid, in the case I mentioned a few pages back when I gave the account of my patient Ann who had involuntarily attended a sado-masochistic orgy, was a symbolic sadist, in so far as she did not inflict actual cruelties upon the others. She carried a whip as a symbol more than anything else, and when she used it she did not inflict very severe pain, but the kind of stinging and tingling sensation that is well known to have more or less aphrodisiac effects.

A.M.'s mental sadism was of the symbolic kind, too, for though he imagined rape and tortures for his 'victims', such treatment was the incidental outcome of their being rendered helpless by various measures of physical restraint. The re-straints were more important to A.M. than the sequel; and the reason for this was not far to seek. He was, as I remarked, afraid of women, and he was only able to allay that fear by imagining them rendered helpless and at his mercy.

Fellatio and *cunnilinctus*, when forced upon partners who do not indulge in them by volition, are also manifestations of symbolic sadism. Again, Astrid provides an interesting ex-ample. These ways of orally stimulating the sex organs of male and female, respectively, represent a token abasement.

GENUINE SADISM AND SEXUAL MURDER

Visual, mental and symbolic sadism are all forms that may be called minor or, as we saw earlier, pseudo-sadism, because they are not truly active aberrations; they are extremely pre-valent and relatively innocuous. They differ from genuine sadism not only in the comparatively little harm they cause, but in regard to the degree of moral restraint exercised by the subject. Minor sadists for one reason or another do not actually practise the cruelties they enjoy watching, imagining or anticipating. They perhaps conform to moral standards that are strong enough to restrain them, or possibly they are held back by fear of the consequences.

We must not leave this somewhat lengthy, yet cursory, study without a mention of those sadists at the other end of the scale who exercise no restraint whatever, even to the extent of taking the lives of their victims. Generally such criminals are devoid of any moral conscience.

We should be careful to differentiate between sex-murders and sadistic lust-murders. Most sex-murders are committed as a result of the fear of detection (often amounting to panic) after the victim has been criminally assaulted. In sadistic murders perpetrated to satisfy the criminal's perverted lust the victim is generally further mistreated, even after death. The murders of Marjorie Gardner and Doreen Marshall by the notorious English sadist Neville Heath were of this kind. Hardened police officers, accustomed to the most gruesome sights, turned pale and vomited at the sight of Doreen's horribly mutilated corpse.

Wulffen mentions the case of an Englishman named Alton who went out for a walk in the town one day and lured a child into a thicket. He returned after a while and went to his office, where he noted casually in his diary: "Killed a young girl today. It was fine and hot."

The child was reported missing and sought for. She was eventually discovered hacked to pieces, but some parts of her body were not found. Alton, when charged, did not show the slightest trace of emotion and gave no explanation as to the motive and circumstances of his monstrous crime.

In May 1966 a young couple, Ian Brady and Myra Hindley, were found guilty of savagely murdering ten-year-old Lesley Ann Downey. Before her death the little girl had been stripped and cruelly flagellated; during this treatment her tormentors made a magnetic tape recording of her screams and pleadings.

Absence of emotion and lack of awareness of any sense of guilt are notable features in nearly all sadistic lust-murders. When one reads the spine-chilling reports of the trial of the mass-murderer Haarmann and his accomplice Grans this appalling coldness is all too noticeable. The same may be said of other notorious cases: Verzeni, Vacher, Menesclou, Kürten, Neckermann, Landru, and many others.[1] It stems from the sadist's terrible feeling of isolation, his alienation and aloofness from the world of his fellow-men, his *Verfremdung*, as Brecht calls it.

It is this 'alienation' that constitutes the greatest threat to society today, for this feeling is by no means confined to crimi-

[1] It should be mentioned, however, that Myra Hindley did show apparently genuine signs of remorse when the tape recording of the child's screams was played back in court at the trial.

nal sadists: it is the attitude to society of many youngsters nowadays. 'Sick' jokes; the 'James Bond' craze; modern theatre like that of Pinter, Becket, Ionesco, as well as addiction to drug-taking, and depraved attitudes to sexual immorality— all have their roots in this 'alienation'. Man must come to grips with it if he is to save himself from extinction.

CHAPTER THREE

Sadism in the Female

ATAVISM AND THE BIOLOGICAL FACTOR

So far, from a purely psychological point of view our enquiry has seemed to lead us into something of a deadlock. If sadism in the male is to be explained as a pathological intensification of the masculine sexual character, then, reasoning in the same way, a pathological intensification of the feminine sexual character ought, one would think, to lead to masochism.

I am afraid that many scientists who apply themselves to these matters are inclined to be too one-sided in their reasoning: that is to say, conclusions tend to be arrived at exclusively from the male point of view. But the act of copulation has not the same meaning and importance for the female as for the male. What for the male is an end is for the female only a beginning. It is very necessary to emphasise that all this must be seen, basically at least, within the framework of the biological mechanism.

The female function in procreation consists in reality of four stages:

Stage 1: Fecundation
Stage 2: Pregnancy
Stage 3: Parturition
Stage 4: Lactation.

To induce woman to submit to the laws of her biological mechanism, Nature has endowed stages 1, 2 and 4 with pleasurable sensations.

How the pleasure mechanism works in the male is sufficiently well known; as to its working in the female, I presume that, originally, ultimate submission to the violent lust of the male was the principal pleasure factor in stage 1. As I have pointed out in my Introduction, in an organised society little

77

place is left for this violent way of courting. Nevertheless, many women still long for it, consciously or unconsciously. This atavistic yearning may, in some women, become indistinguishable from masochism. I shall have more to say about this in Part Two under the heading *Masochism in the Female*.

In the third stage no choice or free-will is involved: the act of giving birth is simply inevitable. But the pain and the unpleasantness are quickly forgotten in the bliss of the fourth stage. The greatest joy, psychically and physically, is experienced when the newly-born sucks at the breast of the mother.

I have purposely so far skipped the second stage because it is precisely here that we find clues that may lead to a better understanding of the phenomenon we are seeking to assess. Once impregnation is a fact, the all-important issue is to create the favourable conditions necessary for the undisturbed development of the fetus.

The first important item in this respect is food. In primeval days the choice of things to be eaten was rather arbitrary; therefore the impregnated female was induced to find pleasure in certain foods which happened to be useful to her own well-being and to that of the developing fetus. The all-but-irresistible and frequently illogical cravings that many women have today for certain foods during pregnancy are presumably an atavistic vestige of this primeval trait. At this stage many a woman experiences feelings of euphoria, brought about by an instinctive awareness of the advancing fulfilment of an inner purpose, her *raison d'être*. We may say that the actions of pregnant women are mainly guided by instinct. It is conceivable that these instincts, through influences of different kinds, mental or physical, may be over-developed and become independent of the condition in which they were originally inherent. This may help to explain such a case as the following, mentioned by Krafft-Ebing, of which he could find no plausible interpretation:

A married man presented himself with the scars of numerous cuts on his arms. He explained their origin in the following way: when he wished to approach his young and highly-strung wife carnally, he first had to make a cut in his arm. She would suck the wound and become, during this act, sexually excited.

This reminds us of the behaviour of the female spider of certain species after she has been fecundated. The male is seized by her and sucked dry. Since it is the general rule that

78

animals do not hunt or eat their own kind without provocation, and the male spider is not attacked at his first approach but only after the act of copulation, we assume that the biological mechanism is again at work here. After the act his only usefulness is to serve as a meal. We find this attitude re-emerging in a moderate form among women who regard their husbands merely as begetters of their children and providers of sustenance. Everything else is relentlessly subjected to the great Cause.

The peculiar propensity of the woman mentioned by Krafft-Ebing is sadistic, notwithstanding that her sadism is deviational and not an end in itself, but a means. Such examples, rare as they may be, are suggestive of an ill-defined cannibalistic trait in the female, descending from earlier and cruder forms of life and still vaguely lingering as a throw-back in certain types of the human female. Even so, such a trait would seem to supervene only when there is something abnormal in the female's nervous or mental make-up; in the case cited above the woman was affected by neurosis: she was "highly-strung". In referring to Krafft-Ebing's suggestion that human sadism probably originated in cannibalism (p. 27) I said that cannibalism might possibly account for sadism in the female but I did not believe that it could provide a satisfactory explanation of sadism in the male.

On the other hand, I personally am inclined to think that sadism in the female is an effect of the continual impingement throughout human history of the handicaps of her biological mechanism upon her insistent quest for unhampered self-expression. In other words, it is due to a thirst for revenge against Nature, against her fellow-creatures, particularly the male (and perhaps other women's children), for the loss of social status endured by woman successively ever since the decline of primeval matriarchy. I shall have more to say about this displacement of women in Chapter Five (*Masochism in the Female*). It is a demonstrable fact that female sadists are seldom, if ever, women who enjoy sexual intercourse on equal terms with a chosen male partner or who are endowed with a wholesome attitude towards motherhood. Women who are sexually frustrated, or who are embittered by a sense of inferiority or of powerlessness vis-à-vis men, or are dispirited by repeated unwanted pregnancies, are those most likely to develop sadistic tendencies. Women who marry a man who

79

already has children by another woman often find it difficult and 'against the grain' to show affection or kindness to the foster-children. 'The cruel stepmother' is a household term of universally sinister implication, and researchers like Magnus Hirschfeld have recorded cases of unbelievable cruelties practised by such women. A woman who behaves cruelly to her own offspring does so, in general, only when the child is unwanted by her or regarded with jealousy as an obstacle to the realisation of some selfish aim that supersedes the function of motherhood.

A more harmless release for the dissatisfaction of frustrated women in a world dominated by men is lesbianism. In the Middle Ages they would probably have sought an outlet for their rebelliousness in witchcraft.

INTENSITY OF FEMALE SADISM

Women who do give themselves up to the infliction of cruelties are frequently more thoroughgoing than men. It is a commonplace that "the female is deadlier than the male". It would seem that the borderline between love and hate, as between meekness and cruelty, is more subtle and intangible in women than in men, and their revenge mechanism is more pervasive and less susceptible to restraint. Everyone is familiar with the saying that "Hell hath no fury like a woman scorned". The cruelties of Juliette and her female companions in de Sade's writings are such as to astound even the most depraved of the male monsters of cruelty, and de Sade himself in a footnote comments: "In *Justine*, certain of our readers quibbled that we had portrayed male villains only. Thanks be to heaven, in these pages we are surely safe from such distressing reproach. Evil, alas, one of Nature's primary laws, is manifest in roughly equal measure in every one of her creatures. The more sensitive a person, the more cruel Nature bends him to the invincible yoke of evil. And so it comes about that the fair sex incline more ardently thereto, and indeed with more refinement than men . . ."

History abounds with instances of sadism in women. During revolutions and civil wars there are always women who earn a dismal notoriety by their cruel actions. During the French Revolution women sat for hours at the foot of the scaffold on which stood the guillotine, peacefully knitting, and occasionally gathering hair from severed heads. Under the reign of

Villa in Mexico there was 'La Goyita'; the Spanish Civil War had its 'La Pasionaria'; among crowned heads we find many examples. Catherine de Medici is renowned for her predilection for the whip. Ladies of the court were flogged in her presence. She was also the instigator of the Massacre of St. Bartholomew's Day in which the Huguenots, with their leader Coligny, were murdered in droves. Charles de Coster relates how, after the slaughter, Catherine de Medici and ladies of her court that night went around gazing at the genitals of the slain noblemen by the light of candles. The Empress Theodora, consort of Justinian I; Messalina in ancient Rome; Queen Caroline of Naples; the Tsarinas Anna Ivanovna and Catherine the Great, of Russia; Empress Tsu Hsi of China, to name but a few, are all known for their cruelty and profligacy. There can be little doubt that they derived sexual pleasure, if not complete satisfaction, from their indulgence in cruelty.

SADISM AS AN ATTRIBUTE OF POWER

I would point out here that the sadistic leanings of these empresses and queens must principally have arisen from the fact that a female in the position of an absolute monarch was an anachronism and an anomaly. Their high office, generally thrust upon them or acquired by chance, they had to maintain in a world that was predominantly and manifestly *a man's world*. In an absolute androcracy they held supreme power, even over men. If these women were strong-willed and identified themselves with the power they wielded it was unthinkable for them ever to become dominated by men, least of all sexually, for, as I have expressed already, copulation is felt to involve subjugation of the female. It is therefore not surprising that many such strong-willed female potentates remained single. If they did marry, for the sake of the dynasty for example, the marriage often resulted in strained and frustrated relations.

Nevertheless, physically they were still women and as such subject to the exigences of the biological mechanism of the female. When, through mental strictures, they had to forgo normal means of satisfying the demands of this biological mechanism (which, however, could not be switched off) other ways had to be found to meet those imperious claims. So it is more than probable that the sexual satisfactions of these

81

women were on a sadistic level. Even if they succeeded in overcoming their mental strictures, only a partial gratification of the sex demand was possible.[1] Kings and emperors could have (and generally did have) illegitimate children in plenty without impairing the esteem in which they were held by their subjects; indeed, on the contrary, they thereby enhanced it with this proof of virile potency. Potency, after all, was an attribute of power.

Monarchs not only had to have power, but had to be seen to have it. The power of monarchs was always closely allied to man's eternal belief in, and hope for, miracles. This superstitious concept was centred in the magic power attributed to kings. To give an example: for long the English kings were popularly believed to have the divine gift to heal scrofula (called for that reason the King's Evil) by touching the sufferer. In this way they were supposed to be able to effect a cure which lay quite beyond the scope of contemporary medical science.[2]

But having illegitimate children did *not* at all suit the public image of a queen. Long-lasting relations with the same man were no less out of the question; which may explain the rapid succession of Catherine the Great's favourites. Men foolish enough to become fractious and demanding, not wishing or unable to recognise the inevitable insecurity of their lot as lovers, were in danger of losing their heads.

Varieties of Sadism in the Female: Visual Sadism

The findings of Dr Alfred C. Kinsey and his team of investigators have amply demonstrated that women generally, in contrast to men, do not derive pleasure from the indulgence of sexual phantasy.[3] It is in keeping with this fact, then, that

[1] Messalina, of course, is a notorious exception. Sexually she was insatiable, a nymphomaniac who on one occasion gave herself to "fourteen young athletes". Mark Antony alleged that Cleopatra once had intercourse with 106 men at a brothel.

[2] For those interested in this subject I recommend the reading of Frazer's *The Golden Bough*. Reference to the miraculous gift of the English kings occurs in Shakespeare's *Macbeth*, Act IV, sc. 3.

[3] By sexual phantasy I mean the kind of reverie dealt with in the previous chapter and known sometimes as the masturbator's 'day-dream'. There are notable exceptions, however, especially among female masturbators who are dominated by a fetishist complex. (Dr Howarth gives a significant example in *Secret Techniques of Erotic Delight*, Luxor Press). For the Kinsey team's findings on this subject see *Sexual Behavior in the Human Female*, W. B. Saunders Company, 1953.

82

among the manifestations of minor sadism in women mental sadism plays an inconspicuous part. Visual and symbolic sadism are the most common forms of minor sadism among the female sex. Flagellomania and the impulse to procure are the principal aberrations of the active, genuine, female sadist.

Many female sadists derive satisfaction (or at least pleasurable stimulation) of their urge from witnessing cruelties inflicted upon their fellow-creatures, including other women. Reference has already been made (in the previous chapter) to spectators of both sexes who obtain pleasure from the witnessing of public executions and displays of violence.

At times the degree of sexual excitation aroused in women by this means is quite intense. Magnus Hirschfeld relates: "A few years ago I witnessed the execution of a murderer. Next to me stood the State Attorney's wife, who followed the horrible scene—the condemned man screamed and fought the executioners who were dragging him to the scaffold—with a heaving chest and ecstatic groans that sounded almost lustful. As the axe fell the woman behaved as though she were passing through the moment of orgasm." Because of the complete reliability of the witness in this case no one can have any reasonable doubt about its veracity. There is no need to suppose that Casanova was exaggerating, either, in the following account, although his notorious bragging about his own sexual prowess might make his testimony more suspect. He was, after all, a shrewd observer of the sexual reactions of his feminine companions. He recounts that he and two women friends were present when Robert François Damiens was put to death with hideous cruelty in 1757 for his attempted assassination of Louis XV. Damiens was finally torn to pieces by horses pulling in opposite directions. He was such a powerful man that the horses had to be reinforced by others and his limbs partially severed with a saw before his arms and legs came away from his body. The whole execution lasted several hours and Casanova declares in his memoirs that his women friends were brought to such a state of sexual excitement that both experienced orgasm.

That this form of sadistic scopophilia is often not without an admixture of morbid fetishism is demonstrated by the following two examples, both cited by Magnus Hirschfeld in the records of his life-long investigation into sexual anomalies and perversions. Referring to victims of the Spartacus rebellion in Berlin in 1918 he reports: "I accompanied a woman to the mortuary where, among hundreds of bodies, some of which were shockingly mutilated or had their throats slit, we discovered her son, who had been shot through the head. In the identification hall an endless stream of people, mainly women, were filing past the unidentified bodies and an attendant who knew me called my attention to some girls who had for several days continually rejoined the queue, evidently because they could not tear themselves away from the sight of the male bodies which lay, entirely stripped, before them. The genital organs of the men—mostly soldiers, sailors and civilian Spartacists—had, owing to hæmorrhages and incipient decay, considerably increased in size and the girls could not remove their gaze from them. To the expert it was clear beyond all possibility of doubt that the behaviour of these young women was largely influenced by sexual factors. The expression on their faces was similar to that with which I had seen the women of Madrid and Seville watch the bullfighters in the ring."

The second instance concerns a sale, in London, of ropes with which criminals had been hanged. "Each rope bore a label made out by the executioner, Marwood, stating the criminal's name, the nature of his crime, and the date of his execution. Thus the public could obtain, according to taste, a souvenir of a poisoner, a strangler, or a patricide. The ropes with which killers of women had been hanged were eagerly bid for, and numbers of gentlemen and poetic-looking young ladies fought for the possession of such treasures. One old maid purchased a whole collection of them. The parts of the ropes which had been in actual contact with the neck were in greater demand than other parts."

SYMBOLIC SADISM IN WOMEN

The most important difference between masculine and feminine sadism is that, as I have already implied, in women sadism is more pervasive: it is what Hirschfeld calls "totalitarian". In common parlance, we may say that with women sadism, by and large, is a matter of 'all or nothing'. This is one of the significant distinctions to be noted between this and the majority of other perversions which, in either sex, do not, as it were, monopolise the subject's life. I mean by this that a man or woman may, for example, have a preference for homosexual practices, or be a fetishist or a secret transvestite, without this

84

aberration affecting his or her day-to-day life in any material way or being apparent to other people. But the woman sadist is conditioned by her abnormality in word, thought and deed. Her whole existence, sexually, socially and professionally, is affected.

For this reason, not only are women sadists unlikely to be satisfied with merely mental experiences, or phantasy, but symbolic sadism has little appeal either, in comparison with the hold this manifestation exercises among males. In the male the 'natural' rôle is to dominate, and to a great number (no doubt the majority) of men in whom this desire prevails it is enough to evoke a token submission in the female: hence symbolic sadism in the male is a relatively commonplace phenomenon. But in the female, as I have already suggested, the desire is not so much for dominance for its own sake as for revenge. Where the desire *is* present in a woman to dominate it is by way of emphasising her revenge, so that merely symbolic surrender on the part of the male is scarcely likely to suffice. After all, although the male likes to see himself as the conqueror of the female, women who are shrewd and competent in love-making can and do exercise the upper hand; and to the extent that the man recognises the importance to their mutual contentment of doing what is pleasing to the woman, it is she who is mistress of the situation. Her man, in fact, does submit to her in all successful cohabitation, lawful or otherwise.

The 'traditional' (i.e. *de rigueur*) habiliment of the female symbolic sadist includes long boots of soft leather, sometimes covering the thighs as well as the lower legs, and with spidery heels inordinately high, a leather jacket, usually tight-fitting and extremely *décolleté*, arm-length gloves, and, often, a neck adornment like a dog-collar. Sometimes she favours a mask, and the preferred colour for all her paraphernalia is black—as though to symbolise the doom of male supremacy. It is true that the female active sadist (almost invariably a flagellant, whose partner is an abject masochist) also attires herself in this way, but the costume is symbolic, and sometimes the symbolism is a sufficient end in itself.

English viewers will remember that long black leather boots and a leather tunic were the stock-in-trade of Mrs Emma Peel (played by Diana Rigg) in the television series *The Avengers*, which came to an end early in 1966. The boots actually figured prominently in the introduction along with the credit titles and accompanied by the signature tune. Mrs Peel was a judo expert (among her many accomplishments) and invariably vanquished her masculine assailants and brought them neatly into submission. The bowler-hat, short overcoat and umbrella of her partner seemed to emphasise the fatuous presumption of the male escort, who would have been powerless without her more forthright and resourceful fearlessness. At the same time the confident widow was portrayed as a *femme fatale* whose good looks and fascinating figure cynically ensnared any opinionated male who imagined he could win her favours.

But less aggressive female sadistic symbolists prefer more femininely seductive attire: sheer nylon stockings, abbreviated skirts, dainty high-heeled shoes. There must be something subtly suggestive about long spindly heels, for every female sadist of the symbolic and flagellant varieties apparently feels incomplete without them: perhaps some inverted phallic mysticism provides the dimly-apprehended illusion of turning the tables on the male with his possessive mania for penetration. At any rate, female sadists of the kind we are now considering sometimes derive pleasure from stepping or trampling upon a recumbent male in their high-heeled footwear, prodding him particularly in the region of the genitals. Hirschfeld cites the following interesting case from Havelock Ellis:

" 'As a boy of fourteen, I was once staying with a family who were very friendly with my parents. My principal playmate was the daughter of the house, a strapping, pretty girl some six years my senior, who was an only child.

" 'The girl was always beautifully dressed and had lovely feet and ankles and was naturally aware of this. Whenever possible she dressed in such a manner as to exhibit her good points to the best advantage, wearing short skirts and small shoes with high heels, and missing no opportunity to display her charms in an amusingly coquettish manner. She appeared to take a certain amount of pleasure in *treading* on things that yielded and collapsed under her feet, such as flowers, soft fruit, acorns, heaps of hay, straw or freshly cut grass. During our walks in the garden, where we were entirely alone, I used to watch her stepping on things and generally teased her on account of this peculiar habit. In those days I enjoyed lying on a hearth-rug in front of a good fire, a pleasure I sometimes indulge in even now. One evening I was in this position and the girl—with whom I was alone in the room—walked across the room in order to get something from the mantelshelf, but instead of stretching out her arm over me, she stepped on me, observing that she would show me how "the hay and the straw feels". I naturally entered into the joke and laughed. Having stood on me for some minutes, she raised her skirt slightly and, supporting herself on the mantelshelf with both hands, held one silk-stockinged and daintily shod foot close to the fire in order to warm it, looking down at my flushed face and laughing at me. She was a very attractive and natural girl, and I am fairly certain that on this first occasion, although she evidently enjoyed the feel of my body under her feet, she did not realise my condition, nor do I remember anything to indicate that, while I myself was almost crazed with the desire for sexual satisfaction, the girl was similarly affected. I seized her raised foot, kissed it, and, moved by an absolutely irresistible urge, I drew it to my erect penis. Almost on the instant as her weight fell upon it I experienced, for the first time in my life, a complete orgasm ... I know that the girl enjoyed treading on me just as much as I enjoyed being trod upon. She had a fairly generous dress allowance, and when she noticed that she was giving me pleasure she bought herself many pairs of smart stockings and dainty shoes with the highest and most pointed heels obtainable, which she displayed to me with great delight, insisting that I should lie down, so that she might try them on me. She admitted that she liked to see the heels of her shoes sink into my body as she stepped on me and she enjoyed the cracking of my muscles when she moved her heels about. On each occasion I drew her foot after a few minutes to my penis. She trod cautiously, but always with her full weight —some nine stone—on my abdomen, regarding me with bright eyes, flushed cheeks, and trembling lips as the palpitation of my penis communicated itself to her foot at the moment of pollution. I have not the slightest doubt that she experienced orgasm at the same time, although we never discussed the matter. We repeated this in the course of several years at every favourable opportunity, and after a separation of one or two months, four or five times daily.' "

Other women prefer to play "gee-gees" with men, as one of them expresses it. They like to pretend that the male partner is a horse and they the rider or driver. One "highly cultured, respectable woman of the highest social class in an excellent financial position" thus describes her preference: " 'He would lean with both hands on a chair, so that he should look as though he had four legs. Naturally, he would be completely undressed. I would place a table behind him, and a chair on the table and I would sit on this chair or box, seize the reins, the other end of which would be in his hands, or in his mouth, tug at the reins a few times, and make a smacking sound with my lips. If this humane method of starting the horse proved unsuccessful, then I would use the whip. The man would have to run, with me regulating the pace . . . Apart from this, I could be very charming to the man of my choice, but he would have to love me in order to be worthy of my affection.' "

The symbolism in the above case is clearly demonstrated: the woman is willing to be "very charming", i.e. to resume her feminine rôle in time and in the 'proper' place, but only after she has thoroughly subdued the male. Here is the revolt of the female sadist in unmistakable guise: first the revenge for timeless indignities and then renewed submission. This rebellion of the woman impelled to assert herself is what Alfred Adler has called "woman's masculine protest". But I do not suggest that such an attitude is found only among feminists or feminine emancipationists. Of course it is 'instinctive', that is to say subconsciously impulsive. Here is an instance of female determination to dominate that first reveals itself in a child.

Emile Zola in one of his novels has created a character called Thérèse who, at the age of six, torments her childhood companion Colombel, who is small and slender. She likes to lead him deep into the garden, jump on his back and make him carry her about. She persists in this sport for hours at a time and while mounted on his shoulders she squeezes his throat and presses her heels hard in his sides so that he can hardly breathe. When, so tired that he almost faints, he stumbles and falls, she bites his ear till she draws blood, and clings to him so tenaciously that her small sharp fingernails penetrate his skin. And thus, by coercion and cruel treatment, she forces poor Colombel to gallop about the huge garden with her on his back like a great lady on her horse.

In this case, however, there is an interesting sequel . . . Ten years later Colombel and Thérèse meet again. They are walking, on a summer evening, in the shadow of the chestnut trees in the old garden. Suddenly, in the darkness, they pause at a narrow path, and Colombel stands aside to let her go first.

She pushes him ahead of her and, with a return of her childhood agility, springs on his back and, in a changed voice, exclaims: "Go on! Carry me!" She seizes the stick he is carrying and strikes him on the thighs. Sitting astride his shoulders and half throttling him with her powerful legs, she forces him to run like a madman through the dark garden. But when she wants him to put her down he grips her knees and runs faster. The horse has bolted and is dragging its mistress. She beats him furiously with the stick and scratches him with her painted fingernails, but heedless he runs on till they come to a shed where the gardener keeps his tools. There he throws her on the ground and rapes her. "At last", writes Zola, "it was his turn. Now he was the master."

Tantalisation is another favourite weapon of female symbolic sadism. We have already seen how the girl who liked to walk and trample on her prone male companion also took pleasure in dressing smartly to incite his admiration, and in displaying her attractive legs by wearing sheer stockings and short skirts. Also she knew that in standing on him and raising her skirt slightly she was enabling him to some extent to look up her clothes and obtain a tantalising view of her limbs. Many an attractive woman, by displaying her charms as brazenly as possible, even beyond the normally accepted limits of respectability, is taking delight in the knowledge that she is inducing an erection in the watching male, who is fettered, as it were, by the obligation to control himself and must languish in frustration.

The Female Flagellant

I have already said that on the whole sadism tends to exercise a more consistent hold in the female than in the male: it is likely to permeate her entire existence. Fortunately, it most frequently expresses itself in an infinite variety of only minor forms, from cynical tantalisation by the seductive but frigid temptress to the domination by the termagant of her henpecked husband: the only common factor is the impulse to dominate in order to annihilate the myth of male supremacy.

But the active genuine female sadist is altogether more formidable. The ways in which her sadistic urge expresses itself may be more restricted in variety than those manifested by her male counterpart but they are not likely to be less intense in degree. Though we may well dismiss as absurd the countless obnoxious 'refinements' described by de Sade in *Juliette* to confirm his point that "the fair sex" commit even more hideous enormities than the other, nevertheless history and the records of researchers in sexual anomalies provide ample proof that diabolical cruelty in any form is not a male monopoly. Even so, atrocities like sadistic lust-murder and necrophilia are almost exclusively carried out by males, whereas female sadists tend to confine themselves to the satisfaction of such urges as flagellomania and procurement. This is not to say, however, that women sadists are devoid of ingenuity in the invention of new cruelties to inflict upon helpless victims.

I suppose the difference between the male and female sadist who are equally immune to any sense of guilt is a difference of motivation. Whereas the male is in such cases perpetrating cruelties with the rapt resourcefulness of a dilettante seeking new sensations, the female is, above all else, consumed with the desire to subjugate absolutely, even to destruction, in order to establish her indisputable supremacy.

When I refer to flagellomania in this connexion I am not thinking, at this point, of the female flagellant who wields her whip against the submissive masochistic male. This class of woman sadist will be considered later. I refer to the urge to subdue persons of either sex by means of chastisement. The motive of punishment provides the usual pretext, of course, but to the true sadist this is never more than incidental: the real aim is subjection, not reformation. In the days when rods and birches were used in girls' schools (a practice now almost universally done away with), it was the custom to make the culprit kiss the instrument of castigation before the flogging began and afterwards to kneel and humbly thank the flogger for the 'salutary' lesson just received. The symbolism in this must be obvious. And indeed, practically all literature on the subject of female flagellation, particularly, stresses the satisfaction to be obtained from reducing an especially proud or rebellious girl to a condition of pleading, tearful, quivering abjection.

There are countless women who, even if they have no overt desire to inflict pain themselves in this and similar ways upon offenders, real or imagined, of either sex, not only would have no objection to such treatment being meted out but would like to enjoy the spectacle. In the days of the bridewells, where prostitutes and other female prisoners were publicly whipped, there were usually as many women among the eager spectators as men, and their number included women of all classes and in all walks of life. Whenever campaigns have been conducted for the abolition of corporal punishment as a judicial measure, women have been as vociferous as men in advocating its retention. In ancient Rome ladies flogged their male and female slaves unmercifully, or ordered them to be flogged in their presence, for any trifling misdemeanour, whether proved or not. Anglo-Saxon women often flogged their servants to death, and Zimmermann in *Travel Notebook*, commenting on the situation of negro slaves in the southern States of America, says: "Negro servants are veritable martyrs to white women". In an autobiography called *Memoirs of a Domestic Servant* (London, 1797) the writer records how he was made by his mistress to whip a page-boy in her presence. Later he was ordered to whip her two nieces, and he did so.

The notorious Mrs Brownrigg, executed at Tyburn in 1767 for the murder of a workhouse apprentice, Mary Clifford, who died from ill-treatment and malnutrition, used to thrash the naked bodies of the girls in her care until she was exhausted. Then she used sometimes to get her husband or her young son to go on with the beatings under her sadistic supervision. Here are clearly demonstrated not only the impulse of flagellomania but the scopophilia related to it, and the urge to procure as well.

By the latter phrase I wish to imply more, of course, than the usual connotation of procuring a person for prostitution: it also may involve the subjection of another to sexual assault or violation, and exposure of another (usually a girl) against her will or without regard to her volition to any form of indecency, humiliation or shame. In causing her husband and her son to take part in the flogging of nude girls Mrs Brownrigg was at the same time satisfying the impulse to procure— which is very strong in some women.

A remarkable case in which scopophilia, the urge to procure, and sadistic violation, are all present came before a German court when a 37-year-old man and his 34-year-old wife were jointly charged with the rape of a young girl who was a frequent visitor to the wife. The man was charged with having violated the girl in his bedroom, while his wife helped him by

91

pinioning the girl's arms. It was revealed at the trial that the couple had committed a number of such assaults.

Another, perhaps the most remarkable, case in which all these manifestations are observable, with the almost paradoxical admixture of female masochism, is the following, quoted from Magnus Hirschfeld's records in *Sexual Anomalies and Perversions*. The case comes originally from Wulffen.

" 'A young widow had two very pretty daughters, aged 12 and 14 respectively, and a 15-year-old son. After her husband's death the woman suffered from intense sexual excitements which evoked sadistic tendencies in her. Making the acquaintance of an unmarried man of mature age, she consulted him in family matters and soon complained to him that her children were misbehaving; they were all indulging in self-abuse and the boy was in the habit of spying on his sisters when they were naked in the bathroom. These allegations were probably wholly untrue, but the woman began to ask the friend of the family to chastise the boy, to begin with, for his misdeeds. The friend at first believed all the mother's allegations and chastised the boy, the mother being present on each occasion. She provided rods, riding-crops, and whips. The boy had to strip, lie down entirely naked on the sofa, etc. His genital member was over-developed for his age, and the friend took a delight in the matter. Later the mother also asked him to chastise the girls, first the younger, then the elder. The two girls had to bend over the arm of the sofa and the mother herself raised their skirts and pulled down their knickers and a whip with twenty-two thongs was used on them. Later the girls had to strip. When the elder girl refused to appear naked in front of the 'family adviser', she was permitted to wear a tiny pair of red bathing shorts which hardly covered her genital organs. The mother held the child, and the chastisement was carried out in such a manner that the girl lay on her back on the sofa and her legs were bent back, towards her head. The mother frequently let the bathing shorts slip off, so that the chastising man could see the girl's vagina. The sadistic mother then invented a still more exciting scene and the two girls, both naked, were chastised together. Finally, she asked the friend, after he had covered the bodies of the three children with red weals, to be chastised herself. She lay down on the sofa and had her wish granted.' "

92

We see, then, that sadism in the female, in its infinite variety of forms, is not less complicated than the corresponding condition in the male. Basically it springs from the urge to dominate, but not (as it is in the male) by way of confirming an established and seemingly immutable right; rather the impulse to dominate in the female is a demonstration of revolt against the existing phenomenon of male superiority which is apprehended as iniquitous and pernicious. Once there is a disposition to indulge the urge, the revolt may take many forms, some of them perhaps hardly recognisable as sadistic at all. Some kinds of dominant women become obsessed by a kind of megalomania, a lust for power for its own sake, and so their aggressiveness is directed against other women also, or against all and sundry who stand in the way of their self-assertion. At other times female aggressiveness against the female sex may be due to jealousy or rivalry or resentment.

If a female sadist accepts the challenge to oppose men's right to dominate women, she may not be content to attack that dominance alone, but may feel impelled to punish other women for their subservience in yielding. The situation is comparable to a total war in which the non-combatant is destroyed as well as the enemy. Her attitude to life may be summed up in the slogan: 'They who are not with me are against me.' Such a female aggressor is prepared to regard the whole world as potentially at enmity with her and therefore as requiring to be subjugated and forced into submission. The male sadist, by comparison, is more directional in his fanaticism.

It is easy to see why women imbued with militantly feminist principles like those I have been outlining become lesbians, especially of the 'butch' (i.e. masculine) type. They are in revolt against men and male dominance, but not against sex itself. Hence they may prefer to satisfy their biological demands in a more or less total negation of the male's right to intervene.

When in a woman an innate sadistic trait combines with homosexual leanings and a strong maternal instinct there may emerge such a figure as Edith Cadivec. This woman ran a school in Vienna, her pupils being drawn from the well-to-do classes. Posing as a philanthropist, she offered to educate a number of poor children without charge and even to adopt some of them. An investigation carried out after certain complaints had been received by the authorities revealed that her exclusive school was actually a flagellating parlour. Among her clients were persons of the highest ranks and social positions in Vienna. The children whom she so magnanimously took under her wing were whipped—for the entertainment of her wealthy customers. She made a full confession at her trial, which took place in 1924, and admitted that she experienced intense feelings of lustful pleasure when chastising children. She was sentenced to six years' imprisonment but was released after four years.

Cadivec wrote her apologia in *Das lasterhafte Weib* (*The Depraved Woman*), in which she gave a glowing description of the sadistic female, in her eyes the most perfect form of womanhood. This 'perfect' woman has no need for such base acts as sexual intercourse with males. She revels in scourging the writhing body of her naked slave until "with an insane outcry of lust his white heart's blood squirts out under the whip". After the scourging the woman says simply: "Come!" The slave must now satisfy the lust that has been aroused in her by the administering of the flogging—but not by copulation as one naïvely might think, but by performing *cunnilinctus* "for hours".

It is perfectly obvious that Cadivec was indeed what her judges designated her—"an incorrigible sadist". Her attitude towards the children in her school was distinctly that of a tireless flagellant; at the same time her conducting of her 'educational' establishment was undoubtedly satisfactory to many, if not most, of her wealthy clients, and allowances must be made for the fact that the school was her principal source of income. In defence of the cruel treatment of her pupils she makes a plea for the right of educators to chastise the children in their care. She maintains that every mother finds a sensuous pleasure in the chastising of her children, such occasions being "much-longed-for oases in the daily humdrum". She comments warmly and at some length on the wonderful *Wonne* (rapture) of both mother and daughter during, and more especially after, a punishment. The prototype of her ideal sadistic female was one of her most intimate friends, and she declares that she had more than once been present at whippings administered by this friend. She herself preferred to whip girls. No doubt the "rapture" to be derived from thrashing a mere male would be less intense!

All the same, the following is a significant abstract from her first novel, *Bekenntnisse und Erlebnisse* (*Confessions and Experiences*), which appeared under the pseudonym of Cadwé, with no place or date of publication mentioned. This episode was once cited by Sigmund Freud during one of his lectures in Vienna as the classical example of the mixture of ruthless egoism, vanity, cunning and bourgeois attitude of mind which typify the average active flagellant. The story deals with the education of a young man called Franz Kilsch.

"After the letter of Franz' father came, I travelled at once to Böhmen to pick up my new pupil. Franz was waiting for me in the station. At first sight we knew we should like each other, as we were of similar age, both of us tall, and without the usual suspicions people seem to be doomed to have of each other.

"As we lived in the same house, made available to us through Franz' father, we soon got to know each other very well, and I realised, what I had hoped and expected from the beginning, that my strong will dominated this man. I took his body and his soul as objects that belonged to me and used them according to my sexual fancies. Franz was by character the masochistic partner who was just waiting to be taken by an authoritarian woman. He used to kiss the hands of his severe mistress with a dog-like devotion, knowing he was there only to provide the erotic pleasures his 'Domina' desired.

"Consequently I educated him in such a way that he did not dare to *share* the feelings of lust I experienced. And when he showed signs of being sexually involved, of being *weak*, I took the whip and taught him to behave. Gradually he became part of me, an extension of my whims, and precisely this extreme submission drove me mad and brought me into ever longer-lasting states of erotic frenzy. One evening I felt completely obsessed. I knew a sublime moment was approaching ...

"I now order Franz to undress entirely and to prepare the whipping-bench. Tonight he shall be a real victim! As he realises my demoniacal intoxication his excitement rises to such an extent that he cannot hide his shameless passion. I whip him to expunge his rut but he lies down with his member brazenly erect, his hands tied together behind his back, and

95

slowly his tongue starts to play with and caress me. The agile movements of his tongue concentrated on the centre of my lust, the knowledge that this creature who makes me undulate in one uninterrupted series of lascivious outbursts is entirely helpless, is unable to satisfy himself in any way whatever, throw me into a heavenly spasm.

"I loose his bonds, tell him to get up and order him, with a command of my hand, to lie down on the whipping-bench. He obeys. I fasten his body with leather straps to the bench and stretch his arms and legs until he cannot move.

"In a shameless way his erect member stands up from his manacled body. Smoking a cigarette, I sit on his face. I don't laugh, I don't show any affection for him. I just rub my body against his mouth letting him feel that he is merely an instrument, a slave to serve his mistress, his goddess.

"This time, however, I want more than oral satisfaction, I want the function of his masculinity . . . But he shall not be a man! His member shall be nothing more than the sheer communication between a powerless and an authoritarian body. I mount him and move. My child-slave groans; he stammers and utters his confession of dog-like devotion and rut. More and more raging I dance on this creature. He cannot move, he cannot regulate his lusts. I sense that his climax is imminent and forbid it. His semen shall not ejaculate before I say so. Not to enjoy but just to function is he there. At last I shout 'now' and like a vampire I suck the life-force out of him with jerking movements . . .

"I sent Franz away and sat down in my room. Looking at the stars, I knew this man was nothing more than the sexual component I needed to become pregnant. From this slave-child another child would be born. Now Franz had become a nothing. He could disappear. I didn't want the man, I wanted to be a mother. All other things were valueless . . ."

PART TWO
MASOCHISM

FEMALE SADO-MASOCHISM: The shaven head, black patent leather, tight corset, and fetters, typical of a sado-masochistic relationship

(Drawing by Wighead)

CHAPTER FOUR

Masochism in the Male

Leopold von Sacher-Masoch was born in 1836. He survived a delicate babyhood to grow up into a very able student, and become a lecturer in History at the University of Graz when he was only twenty years of age. However, he soon made up his mind to devote himself entirely to literature. He composed several historical works of some importance and a number of short stories and other compositions before he became obsessed by the theme that was to dominate the rest of his life and was to bear his name for all time. For his first full-length novel he chose a historical subject (the fall of the Magyar dynasty) and in this work his strange *penchant* is already becoming manifest, in that the women he depicts are resolute and cruel while the men tend to be represented as vacillating and meek.

He was, even at that stage, clearly fascinated by purposeful and unrelenting women, and indeed the theme that came to dominate his thinking and conduct was that a man needs to be humiliated and to suffer physically at a woman's hands in order to experience sexual satisfaction. But the full flavour of his peculiar aberration was yet to be tasted, and its savour became known unmistakably with the appearance of the most famous of all his works—*Venus in Furs*.[1] Actually this was one of six stories making up Part One of his ambitious work *Das Vermächtnis Kains (The Legacy of Cain)*, which was to comprise six parts (dealing, respectively, with Love, Property, The State, War, Work, and Death), each part containing half a dozen stories ; but this project was destined to remain unaccomplished. In this major composition the author set out to

[1] An excellent edition of *Venus in Furs* is available in this same series by Luxor Press, 9/6.

attack the institution of monogamy and purported to show what was wrong with contemporary society and how its maladies could be cured. The first part begins with a preamble in the form of a tale called *The Wanderer*, and this is followed by five other stories dealing with a number of themes. But the most famous by far is *Venus in Furs*, which soon circulated widely throughout Europe and found its way to the United States of America.

The Legacy of Cain was begun during Sacher-Masoch's first experience of sexual bondage—the period of his association with Anna von Kottwitz (or Kottowitz). Her husband was a boor and a bully who was perfectly willing to tolerate a *ménage à trois* provided he was the one to wield authority. Sacher-Masoch, however, would have none of that: although he enjoyed, in fact as well as in fancy, being maltreated by a woman, he would never allow himself to be bullied or even browbeaten by a man—unless this served to intensify still further the humiliations imposed upon him by his mistress. Once he went so far as to challenge von Kottwitz to a duel but the baron declined the challenge. Sacher-Masoch himself was no coward, and even when he accepted a position of subservience to a woman he would never allow her to suppose that she was his superior intellectually. He was always acutely conscious that his peculiar erotic taste constituted a sexual anomaly and voluntarily confessed as much. While his surrender to his women oppressors was complete from the physical point of view, he insisted upon retaining absolute freedom in other respects.

After her husband had refused to defend his honour in the duel to which Leopold had challenged him, Anna von Kottwitz lost all interest in the despicable baron and began to cohabit with her lover. She failed to come up to Leopold's expectations, however, for she proved to be anything but the natural 'sultana' or 'Domina' he was longing for: she was in fact somewhat dull-witted and inclined to nag. Nevertheless, there was one consolation: she was possessed of limitless sensuality (she once told Leopold she could see no reason why a woman of courage should not give herself up to a life of prostitution), and she had no objection at all to flagellating her lover if that was what he wanted and if it enabled her to get her own way, which it certainly did. They frequently discussed, and no doubt she also inflicted, an abundance of heterogeneous torments. Once she even, half-humorously, offered to chop his head off, but this idea was abandoned in consideration of its disastrous finality.

Soon Leopold conceived the idea (or rather gave expression to it, for it had long been in his thoughts) of persuading Anna to give herself to another man. The urge to procure, as we saw, is a frequent enough concomitant of sadism; often, in the case of the masochist, it expresses itself in pleasure at the thought of his beloved being seduced by another man, the more so if he can actually witness their love-making. Whereas the sadist uses the forcible violation of his victim as a means of humiliating her, the masochist cunningly brings about the seduction of his partner in order to humiliate himself. After unsuccessfully attempting to arrange a liaison between Anna and a Habsburg Archduke (no less a personage than the Governor of Graz), Leopold had to come down a peg or two. He finally arranged for her to be seduced by a fellow who called himself a count. Even so, Leopold was denied the pleasure of witnessing their copulation: he was only told about it afterwards. He soon recovered from his disappointment, however, and became immensely stimulated sexually as he dragged out of Anna the somewhat banal details of the affair. The partner proved to be a shameless impostor, a mere chemist's assistant of Russian origin whom the police were after. What was worst, he had infected Anna with syphilis.

Sacher-Masoch responded to this latest indignity with typical chivalry: he challenged the bogus count to a duel, but the offender pleaded a weak heart and declined to fight. (It was this act of craven capitulation, in fact, that first aroused Sacher-Masoch's suspicions about the man's credentials and background). Relieved to find that he himself was not affected by the disease, he nevertheless felt obliged to terminate the relationship.

Afterwards he wrote of Anna in extravagant terms as his first true love, sublimated her beauty and charm into something rich and strange, and lamented her 'betrayal', which, of course, he himself had purposefully engineered. As we shall see, this tendency to dramatise his humiliation and to regard himself as more sinned against than sinning is typical of the male masochist.

Sacher-Masoch's novel *The Separated Wife* is based upon his association with Anna von Kottwitz, and it was this book which brought him into contact with Fanny Pistor, who called herself Baroness Bogdanoff. She wrote to him from Germany in 1869 telling him how much she had enjoyed reading *The Separated Wife,* how highly she esteemed him as a writer, that she sympathised entirely with his tastes in sexual relationships and inferred that she would make a truly satisfying 'Domina'. She sent a bundle of manuscripts, soliciting his opinion of her literary talent. Here, it seemed, was the ideal partner: she gave promise of providing in full the sexual stimulation he craved, and yet she clearly offered no threat to his integrity and independence in the intellectual sphere. At once Sacher-Masoch responded with the utmost enthusiasm, though characteristically tempered with chivalrous respect and propriety.

Fanny proved to be no baroness, but she was imaginative and possessed of a lively enough intelligence to understand exactly what the now famous author wanted. Very soon an arrangement was made between them and ratified in a "treaty" or compact, in which Fanny's own selfish interests were well safeguarded, indicating that she exercised a controlling influence in the compiling of it. For example, the period during which he was to be her slave and to comply unreservedly with all her demands was six months. She was not the sort of woman to tie herself to this crazy kind of life for very long. But while it lasted it could be fun and a great opportunity to pick the celebrated writer's brains, and she intended to exploit him to the utmost.

In their compact Leopold pledged himself to execute all Fanny's wishes to the letter and without question during a period of six months; any favours she might grant him would be in the nature of a gracious condescension; she was not to ask or expect of him any conduct unbecoming to a man of honour and a gentleman of rank; she would allow him six uninterrupted hours every day to attend to his literary work, and she would never interfere in any way with his correspondence or his work as an author; she on her part would wear furs as often as possible and especially when she was about to humiliate or punish him. The whole arrangement would be regarded as at an end when the six-month period expired and everything that had happened between them would thereupon be consigned to oblivion and never referred to again by either of them. The six months need not run consecutively but might be made up of various periods not exceeding six months in all. The document was duly signed by both of them and regarded as binding them equally.

They then went off on a tour of Italy, with Leopold in tow as her valet and porter 'Gregor', travelling in third-class compartments, while Fanny enjoyed all the comforts and attentions his wealth could provide. Now he resorted to the same tactics he had used in the case of Anna: he urged Fanny to give herself to a lover, a suggestion she was more than willing to comply with. In Italy counts and marquises, not to say archdukes, were not easy to come by, and Leopold (alias Gregor) had to be satisfied with her choice of an opinionated and not very talented Italian actor named Salvini. Leopold promptly convinced himself that this popinjay looked positively Apollo-like and referred to him as "the Greek". He, of course, is the Alexis Papadopolis of *Venus in Furs*. Thereafter, whenever Leopold sought a complaisant lover for his mistress of the moment he alluded to the answer to his prayers as a Greek, though to be sure they seldom, if ever, measured up to his optimistic standards.

With unsolicited attentions the untiring Gregor persistently interrupted Fanny and Salvini in romantic interludes, hoping to catch them in the act of making love, and spied through keyholes or hung about outside their room always in anticipation of coming in upon something worth seeing. Once or twice his snooping was rewarded by brutal treatment at the hands of the ever-more-arrogant actor, who pretended to think he was disciplining an insolent menial; and it made the punishment much easier to bear when Fanny urged the lover on to the infliction of fresh indignities.

The truth is, however, that Fanny was at heart a very warm-blooded, highly-sexed woman who liked her love affairs to be uninhibited and straightforward: she found it a bore to have to be constantly playing a part, dressing up in furs, luxurious though they were and a well-worth-while consolation; she disliked having to exert herself in vigorous whipping scenes, though she fully entered into the spirit of the thing while they lasted; above all, she did not care to have to make love under the watchful eye of her slavish admirer. So when the six-month contract expired it was not renewed. Sacher-Masoch was no fool when it came to understanding womanly psychology: he realised unerringly that there was little point in protracting such a relationship *ad nauseam*. Besides, he had not wasted his time. He had enjoyed his moments of very thorough and highly satisfying castigation. What is more, he had religiously performed a full six-hour stint of literary composition every day and added greatly to his output. He had, in particular, produced *Venus in Furs*, which was destined to make a lasting name (of sorts) for him and would prove a highly successful creation, in which his fertile imagination supplied details that had (unfortunately, in his view) been missing from the real scene. In this book Leopold himself emerges as Severin, Fanny as Wanda von Dunajew (pronounced Doonayeff), and, as I have said, Salvini the Italian as Alexis the Greek.

In 1871 Sacher-Masoch, then thirty-five, became involved with Aurora Rümelin, who was to become his wife for twelve eventful years and bear him three sons, as well as bring up Lina, his daughter by a French actress, when the foster-parents tired of looking after her. The exact manner in which their association began is complicated and need not concern us here. It is enough to say that Sacher-Masoch was again taken in: Aurora, who for months kept herself at arm's length, not even allowing him to kiss her, constantly wore a mask to conceal her features, and refused to reveal her true identity, calling herself Wanda von Dunajew—a ruse that the childish Leopold was all too happy to encourage. She pretended to be a married woman, though she·was actually single and twenty-seven years old. She only consented to become his wife when she had made absolutely certain that she could have him on her own terms.

To accomplish this she drew up a "treaty", or contract, insisting upon his acceptance of it in full. This document laid it down that Sacher-Masoch was thenceforward to renounce his individuality entirely and become her slave grovelling in the dust. If he should ever forget his position she was to have the right to punish him in any way she chose. She should be entitled to use the utmost cruelty and if she were even to mutilate him he would have to endure it uncomplainingly and kiss the foot that trampled upon him. If he ever tried to escape she should have the right to torture him to death by every imaginable means. Whatever she might demand of him was to be fulfilled, even though it might involve his committing a crime. His honour, his life, his intellect, his manhood—all were to be surrendered to her entirely. If the day ever came when he felt he could no longer endure such servitude it would be for him to find release by destroying himself: she for her part would never set him free.

It was, of course, an absurd document, clearly devised by a shrewd, scheming, ignorant woman, and what was worse and by no means escaped the notice of Sacher-Masoch, a deliberate and transparent travesty of the agreement between the fictional Wanda and Severin in *Venus in Furs*. What worried Leopold most was that Aurora was commanding him to sacrifice his intellect, his honour and, if need be, to stoop to crime at her behest. This kind of surrender he had always vowed he would never make. He could hardly fail to be aware that she was determined to marry him (he was, after all, a fairly rich and certainly famous writer and she had literary pretensions herself so that he could be of great help to her in this respect), but by now he was completely infatuated and he must have sensed that his total surrender could not be long delayed. He evaded the issue by sending Aurora a guarded and (for him) remarkably cautious reply. His heart and mind were equally full of her, he told her, and though he had not yet seen her face she irradiated a mystic power that subjugated him completely, as though it were something supernatural. His life belonged to her, he assured her ... But their fate, like birth and death, would be fulfilled when the hour came and if either of them tried to accelerate or retard the march of destiny it would be a vain attempt. Not to tell her this would be "a failure of loyalty" on his part.

Not surprisingly this response did not satisfy the new 'Wanda'. She had to have something far less evasive. She allowed a fortnight to go by without deigning to answer. When she condescended to visit him again he was almost out of his mind with neurotic anxiety. She required more help from him for a story she was writing and went so far as to demand a whole chapter of his own composition. When he told her gently that she ought to attempt it herself first and he would be pleased to help by correcting and improving her work, she let herself go. She put on a fur jacket, picked up a whip (there was always one handy) and belaboured him thoroughly until he was writhing and groaning at her feet. Immediately afterwards there was a reconciliation and a new understanding. Aurora had won. He would sign the agreement as she wished, on condition that she removed the offending mask. Even so, he was forced to sign first, and then the moment she had made him wait so long to witness came. She was not a beautiful woman by any means, though he extravagantly extolled her as "dazzling". He later consoled himself by professing that he saw something of a demon in her mien, which there certainly was not. They went through a form of marriage. It was not until October 1873, however, that they were married officially, and she was then introduced to his family who, of course, saw through her at once and strongly disapproved.

It was only when 'Wanda' was completely confident that she could handle Leopold efficiently that she decided she could afford to risk revealing the truth about herself and her background. She had never been married; she assuredly was not aristocratic—she had in fact worked in a factory; she had had four lovers. This last admission delighted her husband, who assured her there would be many more.

It is not my purpose to trace the ups and downs of Sacher-Masoch's matrimonial experiences. During the early years of his life with 'Wanda' he prostituted his unquestionably outstanding literary ability by producing inferior compositions—'detective stories' and cheaply sensational novels—as a means (so he claimed) of keeping the wolf from the door and maintaining 'Wanda' in the manner he considered she deserved. But from the beginning he was obsessed by the idea of further humiliating himself by persuading her to give herself to other men. At first she was reluctant, and even disgusted, especially when the 'lover' he obtained for her at any and every opportunity was evidently not one who appealed to her in the least. But little by little she became accommodatingly promiscuous. Leopold, for his part, never let slip an opportunity of being whipped and ill-treated by any female willing to oblige, whether young or old, including women employed in the Sacher-Masoch household. One good-looking young girl whom 'Wanda' had taken into her service as a lady's maid was summarily dismissed when her mistress discovered that she was dutifully satisfying her master's every erotic whim.

It was inevitable that the course of such a bizarre marriage would not run smooth for long. Leopold von Sacher-Masoch became progressively more and more dominated by his addiction to the lash, and his writings, even when not concerned directly with sex, showed signs of being tainted by this urge.

'Wanda', on the other hand, became increasingly bored by it all: she resorted to the forms of treatment demanded by her husband whenever she wanted her own way, or to restore peace and contentment in the home, or when she wished to have sexual relations with him, for it never failed to arouse his amorous passion. She had long accustomed herself to the realisation that he was in the grip of a pathological abnormality, but regarded it as harmless enough as far as their own relationship was concerned, even though it was at times a bit of a nuisance. What chiefly caused her anxiety was the fear that the children might develop the same tendencies.

The break came in January 1883, when Sacher-Masoch, then just forty-seven, told 'Wanda' and her lover Jacob Rosenthal (known by his *nom de plume* of Jacques Ste Cère) that he was determined to leave her for ever and to cohabit with Hulda Meister, a German secretary whom 'Wanda' had thrashed and humiliated some ten months before when she had learned of their goings-on. The following year Hulda and Leopold were living together in Leipzig and Hulda became a mother, bringing into the world a daughter for Leopold, whom they named Olga. About the same time the death of his favourite son, Sacha, was a cruel blow to Leopold, from which he never fully recovered. It embittered him and made him more than ever determined to persist with the divorce, although both he and 'Wanda' were Roman Catholics and despite the attempts of his legal advisers to restrain him.

At last 'Wanda' was divorced, and shortly afterwards she was deserted by her lover also. She became a pitiable and eventually a rancorous and vindictive creature She resolved to write her memoirs and vowed in the most vituperative terms that she would expose her ex-husband in such a way that people would feel sick to read about him.

It was not until Hulda Meister had borne him a second daughter that she and Sacher-Masoch were able to marry. They settled at Lindheim. With unruffled devotion to duty and certainly with typical German thoroughness, Hulda did her level best to be an ideal wife. But she was completely lacking in the qualities and appearance of a 'Domina'. Although Leopold professed to be idyllically happy with her his old appetites still lurked, all the more troublesome for being unsatisfied, to torture him in daydreams and nightmares. He continued to correspond with 'Wanda', whom he now made the scapegoat

107

for his past behaviour. He alleged to her that he would never have entertained his "fancies" as she called them if she had not, for her own selfish ends, awakened and stimulated them. "If you had loved me I would have wished for nothing more", he wrote. It was her indifference, her ingratitude, her cruelty, he told her, that had given rise to his "fancies", which in any case no one need reproach him with since they did no one any harm but himself. "The real truth", he concluded, was that she understood all too well that the only way she could bind him to her side was with "the devilish fetters of sensuality". We shall see in a moment that this kind of casuistry is characteristic of the ingenuity to which masochists resort in order to show that they are really innocent and that the blame for their perversion lies elsewhere.

Gradually it dawned upon the stolid, unimaginative Hulda that her husband was going mad. When one day she found him wild-eyed and panting, with his favourite kitten newly strangled in his lap, she momentarily lost her self-control. He had always been inordinately fond of cats; and there he was, as she gazed at him in horror, babbling in a queer sort of ecstasy about the "appalling rapture" of rending, suffocating, destroying, annihilating what one most loved—the over-mastering impulse to set the seal of death upon that to which the Almighty Himself had given life. Unable to restrain herself, Hulda asked him outright if he was going off his head. His reaction was alarming. He reeled at her menacingly and shouted in uncontrollable fury that she was never to suggest such a thing again.

But as things went from bad to worse Hulda called in the services of a specialist, who recommended her to increase her household staff by the addition of two powerfully-built male nurses. As things turned out it was as well for her that she took this advice, for not long afterwards Leopold one day seized her by the throat and announced his intention of killing her, after holding forth on the degree of pleasure to be derived from eliminating a soul-mate of whom one was genuinely, in-tensely fond. The frustrated masochist was now a demented sadist. The burly male nurses were within earshot and quickly rescued Hulda. The specialist now decided to take a grave view of Leopold's condition and promptly had him committed to a madhouse. This was March 1895, and his incarceration in the asylum at Mannheim, as far as the world was concerned, coincided with his death, for to safeguard his renown as an author and the honour of his family, it was given out that he had died.[1]

Sacher-Masoch's biography has been detailed at some length because to a remarkable extent his life mirrored his desires.

MASOCHISM AND FETISHISM

It is significant that the goddess of love as Sacher-Masoch saw her—his Venus—should be adorned with furs. The reader will already have observed what a powerful stimulus to his libido the wearing of furs represented. Masochism is very frequently associated with fetishism to some extent, and in a great many instances furs are the ideal concomitant of masochistic acts. Leather (especially black patent leather) is also commonly venerated. Since female sadism and male masochism are often complementary, it is not surprising that the pleasure afforded to the female sadist by the wearing of leather or furs and high-heeled shoes, etc., is generally shared by the male masochist who desires to suffer at her hands. But the fetish may be some part of the body, or something associated with the partner, some article of clothing for instance. As a matter of fact the agent that the masochist envisages as the instrument or means by which his subjugation may be brought about in a manner that yields him the greatest satisfaction may not be anything tangible at all. The fetish may equally well be something intangible, particularly in the case of ideal, or mental, masochism.

Many masochists, more especially males, have extraordinary, and sometimes nauseating, preferences in the matter of the stimuli they find most exciting. The case books of sexologists are full of revolting examples. Some patients derive sexual pleasure from sniffing or licking the perspiration of females; some from consuming feminine urine and excreta; some from the taste or smell of menstrual discharge; and there are an immense variety of other incomprehensible preferences generally referred to in Latin in deference to the listener's or reader's susceptibilities. Krafft-Ebing quotes the case of a Russian civil servant of 24 who every four weeks longed to

[1] One biographer (James Cleugh: *The Marquis and the Chevalier*, Andrew Melrose, Ltd., 1951) states that Sacher-Masoch lingered on in the asylum for ten more years.

have a woman urinate into his mouth. He also mentions a 31-year-old man who liked to lick the perspiration from between the toes of a woman who "but slightly clad stood in front of him holding a whip in her hand, whilst he knelt at her feet like a slave".[1] "A Russian prince, who was very decrepit, was accustomed to have his mistress turn her back to him and defecate on his breast".[2] Wulffen mentions the case of a male homosexual who told him that one of his clients used to make him urinate on his penis while his trousers were undone in front. He quotes the case of a 50-year-old hairdresser who persuaded a girl to make water on his hands, and this gave him complete sexual gratification. Wulffen says there are urine drinkers who consume up to a quart of feminine urine in a single day.

In the former days of Continental brothels, men often paid dearly to be ill-used and would sometimes draw up a programme of the penances they wished to have inflicted. Apart from commonplace floggings, bizarre acts would sometimes take place, such as is mentioned in *La Corruption Fin-de-Siècle*, in which it is recorded that a masochistic man was delighted to lick the seat of a lavatory-pan in a Paris house of ill-fame.

The list is inexhaustible. Magnus Hirschfeld says: "The masochist does not recoil from any of these degrading acts ... I had a case—which is by no means rare—of a man who made a prostitute chew and mix with her own saliva, the food he ate. The licking of a woman's perspiration and lacteal glands ... and ... the sniffing and licking not only of the *cunnus*, but also of the *anus,* are no rarities in the sexual life of the masochist".[3] "Unnatural and terrible as the perversions dealt with here appear to be, they are nevertheless deeply rooted in human nature and are governed by certain laws. Mythology and folk-lore, as well as early childhood experiences, provide ample proof of this statement"[4]

It follows, then, that compared with some of the fetishistic cravings mentioned above, Sacher-Masoch's predilection for furs (which in fact he was extravagant enough to provide at considerable cost to himself) was relatively innocuous, and even wholesome. But fetishistic the preference undoubtedly

[1] *Psychopathia Sexualis,* Case 82.
[2] *ibid.,* p. 193.
[3] *Sexual Anomalies and Perversions.*
[4] *ibid.*

was. By a fetish is understood some object, feature, quality, part, or association, that so obsesses the individual affected by it that he or she is unable to obtain complete sexual satisfaction except in conjunction with it in some way or other. To Sacher-Masoch the furs were as important as the flagellating implement, and perhaps as the flagellation itself. If he could not in reality achieve all the satisfaction he craved, he had recourse to idealising his yearning in his writings. When he and Aurora Rümelin were quarrelling once about the fact that in the opinion of his critics the types of women he portrayed in his novels were not sufficiently varied, he replied cunningly: "If you would wear furs and handle the whip in the right spirit there would be no need for me to depict all those cruel women. You know I revel in being maltreated by you. Do as I say, and henceforth no cruel women shall appear in my novels".

To Sacher-Masoch the experience he sought lacked completeness when the 'Domina' was not dressed in furs. The furs were to him, therefore, an essential part of the ritual. In his best-known novel this fetishism is elaborately pictured. The submissive Severin (Leopold himself) is really thrilled when the merciless, imperious Wanda (i.e. Fanny Pistor) appears fur-clad and ready to inflict a cruel punishment. I should like to quote a relevant excerpt:

"A handsome woman, her face lit by a radiant smile, with rich tresses dressed in old-fashioned knots, and lightly touched with white powder, was reposing stretched on a sofa, leaning on her left arm. She was nude except for dark furs. Her right hand was playing with a horse-whip, while her bare foot was resting carelessly on a man crouched in front of her like a slave, or a dog, and this man of striking and well-cut features, ... was gazing at her with the eyes of an exalted and ardent martyr. In fact the man, a living footstool beneath the woman's feet, was no other than Severin . . .".[1]

Dr Ernst Schertel gives it as his opinion that this passage contains the quintessence of masochism: the radiant goddess functions simultaneously as a cruel though naïve fetish, at whose feet lies the male consumed by passion, grateful that those feet do him the honour of using his back as a footstool. I think that Dr Schertel is here mixing up several perversions accidentally found together in the case of Sacher-Masoch.

Innumerable masochists practise their aberration in such a

[1] *Venus in Furs,* Luxor Press, 9/6; p. 27.

multiplicity of circumstances with such a continual variety of partners and instruments that this element of incessant change demonstrates *a priori* that fetishism is not invariably an inseparable feature of masochism. While the attitude of the fetishist towards his object is basically static, the behaviour of the masochist towards his object is fundamentally dynamic. This dynamism is shown—in the negative way characteristic of the neurotic—by the unceasing tenacity the masochist displays in his determination to attain his goal. Severin does not lie at the feet of Wanda because of *her* whims, as he would have us believe ; he lies at her feet because *he* wants to lie there. With endless cunning he has pushed his way through until finally the situation is accomplished in the manner he has set his heart on from the beginning. In the same way we saw over and over again in our study of Sacher-Masoch's life that it was not a question of his being ruthlessly subjugated by women who forced ther cruelties upon him ; it was rather that he tirelessly left no stone unturned in his quest for women who would be *willing* (even if not eager) to mete out to him the treatment he desired. And this fact is not in the least invalidated by his canting attempt to discredit 'Wanda' (his first wife) by blaming her for his "fancies". Such a disclaimer is a common weapon in the armoury of the masochist.

To revert for a moment to Schertel, it is all the more remarkable that he should link fetishism inextricably with masochism considering he himself indicates that Severin's predilection stems from a childhood experience. Consequently this (and by analogy any other) fetishism cannot be applied to masochism in general. That childhood experience is thus described in *Venus in Furs*[1] :

"One day my parents made a journey to town. My aunt determined to take advantage of their absence to attack my person. Clad in her fur-lined *kazabaika* she entered my room, followed by the cook, the kitchen maid and the little puss I had scorned. Without a word said, they seized me, and, despite my resistance, tied my feet and my arms; then, with a malicious laugh, my aunt rolled up her sleeves, and started to beat me with a large switch, so hard as to draw blood, and, at length, in spite of my courage, I yelled, wept and implored mercy. Then she untied me, but I had to kneel down before her to thank her for the correction and kiss her hand.

[1] *Venus in Furs*, Luxor Press, 9/6; p. 56.

"... Under the switch of that handsome and lascivious woman, who, in her fur jacket, seemed like an incensed queen, the temptation of woman was aroused in me for the first time, and, from that moment, my aunt appeared to be the most attractive woman that God had ever created".

SADISM AND MASOCHISM CONTRASTED

Krafft-Ebing, who coined the term 'masochism' for the particular perversion we are considering, because, as he points out in *Psychopathia Sexualis*, the substratum of the writings of Sacher-Masoch "up to his time was quite unknown to the scientific world as such", defines the essential common element, from the psychopathic point of view, as "the fact that the sexual instinct is directed to ideas of subjugation and abuse by the opposite sex".

Sadism and masochism are not equal and opposite forces in the derangement of man's sexual equilibrium, although one is certainly (at least in most cases) the contrary of the other. Sadism implies the desire to cause or inflict pain, or to contemplate or witness it even to an extreme degree, while masochism is the desire to suffer pain and to be overpowered and coerced into subjection. But whereas sadism, as we have seen, may be totally unbridled and carried to monstrous and lethal extremes, the masochist, as Krafft-Ebing points out, is generally restrained by the instinct of self-preservation from submitting to treatment that would result in death or serious injury.

De Sade, given the type of person he was—inclined to hyper-eroticism and lacking in self-discipline—was, to a large extent, conditioned by the accident of birth and class background to develop as he did. Born and bred in an age of brutal unrest and unrestrained depravity, he was virtually predisposed to prefer the infliction of pain, as a means of gratifying his libido, to normalcy in his sexual appetites. He belonged to the highest aristocracy, which did not attach much value to the lives of the proletariat; the epoch he lived in, which, in its shameless decadence, regarded sexuality only as a means for promoting lust; the trend of his thinking (he accepted sexual impulse and aggression as ineluctable and perfectly natural phenomena): these factors predisposed him to behave like a despot. Sacher-Masoch, on the other hand, was in most respects the exact antithesis of de Sade. True he, also, was born into the ancient nobility, but his family belonged now to a

113

relatively impoverished and declining aristocracy. Born almost a hundred years after de Sade and nearly half a century after revolution had submerged the élite of France in a vengeful blood-bath, Sacher-Masoch had no illusions about the waning power of the class to which, in name at least, he belonged. Highly-strung and somewhat neurotic, he was horrified and no doubt permanently influenced by the scenes of cruelty and bloodshed that accompanied the Ruthenian revolt against the Poles, which broke out when he was at the formative age of ten. Two years later he was in Prague when the Revolution of 1848 took place. His class background, therefore, was one in which his elders and his contemporaries were conducting a losing battle against disruption and disintegration: they were struggling during the so-called *bürgerliches Zeitalter* ('bourgeois epoch') to preserve time-honoured and typical aristocratic and upper-middle-class values in an age of change and dissolution. In sex and morals, then, his effective criteria never surpassed the level of ambivalence. In several of his novels we find the conflict between lust and taboo clearly delineated.

His thinking, though it strove to remain eminently respectable, was constantly overshadowed by his abnormal desire to prostrate and abase himself before dominant womanhood. He was totally averse to any homosexual leanings, and since his warped libido required above all things to be subjugated it was inevitable that this subjection must be imposed at the hands of women (even if, as we have seen, the women concerned enlisted the help of men in humiliating him). Suffering, in fact, seemed to him to be not only the inescapable lot of the discredited male sex but the martyr's road to resurrection.

To a much greater extent than in the case of de Sade, Sacher-Masoch practised what he believed. As we have seen, de Sade gave full rein to his depravity only in his thoughts and writings but refrained altogether from perpetrating the worst of his enormities in his actions. Apart from the Rose Keller affair and one or two other experimental escapades which earned him a measure of notoriety as a practising pervert, he was in his conduct neither better nor worse than others of his contemporaries with strong libidinal inclinations. But Sacher-Masoch was first and foremost a slave to his particular passion. His ideas took their expression from his behaviour, rather than the reverse. In fact, since his wives had little inclination to indulge his whims and his married life was destined to deny him

114

the satisfactions he craved, he consoled himself to some extent in writing about experiences he had had with his mistresses, though much in these accounts was more fictional than real.

AMBIVALENCE, INGENUITY AND HYPOCRISY

I have just said that Sacher-Masoch's attitude to sex (and in large measure the attitude of the entire environment to which he belonged) was conditioned by a certain ambivalence: his sensuality was pronounced and exigent, demanding complete freedom of expression, but his moral judgments were still rooted in religious restraints and primitive taboos. His intense and morbid libido had to find an outlet, and gradually the struggle between the desired and the forbidden resolved itself into a conflict between the sexes, the female (as always) representing the evil forces of lewdness and domination, the male succumbing as the defenceless victim who, through the degradations he is subjected to by his 'Domina', is permitted and enabled to experience sexual fulfilment.

The Marquis de Sade needed no justification for his sexual conduct: after all, he was the superman, aloof from ordinary human beings, whom moral casuistry could not touch. The Chevalier von Sacher-Masoch, on the other hand, could only realise the satisfaction of his sexual fancies as long as he paid for them through prostration and punishment. His sense of guilt demanded expiation, and with the ingenuity of the neurotic he invested the object (and the means) of satisfaction of his lust with the power to provide that expiation by executing the penalty herself. Lust, guilt, penalty and satisfaction are not inextricably interwoven: they have become linked by machinations of cowardly cunning. This gradation is characteristic of the abnormality to which Sacher-Masoch gave his name.

As a sort of extra-compensation for his guilt-feelings Sacher-Masoch interpolated the desire to have his 'Domina' commit adultery. This wish, too, is typical of the cunning of the masochist. By committing adultery the 'Domina' enhances the degradation of her 'slave', which automatically diminishes his guilt in augmenting the burden of expiation. At the same time, the act of adultery moulds the 'Domina' into a more human, more fallible, more tangible being, which not only makes the transition from bondage to carnal intercourse more plausible, but in addition opens up for the wronged one the possibility to feel that in the end it is he who is morally superior.

The sadist, then, may be unbearable because of his total lack of sensibility, his callous indifference, his blunt and arrogant cruelty; but the masochist is hardly less intolerable because of his hypocritical arguments and the whining tenacity he displays in order to secure the upper hand. He may be a sinner, he seems to say, but his oppressor is still worse!

As I believe I have now made clear, the artfulness and disingenuousness of the paranoic neuropath, especially if he is an out-and-out masochist, are not easily surpassed. Even as a literary figure Sacher-Masoch sought to justify his shortcomings at his wife's expense. He knew he had genuine talent as a writer and that he was so highly esteemed in some quarters that he was acclaimed by critics as a potential counterpart to Germany's Goethe or Russia's Turgenev or Dostoievsky. But he was aware, too, that he had prostituted his literary ability by too much harping on a single monotonous obsession. For this he blamed his wife. If she had properly understood him, he alleged, and sincerely loved him, she would have given him what he desperately longed for: then he would have felt free to write with greater variety and versatility. Thus the adverse criticism directed against him as an artist and a craftsman he slyly turned against Aurora. Furthermore, as for the popular (sensational) 'novelettes' he wrote, he claimed that these were potboilers to enable him to earn their daily bread (which was a palpable untruth, for he was a successful writer and they were by no means in financial straits). Pretending to be reluctantly forced into creating what was unworthy of his high reputation, and seeking to incite sympathy for himself as a creative spirit imprisoned by the stark restraints of material necessity—these strengthened his first manœuvre. By such means he was able to achieve what he wanted: humiliation and punishment without culpability; it was the critics and his wife and the cruel necessities of life that must bear the responsibility, for he himself was merely the guiltless victim.[1]

THE LANGUAGE OF THE SADO-MASOCHIST

In the archives of sexologists and psychiatrists there are to be found the most extraordinary examples of correspondence between the masochistic 'slave' and the sadistic 'master' or 'mistress'. Generally the masochist, in such cases, is a male

[1] Hirschfeld called this kind of urge "the impulse to prevail". Alfred Adler has declared that it is a primary symptom of neurosis.

and the 'slave-owner' a female. The female masochist may be equally submissive but is seldom so articulate: she may make illuminating confessions to a psycho-analyst, but she is not likely to express her surrender in writing. The language employed in these exchanges is infantile and often ludicrous.

Most male masochists desire to be treated as slaves or menials by the 'Domina' (servilism), sometimes as servant-girls (incidentally satisfying a transvestite yearning by wearing a maid's uniform, and even feminine underwear); some desire to be addressed and treated as animals (zoömimic masochism); others as schoolboys punished by a strict 'governess' or 'mother' or an 'aunt', etc. (puerile masochism).

Hirschfeld mentions a man who on certain days of the year called on a certain girl at a certain brothel. He would get her to undress him and fetter him in a particular prescribed manner and after remaining alone in that state for half an hour would leave the place completely satisfied. "It is easy to trace in this case", concludes Hirschfeld, "the mechanism of fancied loss of liberty combined with a special fetishist ritual". "The same applies to the man in Paris who enacted a comedy with his mistress, in the course of which he attempted to kiss her on the shoulder, whereupon he was kicked downstairs by a hefty man-servant specially engaged for that purpose". But what about the case mentioned by Hirschfeld from Wulffen? It concerns a homosexual blackmailer. " 'Another man, who took me home with him, had a wooden clip which he fixed to his nose. Then he asked me to pull at a string attached to the clip, so that it became compressed and squeezed his nose. While doing this I had to say: "I hope his nose is going to be so big that everybody will be surprised at it". I did so and the man masturbated during these proceedings'." The childlike ingenuity, the infinite capacity of juvenile make-believe characteristic of the male masochist have, I hope, been amply demonstrated.

And finally, one word more about Sacher-Masoch. Whatever one may think of him as a creative author, there is no doubt that his best-known work, at least, does reflect in a manner very true to life the childish relationship between the male masochist and his mistress. If there is absurdity in it, it is because the situation is itself absurd; but there is nothing grotesque or out-of-this-world, as there is in the narratives of the Marquis de Sade.

CHAPTER FIVE

Masochism in the Female

BIOLOGICAL MECHANISM AND PRIMEVAL URGE

When the Düsseldorf sadistic lust-murderer Peter Kürten was arrested and imprisoned, he received many love-letters from women who only knew him from the horrible tales about his crimes which had appeared in the papers. The same sort of thing has happened time and time again in respect of sadistic criminals. Why is this? Kürten was no play-boy, no ladies' man: he was to all intents and purposes just a commonplace, nondescript member of the working classes. It was not his personal charm that impelled those women to write him love-letters. It seems more likely that they were envious of his victims, that they resented having missed the chance of falling into his clutches. He was to them the perfect he-man. We must assume that these females were unbalanced. Their action in writing the letters was a mentally unbridled outburst of deeply-embedded masochistic instinct.

Masochistic urges would seem to be a component (generally, of course, a hidden component) of the female sex-instinct. Were this not so it would be difficult to apprehend why women throughout the ages have been content to endure their state of submissiveness to the male. Perhaps, after all, masochism in the female is not such a strange phenomenon: it almost certainly has its origin in the accident of biological mechanism. Let us consider this more closely.

It is a proven fact that women have greater capacity to endure physical pain and suffering than men. They have to have. If we reflect, for example, upon what it meant in bygone ages to bear a child—an agonising and unpleasant process endangering life itself—we men cannot help wondering that women in general have always been willing to take the risk.

In my opinion the most characteristic difference between

man and woman is this: the male is primarily concerned with his survival, here and now: the future is to him merely an abstraction, a metaphysical consideration, a dimension for imaginative speculation. The man who is consciously or sub-consciously aware of the limitations of mortality strives for immortality: the artist is born. Artistic creation is man's only means of outwitting, of circumscribing death. One might object to this on the ground that the children a man sires are also a means to that end; but immortality in that sense does not seem to commend itself to him as an irrefutable truth or an ideal solution. In any case, the child is not as clearly related to him bodily, flesh of his flesh and blood of his blood, as it is of its mother. After all, many a man may be a father without even knowing it, and not every man can feel one hundred per cent positive that his children are his own.

Woman's primary concern is the future: the continuance of the human race, the function for which she is biologically predestined. And although man's sperms may be collected and catalogued anonymously in test-tubes, it is still woman who is the matrix of mankind. Experiments with lower forms of animal life have demonstrated that it is possible to procure impregnation chemically with complete elimination of male co-operation. In this way only females were produced. If scientists should one day succeed in obtaining the same results in the human species—which is far from inconceivable—we shall have to envisage a drastic decrease in the number of males, if not their complete extermination, for after all the male is then dispensable, the female never.

This is merely stating that ultimately woman plays the major rôle in procreation. The anguish she endures in labour she undergoes for the great Cause, and she may even enjoy it for the triumph it signifies over death. All her strivings are directed towards assuring the most favourable conditions for this Cause here and now: in reproducing life in her own person she is, as it were, projecting herself into the future, of which she is therefore an integral part. The future, then, is not an abstraction to her, but a palpable reality. Accordingly she does not understand or have much patience with man's eternal fondness for dwelling upon abstract subjects. Women are alleged to have a down-to-earth mentality. This also explains the misunderstandings that arise from the unbridgeable gulf between male and female reasoning.

119

If we would endeavour to understand something of woman's reactions in certain aspects of sex, it is essential to start from a consideration of the biological mechanism.

Theories about the sex-life of our remotest ancestors are conjectural, but presumably it was something like this. The primeval female was pursued by the primeval male; after having brought him to a state of frenzy by her teasing, struggling and resisting, she finally submitted with delight to his blindly violent rage. When she was pregnant she refused further bodily contact, and the male, whose only interest was sexual gratification, went off in search of some other absorbing interest. These actions and reactions were glandularly directed. Both participants in the drama acted on impulse, without any conscious cerebral sublimation. When man began living in communities, prompted by circumstances such as change of climate (the advent of the ice age), by food scarcity, and so on, the female remained submissive to the male, dependent as she was on his abilities as food gatherer and defender against wild animals and hostile strangers.

Later, when the circumstances became less strenuous and the agricultural stage was reached, the female became independent again. Working in the fields was (and still is) the task of women in primitive communities. Gradually she obtained a key position in the community, owing to her mysterious capacity for bearing offspring: mysterious, because we must not forget that it took man a very long time to discover the relationship between copulation and pregnancy; the absence of a distinct mating season in humans and the long period of gestation hampered the discovery of this connexion. In their primitive reasoning they drew the conclusion that the spirits of the dead entered the body of the female to be born anew. Elaborate totemistic rituals came into existence in close association with the miraculous female faculty, again strengthening the vital position of woman in the tribe.

Most probably man discovered the relationship between coition and childbirth when he began domesticating animals (the pastoral stage). He must then have observed that the birth of the young took place at fixed intervals after the mating season.

Gradually women lost their dominant position, which, as it happened, had never had a more secure foundation than the shifting sands of ignorance. Man's attitude had hitherto been inspired by awe and respect for the mysterious creature, woman, who beneficently allowed him to have his pleasure with her in exchange for food and defence. Now man, who had supposed he could never hope to compete on equal terms with this being who had intimate relations with the invisible world of spirits, must have been delightedly impressed by the revelation that in fact it was his act of pleasure that was the source of childbearing, that it was not the work of the spirits after all. Woman's status of demi-goddess degenerated into that of a domestic animal, neither more nor less.

Thus woman, bereft of all her former prerogatives, had to do something to draw attention to herself and to make her importance felt. So she evolved masochism as a defence-mechanism. With the laws and customs of the community against her, she had no other choice. It was no coincidence that it corresponded with her innate desire to be possessed by coercion. She only needed to extend this existing trait and to infuse variety and subtlety into it.

Now this desire to be violated, this capacity for enduring pain with a certain kind of pleasure, or at least of satisfaction, and this indifference to the dangers menacing life, which is implicit in the processes of reproduction, I called, at the beginning of the present chapter, "deeply-embedded masochistic instincts". Cultivated and amplified through ages of masculine brutality, of witch-hunting persecution, of being treated as the inferior sex, this trait is still strongly persistent in many women, sometimes latent but quite often blatant. Women affected by such an urge frequently pester and provoke their husbands, not content until the man loses his self-control and strikes out.[1] This ought then to be followed by reconciliation in bed. But the male in our highly cultivated and civilised society is compelled to use his brains in the daily struggle for life. When he loses his temper and acts impulsively he soon regrets it afterwards and is disgusted with himself, is anxious to make amends and to expunge his boorishness by being more than usually considerate. He is, therefore, least of all in the mood to stage a rape. I am, of course, speaking of the average,

[1] Montesquieu, in his *Lettres Persanes* (1721), alleged that Persian women not only expected but positively desired to be frequently beaten by their husbands. In a letter purporting to be written by one wife to a friend the wife bitterly complains that her husband never strikes her and that her friends and neighbours taunt her for this, saying he cannot love her. She vows that she will provoke her husband at every possible opportunity and thus compel him to beat her. Then, at the least touch, she will scream so lustily that her neighbours will be convinced her husband truly loves her.

121

sociable, cultured man, not the anti-social, bestial or mentally-deficient specimen. Though there are few men who have never contemplated committing rape in any circumstances (for, though he may wish to deny it, the atavistic traits of his arche-typal forebears are also latently present in the man of today) it seems somewhat irrational to expect him to rape the woman he has been leading a respectable married life with for years. Only a man who is something of a connoisseur at love-making will see such a change of procedure as the most natural thing in the world.[1]

The reader should not suppose that I am merely theorising or exaggerating in what I am stating about the importance of 'rape' between persons in love. My conclusions are the residue of many years of psychiatric practice. I have psycho-analysed countless women who were suffering from dissatisfaction born of this tragic incompatibility between past and present. Such women are by no means abnormal: they simply obey the laws of their biological mechanism, or feel impelled to do so. The tragedy lies in the fact that most present-day men have lost sight of the answer to this atavistic challenge.

MASOCHISTIC SELF-EFFACEMENT

There are, however, women in whom this hereditary maso-chistic urge has become over-developed and entirely pre-dominant, quite apart from sex and procreation. When a man possesses them they submit to it as one of the many ways in which they can be debased and humiliated to the point of annihilation. Their only desire is that their personality and individuality shall be submerged and obliterated. Incidentally, in such cases it is not at all necessary that sexual enjoyment, in the commonly understood sense, should supervene. Hirsch-feld records the case of a young woman who kept a French prisoner of war concealed in her room for eight months, dur-ing which time she submitted to sexual acts of all kinds. In-vestigation revealed that the young woman was entirely frigid: the only pleasure she derived from the experience was that of being in a state of sexual bondage. Hirschfeld describes the passive party in sexual bondage as "a will-less tool in the hands

[1] This whole question is very interestingly dealt with by Dr Vyvyan Howarth in *Secret Techniques of Erotic Delight*, Luxor Press, especially in the section dealing with the technique of seduction. See, for example, Chapter 12.

of the active party". He goes on: "It was formerly believed that in such cases hypnotic or suggestive influences were in operation, whereas in reality sexual bondage is due solely to an exaggeration of sexual submissiveness, that is to say, degeneracy of the submissive impulse." He mentions as examples prostitutes who surrender their individuality entirely to their 'bullies' and are "like wax" in their hands. This sort of thing is not uncommon among homosexuals either: Hirschfeld himself had a patient who engaged in shop-lifting on the orders of her lesbian friend to whom she was in a condition of sexual bondage.

What causes this distortion and overgrowth of an originally normal sex-instinct I cannot say. It may be that some disturbance of the glandular equilibrium is at the root of the trouble. But that is merely conjecture. I personally have not met such a woman in my own clinical experience. What I know about them I have only from hearsay and reading. It would seem that these poor creatures, unless they meet the cold and cruel master they long for, are morosely dreaming their lives away, always vaguely unhappy, sometimes contemplating suicide but never actually committing it.

The self-chosen martyrdom of a woman who longs to be 'disciplined' by others (especially by someone of the opposite sex) and who finds ultimate satisfaction only in total surrender has been described in a compelling story that was published not long after World War II. The story, called *L'Histoire d'O* (which has been translated into English), was published in Paris and was ostensibly written by Pauline Réage, but there is reason to believe that Jean Paulhan, who wrote the introduction, is the real author. It is regarded by many psychiatrists as an eloquent but extreme example of a female masochist's self-immolation, but it seems to me that it may equally well be seen as the epitomisation of a male sadist's dream wishes. The gist of the story is the progressive destruction of a human personality, entirely without any semblance of resistance on the part of the victim. The awful thing is that, despite its evident lack of authenticity, the tale, as one reads it, seems entirely credible: it fascinates and captivates, and finally suffocates, the reader with the sinister, sickly, cloying subtlety of poison gas. In contrast to de Sade's nightmarish fantasies, this story is somehow horrifyingly true to life. Moreover, in spite of its sexual and moral depravity, it breathes a kind of insidious apologia, since everybody concerned, including the victim herself, casually agrees to the acts performed, however repulsive they may be. The girl's lover, when he is satiated with her, hands her over like a pimp or procurer into sexual bondage, heaping humiliation upon humiliation, which the girl accepts with the resignation of a zombie.

To show how the strange yet realistic atmosphere that pervades this 'classic' of sado-masochistic literature is created, I append an excerpt taken from the opening pages of this disturbing novel:

"Her lover one day takes O. for a walk, but this time in a part of the city—the Parc Montsouris, the Parc Monceau—where they have never been together before. After they have strolled awhile along the paths, after they have sat down side by side on a bench near the grass, and got up again, and moved on towards the edge of the park, there, where two streets meet, where there never used to be any taxi-stand, they see a car, at that corner. It looks like a taxi, for it does have a meter.

" 'Get in', he says. She gets in.

"It is late in the afternoon; it is autumn. She is wearing what she always wears: high heels, a suit with a pleated skirt, a silk blouse, no hat. But she has on long gloves reaching up to the sleeves of her jacket. In her leather handbag she has her papers, and her compact and lipstick. The taxi eases off, very slowly; nor has the man next to her said a word to the driver. But on the right, on the left, he draws down the little window-shades, and the one behind too. Thinking that he is about to kiss her, or so as to caress him, she has slipped off her gloves. Instead he says:

" 'I'll take your bag; it's in your way.'

"She gives it to him. He puts it beyond her reach; then adds:

" 'You've too much clothing on. Unhitch your stockings; roll them down to just above your knees. Go ahead'; and he gives her some garters to hold the stockings in place.

"It is not easy, not in the car, which is going faster now, and she doesn't want to have the driver turn round. But she manages somehow at last. It's a queer, uncomfortable feeling, the contact of the silk of her slip against her naked and free legs, and the unattached suspenders are sliding loosely back and forth across her skin.

" 'Undo your suspender-belt', he says. 'Take off your panties'.

124

"There's nothing to that: all she has to do is get at the hook behind and raise herself up a little. He takes the suspenderbelt from her; he takes the panties; opens her bag, puts them inside it. Then he says:

" 'You're not to sit on your slip or your skirt; pull them up and sit on the seat without anything in between'.

"The seat-covering is a sort of leather. It's a very strange sensation the way it sticks and clings to her thighs.

"Then he says:

" 'Now put your gloves back on'.

"The taxi goes straight on and she doesn't dare to ask why René is so quiet, so still, or what all this means to him: she so motionless and so silent, so denuded and so offered, though so thoroughly gloved, in a black car going she hasn't the least idea where. He hasn't told her to do anything or not to do it, but she doesn't dare either cross her legs or sit with them pressed together. One on this side, one on that side, she rests her gloved hands on the seat, pushing down.

" 'Here we are', he says suddenly. 'This is it'. The taxi comes to a stop on a fine avenue, under a tree—these are plane trees —in front of a small mansion. You could just see it, nestling between courtyard and garden, the way the Faubourg Saint-Germain mansions are. There is no street-light near by. It is dark inside the cab, and outside rain is falling.

" 'Don't move', says René. 'Don't move a muscle'.

"He extends his hand towards the neck of her blouse, unties the ribbon at the throat, then undoes the buttons. She leans forward, ever so little, and believes he is about to caress her breasts. But no; he has a small penknife out: he is groping for the shoulder-straps of her brassière. He cuts the straps, removes the brassière. He has closed her blouse again and now, underneath, her breasts are free and nude, as her belly and thighs are free and nude, as all of her is, from waist to knees.

" 'Listen', he says. 'You're ready. Here's where I leave you. You're going to get out and go to the door and ring the bell. Someone will open the door. Whoever it is you'll do as he says. You'll do it right away and willingly, of your own accord, or else they'll make you. If you don't obey at once, they'll make you obey. What? No, you don't need your bag any more. You don't need anything. You're just the whore; I'm the pimp who's furnishing you ... Yes, certainly I'll be there. Sure. Now go'." (*Slightly adapted*).

I believe this kind of book to be of far greater danger to the reading public than the sadistic 'strips' emanating from the U.S.A. Undoubtedly these reflect evil too; but owing to the commercial greed and moronic lack of discernment of the minds behind them they are so primitive and crassly absurd that their main result is only a temporary shock-effect, while the damaging outcome of a novel like *L'Histoire d'O* lasts much longer and is more far-reaching, as the content is brought home with the cunning sophistry of the neurotic and has the appearance of being literature. One book like this implies more danger to unstable minds than all the semi- or pseudo-scientific literature about sadism and masochism that has been published in the past century or so. It is all too painfully reminiscent of that *Verfremdung* (alienation) I referred to (on page 75) as the great lurking menace challenging society today.

In the "Traveller's Companion" series of the Olympia Press in Paris another book has been published, called *Thongs*, written over the pseudonym Carmencita de la Luna, although I am pretty sure the writer is really a man, and not even a masochist at that. Some parts of the story are well written: for instance, the description of a brawl in the slums of Glasgow, ending with the death of the heroine's father. However, I do not think that sado-masochists will find it very stimulating reading; I am afraid the analysis may be a little too penetrating for them. I mention it, in fact, because it seems to me that the person who wrote it has been doing some thinking (not very constructive perhaps) about this subject, which was apparently alien to him (or her) before.

The writer has been concerned in *Thongs* to capture realistically the cynical attitude to 'normal' sex relations which the female masochist evinces, and to convey the impotence of defeatism, the utter hopelessness of willing surrender. This time, however, the surrender is not to an individual (the man is even reluctant to accept the rôle the woman wants to assign to him), but to life itself; the alternative to voluntary self-extinction through suffering is seen as slow death from boredom, from monotony, from the sheer purposelessness of existence. Clearly this paralysing lack of faith in anything, including the future and in human beings' *raison d'être*, is another disturbing symptom of our times and is closely related to that other attitude—of alienation (or *Verfremdung*).

These 'examples' of feminine masochism are taken from literature (of a sort) but are not necessarily reliable: they may give food for thought but they can scarcely be regarded as scientific evidence by a serious student of sexual aberrations. Perhaps it is extremely improbable that we shall ever have a *genuine* confession, in the form of an ordered narration, of the absoluteness that characterises the 'suicidal' female masochist's determination to immolate herself—for the perfectly good reason that the very nature of her obsession precludes that possibility. To perpetuate herself by the extrovert means of literary creation of any sort is a negation of her purpose and therefore of herself as what she is or believes herself to be. In telling others of her feelings she would be admitting that she does have feelings, which is the very contention she exists to refute: it is only in the surrender of all right to have feelings that she believes she will find satisfaction; but a feeling-less existence has no content, in describable terms, and therefore cannot be conveyed by the subject herself. It is like expecting a spiritualist medium to describe what he feels while in deep trance, when the very nature of trance is supposed to be the sacrifice of human faculties to extra-terrestrial agencies. Therefore, descriptions of such extreme masochistic attitudes as we are at present considering are bound to be synthetic and nugatory, for they are not written by those who hold those attitudes but by others who only *think* they know what it is like to be so conditioned.

Nevertheless, sufficient evidence abounds to prove beyond all reasonable doubt that such self-extinguishing masochists do exist. That they are not so forthcoming as other types of patients in the information they give concerning their anomaly is itself, unfortunately, a symptom of their malady. The tragedy of their situation is that their implacable resolve to be submerged, or their irrational lack of will to be rescued, inevitably makes treatment difficult and cure virtually impossible. They exist only in order to cease existing, as individuals with a will and a personality of their own.

SURRENDER WITHOUT SELF-EFFACEMENT

Less extreme forms of submissive masochism are, of course, common enough. We do not need to have recourse to imaginative literary effusions to confirm this. I myself witnessed the revelation some years ago of a case in point while I was living in Holland. A Dutch magazine printed an exposure of a certain type of correspondence that had been going on in public and, by way of example, revealed the sequel in one particular case

One of the advertisements which were displayed in the window of a small undistinguished-looking shop ran: "Married couple would like to contact young girl of submissive nature. Please reply to No. ———." The reply to this peculiar announcement was printed in the magazine also; it consisted of a few non-committal words only: "Have read your advertisement and would like to make your acquaintance. All my friends praise my submissive character."

The following reply was received by the applicant:

"Our little slave!

It was with great interest that we read your letter which arrived yesterday.

We shall be glad to receive you as a boarding-school pupil and we propose to discipline you into an obedient girl who will carry out any order we may give her. We (that is to say the school) will aim at educating and forming you into an experienced servant of love, which any *good* woman ought to be. You must be able and willing to provide the highest pleasures imaginable. The task of our school is also to make of you a modern, sophisticated slave, etc., etc. Naturally we shall not be able to do this without using the whip (not inflicting corporal injuries however) and many other forms of treatment (binding, horse-riding, etc., etc.).

Make an appointment with us.

We remain
Your Master and Mistress,
Thea and George.

P.S.:
Next Saturday we shall expect a letter from you at the ——— kiosk in the City."

Following the success of Sacher-Masoch's novels, particularly *Venus in Furs*, many novels dealing with the same kind of theme were published by authors of inferior talent. One of these epigones produced a book called *Diary of a Lost One*, in which a typical 'example' of female masochistic emotion is combined with hand fetishism. A good-looking girl, named Thymian, is so fascinated by the "soft, white, beautiful hands" of a man named Osdorff, although he has a "stupid, dull face with those light-grey fishy eyes", that she cannot forbear begging him, "Slap me, scratch me, pinch me,—please! I want your hands to hurt me!"

But the female masochist does not always feel the need of a partner: the agent for the infliction of suffering need not be external at all. Giese gives some examples of cases in which women inflict pain on themselves to such a degree that death ensues.

REFLEXIVE MASOCHISM

A remarkable case in which a woman devised and controlled the manner and extent to which pain was inflicted upon her, although she was obliged to call in the assistance of another person in so doing, is mentioned by Charles Virmaître who is generally regarded as reliable. He tells of a female inhabitant of the Basque fishing village of Ciboure near the town of St Jean-de-Luz. This woman, who was very rich, lived alone with her maid in a house close to the beach. Whenever there was a gale blowing, the maid was sent upstairs to prepare 'the black room'. All the windows of this room had to be opened wide to enable the raging wind to blow through the gloomy apartment. While the maid went down to the beach her mistress took herself to the black room, stripped and stretched herself full-length on a bed, face downward. There she waited till the maid returned with a carefully-closed bucket and a number of strands of soaking wet seaweed.

The maid had to thrash the woman with the seaweed till her back was bloody. After that she had to open the pail and take out of it crabs she had collected on the beach, and apply them to the weals on her mistress's back. The crabs crawled over the woman's bleeding back and buttocks and dug their pincers into her flesh. The maid's task, then, was to put back on the wounded flesh the crabs that slithered off her mistress's body. Only when the pain caused by the lacerations and the biting and pinching of the crabs became unbearable did the woman reach an orgasm.

This can scarcely be explained as any innate or unconsciously-induced form of masochism deriving from a distorted manifestation of the sexual instinct. Personally I am inclined

129

to think that this was a case of what may be called 'acquired' masochism. Note that the action is 'reflexive' rather than merely submissive; whereas the submissive masochist subjects himself or herself to the endurance of whatever ill-treatment the persecutor chooses to inflict, the reflexive masochist is both the subject and the object of the infliction. This woman chose with conscious deliberation the treatment she intended to suffer and would be satisfied with nothing less. There may even have been an element of active sadism in her behaviour, for she obliged her maid to perform tasks which may well have been utterly distasteful to her.

DIFFERENCES IN CAUSATION OF MALE AND FEMALE MASOCHISM

A man's sexual preferences are often influenced, if not dictated, by parental imperatives. One of my patients once told me that his parents kept very strict vigilance over him to prevent him from masturbating. Every time they caught him in the act he was given a sound thrashing. The only result of this ill-conceived attitude on the part of his parents was that to this man lust and pain became inextricably interrelated. Forbidden fruit tastes best, but one has to pay a heavy price for the precious fruit: this became his conviction. Women masochists are less likely to owe their anomaly to any traceable factor that can be so easily pinpointed. We have seen that in the female the foundations of a masochistic predisposition are to be glimpsed in 'natural' and biological antecedents. This tendency, which I have suggested comes from "deeply-embedded instincts", is what Hirschfeld calls "the submissive impulse", and all known forms of female masochism derive, or seem to derive, from distortions or exaggerations of that impulse, though they may frequently be complicated by other anomalies that tend to make recognition and diagnosis difficult.

130

CHAPTER SIX

Causes and Complications

CAUSATION OF MASOCHISM IN THE MALE

We have, within the limits of reasonable speculation, traced back the origin of masochism in the female human being and found that it is most probably an exaggerated manifestation of the normal female sex-instinct, which has—in its most extreme form—become detached from the sex-complex as a whole and acquired independence. I can therefore agree with Krafft-Ebing when he states that sadism in the male and masochism in the female find their origin in natural components of the respective sex-instinct. But how can we explain masochism in the male? It cannot be inborn, so we must conclude that it is acquired. It is quite certain that the foundations of a man's masochistic inclinations are laid in his early youth. (It will be remembered that we noted certain causative elements in the early experience of Sacher-Masoch).

An excessively strong attachment to his mother, at first cultivated by the mother herself, will undoubtedly result in more or less latent incestuous yearnings in the young boy. When this boy grows older, his too-ardent affection, especially if evinced in public, may repel the mother, partially out of shame towards others, partially because she feels intuitively the unhealthiness of it. In an effort to establish more normal conditions she draws back completely, leaving the boy in the cold. She has changed from a loving mother into a severe mistress. As this generally happens at an age when the child is still very impressionable, it is likely to occasion serious mental troubles. He cannot restrain himself from longing for the endearments he has been used to, at the same time recognising them as wrong because the mother has made it clear that they are impermissible.

There is a stage in the relationship between parents and

131

children when the former seem to the latter no less than gods: they are omniscient, omnipotent. Under normal conditions the child becomes critical at a certain age and begins to evolve his own judgments.

With the imaginary boy whom we are now considering the goddess-status of his mother has become fixed. He cannot see her as a normal human being; what she says is imperatively, categorically true. The fact that he has been pushed back does not cool his ardent longings: on the contrary, they are enhanced by that treatment. At the same time he develops a strong awareness of guilt, without being able to relinquish his 'sinful' yearning. He becomes difficult, sulky, trying to attract the attention of the beloved mother by fits of temper and tearfulness. Most probably she will respond by boxing his ears. He may feign illness, which will bring back temporarily the loving care and attention he craves. But it does not last. The mother becomes increasingly more easily irritated. The boy provokes a spanking. In his primitive childish reasoning he comes to the conclusion that he can nurture his sinful yearning and commandeer his mother's undivided attention only as long as he takes the punishment that goes with it. The pleasure-pain connexion is established and is destined to develop in time into an all-pervading masochistic complex.

ABERRATIONAL COMPLICATIONS

In the same way as is the case with sadism, masochism is generally linked with other aberrational inclinations. Homosexuality, zoöphilia, exhibitionism, scopophilia, pluralism, gerontophilia, paedophilia, fetishism, transvestitism—are all anomalies or perversions to be found among masochists. The reader will no doubt have noted that, with the exception of transvestitism, they are the same deviations as can be found among sadists. That transvestitism is found among masochists and not among sadists is not difficult to understand; but there is another significant difference: there have always been religious masochists but the religious sadist does not exist. I will endeavour to demonstrate this later. But for the moment I propose to confine myself to a consideration of the catalogue of combinations I have enumerated above.

MASOCHISM AND HOMOSEXUALITY

Rudolf T., a man of 54, who was a patient of mine, told me

132

a strange story of how for the greater part of his life he had been fascinated by a nostalgic attachment to a tutor he had had in his boyhood, named George ———. The tutor, a man in his forties with old-fashioned ideas, believed in the efficacy of corporal punishment. The boy really believed him when he assured him that the chastisement was more painful to the tutor than to Rudolf T. himself, and accepted it gladly as being for his "own good". Little by little a very close friendship developed between tutor and pupil. Rudolf grew to like the thrashings he was given, and even at times deliberately provoked punishment in order to enjoy the moving scene of reconciliation that inevitably followed.

When Rudolf reached the age of 17 the tutor left, and for years afterwards the young man found himself yearning inconsolably for the fatherly companionship he had lost. He shunned women.

One day, many years after this, he came across the following advertisement:

"Strict teacher seeks pupil. Old-fashioned methods.
Send letter to this shop, addressed to Gerhard."

Rudolf eagerly got in touch with this Gerhard, hoping that at last his cherished dreams were about to be fulfilled. The fellow turned out to be a pot-bellied middle-aged sadist, with cruel eyes, quite incapable of showing the slightest sign of paternal affection. He soon had Rudolf T. in his power, and used to beat him once or twice every day for any trumped-up misdemeanour. It was a long time before Rudolf could break free of this unpleasant association. I was finally able to convince the patient of the fact that he could never recapture the bliss of those days with George and that he must adjust himself to living without him.

MASOCHISM AND ZOÖPHILIA EROTICA

The term *zoöphilia*, properly used, indicates no more than an exaggerated fondness for animals, without any sexual connotation. When the fondness for animals does have a strongly sexual significance, the condition may extend to *bestiality*, which implies unnatural sexual intercourse between humans and animals. Perhaps the most correct term to suggest a sexual attraction towards animals without any implied genital contact is *zoöphilia erotica*. There is evidently a close connexion between masochism and bestiality, particularly if the masochist is a female who allows an animal to excite or satisfy her sexually, whether by oral or genital contact with her own body. We have already seen (p. 58) that males are also sometimes given to unnatural sexual contact with animals. A good deal less common is masculine predilection for deriving sexual stimulation from animals without any genital or anal contact. One interesting case came to my knowledge, however, through one of my women patients.

Mrs Y. had been sent to me by her doctor for treatment of some disorder the source of which the practitioner had diagnosed as probably being due to mental causes. I soon discovered that in fact the woman was suffering from a tumour of the brain. But before I could send her to an appropriate specialist she had found occasion to acquaint me with the details of an extraordinary habit of her husband's that had worried her for a long time.

They lived on the outskirts of the town and kept chickens. It seems that at certain times the woman had to bring the birds into the kitchen. Her husband would undress and lie down on the kitchen floor stark naked. The wife was then ordered to strew chicken feed all over him, which was eagerly pecked from his body by the chickens. The scratching of their claws and the pecking of their beaks induced a powerful erection and finally brought about an orgasm, phenomena which, the woman observed rather bitterly, she had not known to occur otherwise for a good many years.

Another patient of mine, Albert B., experienced his favourite pleasure in phantasy. He imagined himself caged in an iron contraption, closely confining his body. This cage was subdivided into compartments. Hungry rats were then put into the cage. They gnawed their way through his body. When they reached his genitals and started gnawing at them he experienced orgasm.

I had little difficulty in finding out where his phantasy came from. I remembered having read it somewhere, probably in *Le Jardin des Supplices*. Probing in this direction soon brought to light that he had read the story as a boy. The title of the book he had forgotten, but this particular story had left a tantalising impression upon him.

Masochism and Aggressive Exhibitionism[1]

One day I was required to give expert evidence in the case of a man who had been arrested and charged with having made improper suggestions to several market-women. The presiding magistrate was greatly puzzled about the case because the plaintiffs and the witnesses for the prosecution alike were most vague and contradictory when questioned. The defendant, a soft-voiced, mild-mannered individual, denied ever having made any indecent proposals. He maintained that all he had done was talk about the produce that was being offered for sale, a fact the prosecution had to admit. It was not *what* he said, but the way he said it, was the nearest description one woman, a greengrocer, could give. When pressed for details, she could only state that he had a lewd way of talking. The magistrate wondered how one could possibly talk lewdly about leeks; the woman was at a loss to make this clear. What she did make clear was that she had become very much enraged and shouted things at the man, which soon attracted a crowd, and in the end she had shoved a bunch of leeks in the face of the accused and, not content with that, had boxed his ears with it right and left, much to the hilarity of the onlookers.

The accounts of the incident as given by others approximated fairly closely to this version. This man had perfected a technique of putting questions that made the blood of these simple quick-tempered women boil. It was his greatest joy to be insulted and abused in the presence of a crowd, particularly so when the women became physically violent. Juridically the man had not done any palpable wrong. The case was dismissed and the man cautioned to avoid frequenting the market-place.

Masochism and Voyeurism (or Scopophilia)

Masochistic *voyeurs* (scopophils) are really passive. They reach their highest peak of sexual excitement when witnessing the pain of others and identifying themselves with the victims. In the past they had ample opportunity to satisfy their cravings because the punishments and executions of criminals were staged as a public entertainment. But the golden days of the

[1] The term 'exhibitionism' is here used (for want of a better) in the broadest possible sense, as will be seen from the case cited. The man was aggressively determined to draw attention to himself in order to be ill-treated by women. (See my explanation of the term on pp. 47-8).

scopophil masochist are over: nowadays they have to content themselves with watching wrestling- and boxing-matches, bull-fights, etc. Sometimes they succeed in sneaking into sado-masochistic orgies but they are not welcome there, which is not strange when we bear in mind that they contribute nothing to the build-up of communal ecstasy. Being completely passive, they are justifiably regarded as parasites.

COLLECTIVE MASOCHISM

What has been said of pluralistic, or collective, sadism may obviously be taken to apply, inversely, to collective masochism. Nor need enjoyment be confined to imaginary identification *en masse* with the victims of suffering: group masochists may also take pleasure in actually (physically) undergoing collective sufferings or humiliations.

MASOCHISM AND GERONTOPHILIA

Since over-veneration of the mother-figure is often to be found as the origin of masochism, the preference of masochists for elderly women is understandably a common phenomenon.

MASOCHISM AND PAEDOPHILIA

The theme of the trials and tribulations of an old husband married to a young and beautiful wife has found favour with many novelists and playwrights. It is always the story of an elderly or middle-aged husband or lover who endures countless humiliations and mental sufferings through the indifference and wantonness of a much younger, capricious and unfaithful wife or mistress.

Though the male partner is in such cases sometimes a masochist, he does on occasions strike back. It is, for example, claimed that the notorious Dr Crippen found an outlet in violence for the indignities he so long suffered in silence. Vladimir Nabokov used this theme in an extreme form in his best-selling novel *Lolita*. The middle-aged man, infatuated to distraction by the adolescent girl, complains bitterly about her whims and caprices, but when she abandons him he is distraught. His wrath is directed against a man who has seduced the girl at a party. He kills the seducer for this act of 'sacrilege'. Familiar masochistic tendencies are clearly apparent here. The well-known story of the old philosopher Aristotle and the youthful Phyllis belongs to this category of phenomena also. Nevertheless, on the whole such cases are rare.

Not so rare are cases in which elderly men allow themselves to be tyrannised over by young boys. Details of such cases can be found in abundance in records of law-court trials. I should like to relate here the outline of such a case. It is the tragic story of a man of aristocratic origin, a talented painter and a gifted poet. He seemed destined for a brilliant career, but all his opportunities were nullified by his one fatal weakness: to kneel at the feet of a young, hefty boy.

When I first met this man he was in the hospital of a prison where he was serving a term of penal servitude for the third time. His life had been a continual series of flights from one country to another, trailing scandals in his wake, spending his considerable fortune on his young, capricious companion of the moment. Penniless, tired and in broken health, he returned at last to his native country where he lived on the proceeds of the sale of his paintings and the charity of his reluctant relatives.

He told me with elation about the whimsical behaviour of his latest boy-friend. Sometimes, while he sat working, this youngster would climb stealthily on a chair behind him and urinate on his head. Then the boy would fly into a fit of rage and order him to clean up the mess on his knees, kicking him wherever he could.

At other times this boy would bring a friend in for fun and games. The old man then had to crawl round the room naked, barking like a dog, while the boys kicked him and smeared his body with paint. Then he had to go out into the street clad in his pyjamas and buy sweets and ice-cream for them, while the boys hung out of the window roaring with laughter. Of course this attracted the attention of the neighbours. The parents of the boys got wind of it and filed a complaint against the old man for corruption of minors. He was condemned to two years' imprisonment and confinement in the psychopathic observation ward afterwards.

There he met a young criminal who had been in penal institutions and reform schools since his fourteenth year. This sinister-looking, ferocious-natured youngster became curiously attached to the old man and remained with him till the man died. It seems that the old debauchee, who could not paint any more, because he had practically lost his eyesight,

137

aroused in the young man all the generous and tender traits that had lain dormant; he worked for him, cared for him, and remained honest so as not to run the risk of being separated from his protégé. After the old man's death he went astray again and soon landed in jail once more.

What prompted this well-born, nice-mannered, erudite man to submit to coarse and callous youngsters? I had no special commission to look after him, so I had only now and then an opportunity to have a talk with him. Probing more deeply into his past might have revealed the source of his trouble. With the scant data I possess I can only hazard a suggestion. There are three facets to this anomaly:

(a) Plain masochism—the origin of which might be found in some such set of circumstances as those suggested earlier in this chapter.

(b) An inclination to identify himself with young violent-natured boys—a revolt against the narrow-minded code of conduct by which he had been brought up, with all its restrictive taboos, in which code there was no place for spontaneous outbursts of rage or joy or any display of emotional feelings. Being of an emotional temperament, he underwent the process of 'breaking-in' and 'bringing to heel' during his formative years as a violation of his personality. The licentious wildness of the boy he chose caused him shudders of delight and fear as he identified himself with the boy's rebelliousness. Such wildness had been absolutely denied to him in his own youth. To his mind this conduct commended itself as daring, adventurous, resourceful, irresponsible: attitudes he had always subconsciously longed to express but which had been precluded by circumstances too strong for him to oppose.

(c) The homo-erotic trend—which must not be seen in this case as an independent predilection but as a superimposition of (a) on (b).

MASOCHISM AND TRANSVESTITISM

Transvestitism, or transvestism, must not be confused with *travestisme*.[1] The latter is prompted by theatrical necessity or

___

[1] *Travestime* is a French term, from the verb *travestir* (the English word travesty' derives from the same root)—meaning to disguise by reversing masculine and feminine clothes.

138

expediency. In past ages women were not allowed to appear on the stage, in many countries. In England, for example, in the theatre of Shakespeare's day, women's parts were played by boys whose voices had not yet broken. Sometimes the rôles of women were played by slight, rather effeminate young men. Famous Japanese painters like Kuniyoshi, Utamaro, and Hokusai, to name only a few, have made drawings of well-known *travesti*-players of their time. *Travesti* has always been very popular in Japan and China, and remains so even today. Some years ago I saw a Japanese film in which a man was able to enter the palace of the son of the shogun (an impostor) in the disguise of a beautiful woman. Later he turned out to be a skilful swordsman. In China during the 'thirties their most famous *travesti*-player was Mei Lan Fan, whose name was such a household word that cosmetic products were named after him.[1] The custom has been widespread in Italy, too, since ancient times. In later centuries young boys were frequently castrated so that they could continue to sing soprano in church choirs. In several of Shakespeare's plays the success of the plot depends upon the skill with which the actors perform their *travesti* rôles: in *Twelfth Night* everything turns on Viola's being accepted as the man Cesario; in *The Merchant of Venice* Portia and her maid Nerissa are supposed to be so convincing in the guise of a beardless young lawyer and his male clerk that they deceive their own suitors to whom they have become affianced only hours before. On the stage today the parts of young boys, pages, etc. are often played by girls; and in English pantomime the 'Principal Boy' is invariably a girl and the 'Dame' as inevitably a man. *Travesti* rôles of a burlesque character are perennially popular, like *Charley's Aunt* or Billy Wilder's *Some Like it Hot*. The same kind of entertainment is common in cabaret: "Madame Arthur" in Paris and the cabaret of the same name in Amsterdam are famous for it. In the last-named example we can say that there is a combination of *travestisme* and transvestitism; but I shall have more to say on that score later.

Summing up, we may say that *travestisme* is sometimes a matter of necessity, sometimes a means of exploiting a preference on the part of the public. In such a preference we can discern a link with transvestitism, in the partial satisfaction of

[1] Another, perhaps equally talented, called Wan Ciun, is referred to in an episode in *Oriental Love in Action*, Giovanni Comisso, Luxor Press, 9/6

a secret and unsuspected urge to change sexes. Transvestitism, on the other hand, is indulged in primarily to satisfy the urge of the transvestite.

The word 'transvestitism' was coined by Hirschfeld, who presumed that the inner urge to resemble a person of the opposite sex was of homo-erotic or auto-erotic origin. Although I admit that this tendency is often present in homosexuals and auto-erotics, I find myself obliged to object to its being regarded as a general rule. Limiting myself for the moment to the inner urge in some males to resemble females, I must relate here some evidence I have found to sustain my thesis that this urge is in fact universal and belongs to all times, quite apart from whether a man's sexuality is inversively directed or not.

Under the heading Masochism in the Female I have referred to a time when woman occupied a dominant position in the community, which was prior to the discovery of the relationship between coition and pregnancy. The male looked up to this creature with awe and envy: awe for her miraculous ability to bring forth life, envy of the finer bodily qualities that were yet adapted to this miraculous function and that also made the difference between him and her visible. Magic power was associated with another feminine peculiarity—menstruation. With the menses she procured power over males. (This is still believed in some parts of the world: the menses form an important ingredient in the charms and spells of witch-doctors).[1]

In my opinion it is this vagina-envy that gave rise to the bloody and painful ritualistic mutilation of the male genitals during initiation rites. Best-known in this respect is the practice of circumcision—the surgical removal of the prepuce; the blood that flowed was most probably regarded as an equivalent of the menses. Elaborate precautions were taken to prevent this blood from being wasted: among the orthodox Hebrews it was sucked up by the Rabbi who performed the operation. But the ritual that seems to leave no doubt in this respect is subincision—the cutting open of the urethra from glans to scrotum, as still practised by Australian aborigines. The fact that for these operations metal may never be used

[1] An interesting traditional Gaelic belief in the power of a woman's menstrual blood over a man is mentioned in *The Merry Muses*, Luxor Press; 9/6; p. 169.

but always stone or bamboo may be an indication that these customs must indeed be of vast antiquity. Initiation rites are really transition rites (*rites de passage*) marking the passing from childhood into adulthood; they are generally accompanied by other symbolic actions, all aimed at "trying to take over the functions of the female" as Margaret Mead puts it. We may assume that all the mother-goddess cults found their origin in gynaecocracy. At the annual feasts of these goddesses those who were to be priests or temple eunuchs brought themselves to a state of frenzy through the traditional media—rhythm, chanted mumbo-jumbo, dancing, stimulants—and in that state cut off their genitals with their own hands. In the cult of Ashtaroth the self-castrator ran yelling into the town and threw his amputated parts into an open window. The owner of the house thus honoured found himself under the obligation to supply the initiate's vestments. *These barbarous and bloody customs and transvestitism have a common origin.*

The boy's mother is his first attachment. He does not understand why he is different from his mother and feels it as an injustice. In his primitive way he tries to get 'even'. Every boy who has known this attachment shows this urge to get even, to resemble the mother, at least once. That is why I have said that transvestitism, traced back to its origin, has nothing to do with homosexuality. I would not even say that it is innate or hereditary or congenital: it is just that man everywhere and at all times has consistently reacted in the same way to basic needs and problems. In this sense it is perfectly natural: so far so good. Under normal conditions the boy grows out of it. When he is adult he may still enjoy a *travesti* show, because consciously or subconsciously he recognises something of himself in it. But when the male does not succeed in outgrowing this childish urge it is no longer natural. This may happen if he is a masochist. Because (as I have explained before) the masochist never gets over his adoration of the mother, it is conceivable that his urge to resemble her is also a lasting trait.

Since masochism is also a favourable condition for the development of homo-erotic tendencies, transvestitism and homosexuality are often found together. But because of the entirely different origin of masochistic tendencies in male and female human beings respectively, there is far less likelihood that there will be any discernible link between feminine masochism and lesbianism than that there will be some such cor-

141

relation between masculine masochism and male homosexuality. The female masochist, as we saw, is suffering from an exaggeration of the submissive impulse: even as the passive partner in a tribadic association she is less likely to satisfy her desire to be humiliated by submission to her female 'lover' than she would by surrendering her personality to the whim of a male 'conqueror'. The possibility of any link between feminine masochism and transvestitism is a great deal more remote still: a woman dressing herself in men's clothes is much more likely to have sadistic leanings. The male being the traditionally dominant sex, there is an evident incompatibility in using masculine clothes to indulge a submissive instinct.

I still owe the reader an explanation of my statement that in the "Madame Arthur" shows we can speak of a combination of *travestisme* and transvestitism. The audience see a *travesti* show that may bring back reminiscences of their own puerile transvestite longings; the performers, on the other hand, are generally in deadly earnest when they impersonate women. In their transvestitism they are indulging a powerful inner urge. Some of them, I have been told, even go so far as to make use of injections of female hormones in order to develop feminine curves.

About ten years ago a great sensation was created by the GI, stationed in Germany, who had his sex changed by a Danish surgeon. He, or rather she, then returned to the United States as Christine. There is also, of course, the still better-known case of "Coccinelle" (Jacques Dufresnoy), who has been called the best *travesti* in the world and whose superb female figure has delighted millions in strip-tease acts during the past few years.[1] But clearly these, and other, amazing cases of sex transformation do not properly fall within the scope of this work at all.

I know a man, in his daily life a well-known fashion designer, who at times cannot resist the temptation to don one of his own creations, complete with jewels, make-up and a fashionable wig. In this attire he visits bars, accepts the homage of male guests, and generally goes away with one of them, and gets quite a thrill out of the treatment meted out to him (and which he fully anticipates) when his true sex becomes

[1] Coccinelle underwent a successful operation for change of sex at a Casablanca clinic in 1958, but it was not until December 1961 that the Paris press was able to reveal that she had been granted the legal status of a woman.

known. He has been pushed out of moving taxis and thrown downstairs, sometimes having had to undergo a prolonged stay in hospital after one of these adventures.

An equally remarkable case was brought to my notice when I was on a visit to Latin America some twelve years ago. No less a personage than Her Britannic Majesty's Ambassador to one of the South American countries was found to be both a practising homosexual and a transvestite when he was involved one night in a most unsavoury brawl in the dock area of the city. Prostitutes attacked him, while he was dressed as a woman, for 'poaching on their preserves'. In the fight that followed he was taken into custody by the police. He protested: "Do you realise who I am? I am Sir —— ——, British Ambassador here!" A policeman, who evidently construed this as tantamount to resisting arrest, struck him over the head with his truncheon, saying, "Yeah, and I'm King Kong!"—or words to that effect. Naturally the incident was hushed up afterwards and the ambassador was bustled out of the country as soon as possible. (The story was related to me in confidence by an official of the hospital where the man was treated for a head injury,—and I can vouch for its veracity.)

A certain Dutch periodical some time ago published a series of advertisements and the correspondence that followed. As this kind of procedure is of common occurrence in many parts of the world, I will now give an example, taken from this published source, of such an exchange of letters, and the reader will be able to observe the evidence of strong transvestite and masochistic inferences it provides.

"Middle-aged gentleman of very submissive character desires to make the acquaintance of a lady of really imperious nature".

After the man received a reply, he wrote the following letter:

"Very honourable Mistress,

Herewith the undersigned thanks you for your letter, in which you state you are prepared to undertake my education with a powerful hand. I intend to write you an honest letter and I would like you to send me an honest reply in which you

143

tell me exactly what you want to do with me.

When I visit you I want you to take away all my possessions and my clothes. They are to be put under lock and key, even my shoes and socks. After you have done that you must dress me as a girl—underwear, skirt and blouse, if possible earrings and necklace, etc. I am 47 years of age but I am very slim and my figure is youthful. All female clothing in the sizes 42–44 can be used. I must be your girl-slave. I offered myself by means of that advertisement and so I am nothing but a whore! I beg you to teach me what being a whore means! Swear at me, call me names if you want to. Tell me I am a whore and nothing better than a bitch,—so long as you never address me as a man during the time I am with you. Naturally you can ask any other woman to come and do with me as she pleases; that woman must pay you for the services I render.

Those services will consist of immediate obedience on my part after you or she have given me orders. It doesn't matter what you have ordered me to do. The most perverse is suitable for your whore. And if I am not willing or if I am not good or quick enough, then punish me without mercy!

Use the whip often and thoroughly. Tie my hands and feet and whip me.

I once had a mistress who tied me to the banisters and let my female clients do with me what they wished.

Some spat into my mouth because they thought it contained female hormones [sic.] At the same time they pulled and twisted my tits. (I do have rather loose skin on my chest). If I groaned or whimpered they popped a pair of panties into my mouth and whipped me, after which they locked me in a cupboard. I have several photographs of these scenes that I will show you when we meet.

So you see, there is only one thing to do: be severe and treat

144

me very harshly and whip me into doing anything that you fancy at the moment.

I am fully prepared to have you make me do the work of a charwoman or maid (polish the floors, clean the windows, make tea, and serve you). Make me, before you start, sign a note in which I state that I am your slave.

Awaiting your reply, I remain in deepest humility,

Your girl-slave
Gerda.

Humiliate me as much as you can.

P.S.:

Be imperious even in your letter of reply. If you would like to meet me, I am free between the hours of 12 and 1 and from 5.30 to 6.30. to go to any meeting-place you have fixed. You tell me where to go; but I must say that I'd sooner remain in the City as I am employed by an office on one of the canals. Since your letter comes from Haarlem I presume that you too work in Amsterdam. We can have a cup of coffee and talk over the details. I am married so you can be sure of my discretion!

Mistress! Tell me how I can meet you and how to recognise you. I shall be dressed in a dark-blue raincoat and I shall not be wearing a hat."

This *document humain* (which in so many ways reminds us of the absurd 'treaties' drawn up by Leopold von Sacher-Masoch and 'Wanda von Dunajew') is all the more grotesque for being written after the man 'Gerda' had received only a short, non-committal note that ran:

"Have read your advertisement and would like to make your acquaintance. Am of a dominating nature and used to being obeyed."

145

It is clear that this man felt his wish to resemble venerated woman as sinful. (Note the emphasis upon wanting to be treated like a whore and a bitch). In accordance with the masochistic attitude as we have come to know it, he did not restrain his wish but persisted in seeking to gratify it, at the same time asking for punishment and humiliation. (The reader will recall that we found evidence of the same kind of unregenerate persistence in the conduct of Sacher-Masoch—the continual demand for correction coupled with a firm resolve to remain incorrigible.)

Sadism and masochism may both originate from an under-developed emotional life, caused through lack of affection on the part of the parents for the child. The sadist wants to exact revenge for it; the masochist will long for the missed affection all his life. We can compare this with the primitive's attitude towards the dangers and uncertainties of life. He may try to master the dangers through recourse to magic, or meet them with the passive attitude of appeasement, sacrifice and submission, the religious attitude. In fact both attitudes are religious: the weird antics and esoteric mumbo-jumbo of the witch-doctor are in essence not very different from the ministrations of a priesthood-élite; the prostration and obeisance of the humble are at one with the unquestioning self-abnegation of the faithful. All believe they are motivated by the same intention—to placate an unknown and vaguely apprehended deity.

RELIGIOUS MASOCHISM

The religious masochist regards himself as unclean in the sight of the Almighty, abject, sinful and unworthy to be one of God's creatures. He constantly begs forgiveness for the fact that he exists: he believes he was born in sin and nurtured in corruption, and he is always trying to prove that he really wants to purge himself. He puts on sackcloth and ashes and mortifies the flesh, holding his body in contempt (notwithstanding that his tenets tell him it was made in the likeness of his Creator), and he prays and fasts and strives to cast out evil spirits. Hair shirts, worn under the other garments in contact with the flesh, cause constant irritation, especially of the nipples and other erogenous zones. In addition to this, sometimes the penitent wore a girdle or necklace set with sharp spikes. Those who were more hardy might take to a bed of

146

nails. Flagellation, whether self-inflicted or administered by others, was considered a highly salutary means of disciplining a sinful body. The most ardent self-chastiser would go further in the invention of fresh sufferings, even resorting to self-mutilation.[1] For these extreme forms of self-discipline they found justification in the Bible (Matthew v, 29–30)[2].

In the Middle Ages they could aspire to canonisation by such means. It would be idle to doubt the sincerity and devoutness of such people, who earnestly believed in the beneficial results to be derived from torturing themselves and never for a moment suspected that they were merely obeying their own subconscious masochistic inclinations. But one cannot help frowning on their cranky reasoning. By all these means it was intended to mortify the flesh, while every normal-thinking man and woman must be well aware that only the precise opposite could be accomplished: instead of being able to forget and ignore the body, by these titillations, irritations and stimulating flagellations they were simply made hyperconscious of it. They were constantly aware that they *had* a body. There are many eye-witness accounts extant of the state of ecstatic frenzy self-flagellants attained to, ending up with orgasm. And to think that benevolent Nature has provided so much easier and pleasanter ways to arrive at the same result! This is certainly one of the most peculiar differences between man and beast: man begins by denying himself the greatest pleasures, and then proceeds to invent intricate means and pretexts for producing the same effects; the beasts do not feel the need to conceal or disguise their procreative instincts.

As I have said before, sadists are never religious. What I mean by this, of course, is that religion is never the motive force of their sadism, though it may supply a pretext; nor does any theistic religion overtly enjoin sadistic practices on its priesthood or the faithful in the way that it prescribes practices that are certainly masochistic in effect. The only relation

[1] In the past few years, through pictures in the newspapers and on television, the world has become almost inured to the sight of Buddhist monks and nuns burning themselves to death in the streets of Saigon as a form of public protest.

[2] "And if thy right eye offend thee, pluck it out and cast it from thee: for it is profitable for thee that one of thy members should perish, and not that thy whole body should be cast into hell. And if thy right hand offend thee, cut it off, and cast it from thee: for it is profitable for thee that one of thy members should perish, and not that thy whole body should be cast into hell."

147

between sadists and organised religion in the past consisted in the fact that the Church afforded them an opportunity to indulge their sadistic bent. With such fanatics as Torquemada one might venture to suspect that his inhuman, unbelievable cruelties were staged as an act of defiance against God, to challenge Him to reveal Himself by direct intervention. But that, it seems to me, would constitute the only relationship, in any acceptable sense, that might have subsisted between his diabolical actions and the religion he pretended to uphold.

THE MASOCHISTIC DAY-DREAMER

There are masochists, probably a majority, who never give active expression to their secret longings. They content themselves with building up a dream world wherein the most improbable humiliations and cruelties are inflicted on them. Some of them write down these phantasies; others, who perhaps lack the imagination to invent phantasy, merely read them. There are, it seems, plenty of writers willing and eager to supply material for this voracious readership. On the whole the stories are of execrable workmanship, constructed with little or no literary talent, and generally the writer prefers to remain anonymous or to use a name that is evidently a pseudonym. Just to give the reader an insight into this mass-manufactured dream-world of the insatiate non-active masochist I propose to conclude this chapter with some excerpts (suitably adapted) from typical examples of such writing. The first book in question is *Die grausame Lady* (*The Cruel Lady*) which is the work of an anonymous author and was privately printed (in German).

"James Stewart discovered his perverse inclination when he was already a grown-up man. True, as a child, he had revelled in the sufferings of others—especially when inflicted by the History teacher Miss Morgan. For the least offence she dealt out canings with relish. James gave her occasion as often as he could. He even gave wrong answers intentionally, when he knew the right ones . . ."

On his twenty-first birthday he has a party. When his friends find out that he has never had sexual intercourse they take him to a brothel and entrust him to the care of a good-looking young whore named Christa . . .

"James was filled with conflicting sensations. He experienced lust when he saw the exciting sweetness of the naked girl, and desire became overwhelming when she touched his member. He lost his self-control completely and fell on his knees, embracing the knees of the woman. The experienced whore knew at once what was the matter with her client.

" 'Aha,' she murmured, almost inaudibly,—'so you are that way, are you? . . . Well, I am prepared for it!'

'Brutally she pushed him away with her foot and yelled at him:

" 'You dirty lout! Having the boldness to touch me! How dare you!'—the same words she always used when dealing with masochists.

"While James was still kneeling on the floor, she suddenly produced a pair of handcuffs, the sort that are used by the police.

" 'Hold up your arms, and don't you dare to answer me back!' With a slow gesture of surrender James stretched out his hands and the steel handcuffs clicked round his wrists. The young man, now defenceless, had to kneel in front of the bed and await what was coming to him. And he found himself anticipating it with pleasure, with a concupiscence he had never felt before.

" 'You wretched boy! Admit that you have offended me. Do you realise how badly you have behaved towards a lady? You lout! Do you imagine it is permissible to touch a lady with lecherous intentions as you did?'

"With this incongruous torrent of words she excited the young man's perverse desire. He remained motionless in his abject posture. She slapped his mouth with her open hand.

" 'Answer me, you scoundrel!'

"With bowed head and in complete surrender James answered trembling:

" 'I am guilty, Miss Christa: I deserve to be punished'—almost the very same words he had uttered in his early youth, before the teacher chastised him.

"The prostitute, well educated in the way to treat masochists, looked down upon the kneeling man, standing spread-legged, hands on hips.

" 'Bow your neck, slave. I will show you how I despise you. I will humiliate you. You shall know that you have insulted a lady!'

"When the boy bowed his head between her legs in mute obeisance, he suddenly felt a warm wet stream on his neck.

The whore emptied her bladder on him.

"While undergoing this mortification, feelings of unfamiliar lust arose in him. He uttered no words of protest. Only a slight groaning proved what profoundly voluptuous sensations he was experiencing.

" 'After having dried herself with a handkerchief, she took a supple instrument out of a drawer next to the wash-bowl. It was a birch, specially made for the chastisement of recalcitrant lovers; she made it swish in the air. Then, rudely, she pulled his head up by the hair and looked malevolently into his eyes.

" 'Have you deserved a whipping?'

" 'Yes, mistress, yes, I deserve it!'

"Christa let the birch come down on the back of her victim. Under this first blow from the hand of a beautiful woman James writhed. He was far from any awareness that he was in a brothel with a paid prostitute. The blow hurt him terribly, but he experienced at the same time a feeling of lust he had never known before."

Later, he has to perform *cunnilinctus* on the girl as a final humiliation.

Subsequently he encounters a Lady Elena Fay, who proves to be the perfect Mistress. When he visits her house, she induces him to kiss her. But when he does so, she appears to be highly indignant.

" 'What! You allow yourself to take liberties, do you? Little buffoon! Are you out of your mind? Or is it the wine? ...'

"She lashes out and strikes him in the face with her right hand. James is petrified. This sudden change of attitude takes him completely unawares. But when Lady Elena takes hold of him by the hair and orders:

" 'On your knees! Beg forgiveness for your impertinence! ...' he found himself again. Like a slave he threw himself at the lady's feet, embraced her legs and stammered:

" 'Lady Elena ... I am desperate ... Never again ... never!'

"A kick with her foot sent him sprawling backwards. Elena stood like a fury over him, stretched out one foot and ordered:

" 'Kiss my foot, servant!'

"When he obediently does so, she orders him to repeat after her the words 'I am a dirty servant—a filthy slave ... I have dared to bother my Mistress. I have dared to kiss my Mistress'. He dutifully repeats the words. She looks at him with unconcealed cruelty, and continues: 'I have deserved a punishment

150

and I will endure the torture patiently'. As he repeats these words also, he adds eagerly, 'Yes, yes ... I will ... I will do anything to make amends,' and he cringes before her.

"Then she singes his armpits with a lighted candle. After singeings on other parts of his body too, he is ill for several weeks. But the lady, who seems to have plenty of influence, arranges with his employers for him to be absent on sick leave.

"Every time she orders him to come to her home he obeys. He has no will of his own. He cannot conquer his infatuation for this dangerous woman.

" 'I will come, love, I will always come ...' he said, and even as he said it he knew that one day he would perish through this woman."

Incidentally the act of submitting to being urinated upon is commonly encountered among the predilections of masochists. Indeed, as Hirschfeld has pointed out, "defecation, micturition, and flatus ... play a considerable part in the folk-lore of civilised modern nations and are nearly always connected in some manner with sex ..."[1] The practice is particularly common among male masochists who enjoy having a woman make water on them.[2] Much less common are cases in which the masochist with this preference is a woman. Nevertheless, Hirschfeld relates the following case from Stekel ...

" 'I am in a wood or in a narrow gorge, with some exposed points; often there is a pond or flowing water close by. It is summer. I am lying in the grass on my back. The stranger comes. Although he is a stranger, I feel that he is nice. He sits down by me and talks to me, but at first I only listen absently, because I feel that his presence induces a vague sexual sensation in me, which I am unable to resist. He seems to sense what is happening within me. Morality and convention cause a woman to be afraid to admit that she expects something from a man, but as this is a secret day-dream I frankly confess that I desire that he should urinate upon me. He senses this

---

[1] *Sexual Anomalies and Perversions.*
[2] As a matter of fact, this practice is not by any means confined to masochists. Many men with powerful natural sex instincts are interested in female micturition, like a friend of mine (in whom I am sure it was not an anomalous condition) who confessed to me that he liked to get his wife to make water on him while he was in the bath.

In *Walter, The English Casanova,* Luxor Press, the Victorian diarist recounts several episodes in which he enjoys making a woman urinate in his presence, and in one case he puts his fingers against the girl's vulva while she is passing water in order to feel the warm flow on his hands.

151

and expresses an intense desire to do this, but I must undress, in order to feel the flow on my naked body and also in order not to wet my clothes. This is somewhat repulsive to me, but he helps me, and his touch makes me shiver. The more clothes I take off the more helpless I feel, but the stronger does my sexual sensation become. Finally, when I am quite naked, I try to hide in the grass; I feel at a disadvantage and uncomfortable. He is dressed, and *that underlines his masculine superiority, while my nakedness accentuates my feminine inferiority.* This intensifies my sexual excitement, *which is based mainly on the difference between the sexes.* He does not seem to be in a hurry. When he touches my thighs and his hand lingers on them, I shudder with pleasure. Then, lying in the grass and half hidden in it, I await the moment when he is going to start. This critical moment has never been imagined to its conclusion even in my day-dreams. I have never dared to finish it in my imagination. I can quite imagine that in such circumstances a degree of appreciation of the phallus might develop.

" 'I imagine the stranger in various positions—standing, kneeling, reclining, always in a position to enable me to enjoy the benefit of the warm, soothing flow. He turns me round, so that I can feel it everywhere; it is sheer delight; I feel it on my breasts, on the thighs, the arms. Sometimes I imagine him naked, then he stands barefooted on me, or straddled over my thighs. Sometimes I am standing, while he is standing or kneeling, and he puts his hand between my thighs and this intensifies my pleasure. The peak of pleasure is reached when I am lying face downwards and he pulls my legs apart, then kneels down and urinates into my vagina. Sometimes he does it in such a way that I am obliged to look into his face; it is the peak of emotional stress and I want more and more. The sensation in itself is sweet, then there is the fact that the precious fluid flows out of him over me. In these day-dreams I have olfactory hallucinations. I can smell the urine, although I know that it is an hallucination. In my daydreams I also like to see the way the fluid comes out, although this vision counts for very little as compared with the joy I feel when the urine splashes over my naked flesh' ".[1] (My italics).

As my second, and final, example of the sort of fare that is

[1] *Sexual Anomalies and Perversions.*

152

liberally provided for the inactive masochist I would refer the reader to a French *roman masochiste* by Jean de la Beucque, called *Despotisme Féminin*.

One of the passengers on the mail-boat *Excelsior* is the beautiful Mme Hernández, the Paris-born widow of an Argentine *latifundista*. She is accompanied by a black female slave, Melbah (also beautiful), whom she treats in public in a most humiliating manner. This attracts the attention of another passenger, Philippe des Roches, who becomes acquainted with Mme Hernández. She resolves to tame this young man. The prospect seems to excite her to such an extent that she makes up her mind to torment Melbah by way of giving herself a pleasing foretaste of delights to come.

Back in her cabin, she sits down, and the slave, after kneeling before her and kissing her feet, takes off the rich woman's shoes and her fine dark silk stockings. Mme Hernández lights a cigarette. Placing a foot on "the heap of black flesh crouching before her" she delivers her other foot to the caresses of her servant, who starts licking it meticulously. While she "undergoes this caress of an agile tongue", the widow shivers with pleasure, dreaming of the next day when the young man she has chosen for her plaything will pay her the same servile homage. What great delight it will give her to break his will and make it lose itself in hers! (The characteristic dream-wish of the sadist). What a refined joy it will be to feel his rebellious body tremble under her feet when she tramples upon him and belabours him with her heels! How delicious it will be to place upon his lips the sole of a shoe which he must lick with the respect becoming in a slave!

After half an hour's meticulous foot-licking by the dutiful Melbah the negress has to lie down naked on the floor like a door-mat while the wealthy widow wipes her feet on her breasts and face. And at last, presumably satiated by many other bizarre rituals, the lecherous widow goes to bed. But, no, she is not satiated: she cannot sleep. The anticipation of coming events keeps her in a turmoil of sensual excitement, makes her brain feverish. She gets out of bed, seizes a whip and shakes the sleeping negress. It doesn't take Melbah long to realise that she is about to have to endure another flagellation orgy which her mistress's imperious caprice imposes upon her from time to time.

In no time Melbah is stark naked, trussed up on the bed,

exposing her genitals to the avid sight and touch of her depraved mistress. De la Beucque regales his readers with a detailed description of Melbah's vulva and of Mme Hernández's probing: the lady is satisfied that her slave is still *virgo intacta.* But, as if by way of recompense for her continence, she now lambastes the poor creature until she "writhes with rapid convulsions". This is apparently the sign that Melbah must "play or die." At this stage, therefore, Mme Hernández, who can clearly read the signs, throws aside the whip and masturbates her long-suffering slave to orgasm. De la Beucque's description of Melbah's crisis is so long, so unnecessarily detailed, and so obscene, that even an experienced researcher like me almost blushed to read it. It would certainly be, in almost any country, an indictable offence to print it. No sooner is it over, however, than the redoubtable Mme Hernández picks up her whip again and flogs the poor negress until the victim lies panting and exhausted on the mat. Then, at long last, she calls it a day and turns in.

By the time we get to Chapter XVI Mme Hernández and her slave, who is also her faithful ally, have completed the conversion of the insolent Philippe des Roches into a masochistic boot-licker ...

"They were now alone in the apartment in the Majestic Hotel on the Prado. It comprised two bedrooms with annexes. The woman wore a delightful beige two-piece, which suited her marvellously. Her dainty feet were imprisoned in elegant black patent leather shoes with Louis XV heels that well matched the archings of her imperious feet (*sic*). She stood erect, proud, nonchalant, fixing with her eyes the young man who was about to fall on his knees and was lightly advancing to one of her divine feet.

"Filled with a holy intoxication for what for him was the most imperative of orders, Philippe threw himself at her feet and began licking and kissing the magic shoe from the point to the back of the heel, shuddering lustfully from the contact with the leather he tasted with his feverish mouth. At last the divine moment had come to humiliate himself freely at the feet of his Idol, and he continued to steer his tongue over the patent leather while Yvonne (Mme Hernández), with a triumphant smile on her cruel lips, let herself be rendered this passionate homage.

"She withdrew her foot and advanced the other, to which

154

his servile mouth adhered with the same ardour. She placed her other foot on the head of her slave, crushing his lips against the point of her shoe. At this brutal shock of the feminine foot on his skull, at this contact so passionately longed for, Philippe gave a long shudder. She held him in this position for some minutes, then she let the point of her shoe that she had first put on his head glide down to his throat, rudely tearing loose the collar of his shirt, exposing the neck. She amused herself belabouring his flesh with the sharp sides of her heel, filled with lust at the uncontrollable shudderings of the suffering slave.

"Next, she put the point of her shoe against his temple and pushed his head in such a way that one of his cheeks was being ground into the carpet. Then she trampled his face with vivacity. Then she kicked his sides. She ordered him to strip completely and kneel down in front of her. Hastily he obeyed, while the young woman, comfortably seated in an armchair, peacefully smoked a cigarette."

And so it goes on ... He licks her hands and she tickles his torso with her shoes, which he then has to kiss all over again. But there is a prize awaiting him:

"'You will see: I shall keep my promise. I have said that you shall be my lover and you shall, this evening ...'" However, it's not as easy as all that: he has to go through some more yet. "'... first you will have to submit to the chastisement I have promised and you are going to receive this correction now!'"

After pulling a whistle out of her beautiful bosom and blowing it, the formidable termagant orders Melbah, who has appeared in answer to this summons, to thrash Philippe while she herself sinks back in luxury to enjoy the spectacle and listen to his groans and sighs. As she does so a brilliant idea dawns upon her. When she has had her fill of him she will have him deflower Melbah! But before that there is more trampling, and of course a great deal more foot-licking.

The whole story is, of course, sheer arrant nonsense, written by a person of no literary talent and who does not even know what he (or she) is talking about. For example, at one point we read: "... the rich South American lady sinks back [absorbed] in reveries of all the times she had let Melbah administer lashings to the *gauchos* on her *hacienda*." Now in the first place, the ranches in Argentina are called *estancias*,

155

not *haciendas,* which are found in Spain. And, secondly, the idea that Argentine *gauchos* would allow a woman (particularly a negro servant) to beat them is quite ludicrous to anyone who knows anything at all about Latin America. The *gauchos* are invariably tough, virile, and independent, the very backbone of the nation, and implacably aggressive when provoked: they would, in fact, be much more likely to administer a salutary thrashing to Mme Hernández herself! But, as the reader can see, here is a pornographic extravaganza, a hotch-potch of every conceivable aberration and perversion—sadism, masochism, flagellomania, masturbation, fetishism, voyeurism, the urge to procure, defloration mania—the lot! And as for foot-licking, enough lubricating energy for this purpose has been expended in the space of ten pages to clean the British Museum from end to end.

PART THREE
FLAGELLATION

CHAPTER SEVEN

Flagellomania

DEFINITIONS

The Latin word *flagellum* means a scourge or whip. To forestall confusion of ideas it is necessary to define properly what we mean by the words we are about to use.

Flagellomania: excessive partiality to the whip.

Flagellant: person given to flagellation.

Flagellation: the act of whipping, scourging.

The pornographic literature on this subject is disproportionate. In psycho-medical literature the word 'flagellomania' and its derivations are frequently used, but explanations of this particular aberration are still vague. It is generally treated as a part of the sado-masochistic complex. But why then did it receive a special name? Other preferences of sadists and masochists are as frequent as flagellomania. I will name only being kicked, and the licking and kissing of feet and shoes. It would have been easy to invent Latin words for these likings too, and no doubt some authors have attempted to do so. But such words have never been adopted into the language. Long ago I came to the conclusion that there are good reasons to regard flagellomania as distinct from other sado-masochistic preferences. I will now try to explain the conclusions I have reached.

Instruments used for flagellation are whips of all forms, sizes and materials, switches, especially birches, rods, thongs, slippers, canes, belts, rulers, and all the materials and objects that can produce painful burning sensations, and sounds, causing feelings of excitement.

FLAGELLATION AS AN APHRODISIAC

To understand this we must take into consideration that the genitals are not the only parts of the body in which feelings of sexual excitement are readily aroused. The mouth, breasts (especially the nipples), and the anus are also erogenous zones, which may include other parts of the body too. Krafft-Ebing writes in his *Psychopathia Sexualis*: "In men, as well as in women, erection and orgasm, or even ejaculation, may be induced by irritation of various other regions of the skin and mucous membrane". And again—"Libido sexualis may also be induced by stimulation of the gluteal region (castigation, whipping). This fact is important for the proper understanding of certain pathological manifestations. It sometimes happens that in boys the first excitation of the sexual instinct is caused by a spanking, and they are thus incited to masturbation."

We must keep in mind that Krafft-Ebing wrote his *Psychopathia Sexualis* in 1884. He was a pioneer in a field that up to then had been circumvented as a result of the prudishness about everything pertaining to sex. Masturbation—in his days —was looked upon as something very dangerous to the health of a person. In the light of the experience of psychiatrists of the last decades, many phenomena he called 'pathological' have been proved to be quite normal.

Anyhow, it is a fact that the more or less violent irritation of certain parts of the body gives way to emotional feelings, directly affecting the central erectile power. Every prostitute has or has had clients whose diminished sexual powers have first had to be stimulated through whipping. We may say that as long as flagellation is only a (necessary) means to produce an erection which enables the person to perform coition, it is just a sort of aphrodisiac.

Of course a phenomenon like flagellation has been, and still is, commercially exploited. Pisanus Fraxi gives details about provisions for flagellants found in Victorian London brothels. The famous queen of the brothels, Mrs Berkley, constructed for her flagellant clients a contraption called 'The Berkley Horse'. Passive flagellants were fastened to it and flogged. A picture of 'The Berkley Horse' can be found in one of Pisanus Fraxi's books.

In this modern age most big brothels have the necessary equipment dear to flagellants the world over. Some of them have 'torture rooms' too. Friedrich Thelen draws attention to the existence of secret societies of flagellants, and Ulrich Mechler gives detailed information about the 'salon' of a 55-year-old widow in a Viennese suburb where flagellants meet twice a week. All of them are middle-aged gentlemen with

160

high annual incomes and the best positions in the social life of the capital. Monthly subscription is as high as 1,500 schillings Before being admitted, members have to pronounce a secret password that is changed every month. At a rough estimate the club has forty members and that ensures the merry widow a monthly income of 60,000 schillings.

Six young females play the part of 'mistresses' at the meetings of the club. On most evenings four of them are present. In daily life these 'mistresses' work as a secretary, a teacher, a student and a chemist respectively. One is the wife of a consul. The eldest is 40 and the youngest is 21 years old. Only the secretary and the student are single; all the others are married; the teacher to a well-known journalist and the chemist to a famous scientist.

The widow always draws up the programme for a meeting and every time the highlight of the evening is a general 'flogging orgy'. She seldom takes part herself in the floggings. Most often she leaves the flogging to her 'mistresses' who are paid a large monthly salary for their trouble. Sometimes the 'mistresses' wear riding-breeches, at others they appear dressed for a fancy-dress ball, or they wear an evening-gown. During the meetings the members are naked. Only when they play the part of 'disobedient schoolboys' they wear shorts and sweaters. They undress in changing-rooms. The 'mistresses' all have their private rooms where they can retire with their favourite slaves.

In certain cases a mild flagellation given not in seriousness but in a playful mood can be an introduction to love-play. Nobody would think of calling this a perversion, which is something that has taken the place of normal coition. In this case fetishism scarcely plays any part.

THE MEANING OF FLAGELLATION TO THE SADIST

The man with a whip in his hand is the perfect symbol of the 'master'. Sadists who are nates-fetishists may like to whip buttocks, because they resent the power of attraction these objects (to the fetishist the fetish is an object) have over him. Sadists do not want to be subjected, no matter to what. Given their attitude to life, it is quite understandable that they want to establish their mastery over the enchanting objects by whipping them.

161

It is a short step from over-zealousness about flagellation, whether from the point of view of the active flagellant or the passive scopophil, to an extravagant and disproportionate admiration for the nates. Interest in the human backside, amounting at times almost to veneration, is no new thing. The ancient Greeks esteemed the rotundity of a woman's buttocks far more highly than the shapeliness of her breasts, and Greek girls would compete with each other in beauty contests for the title of Miss Beautiful Buttocks (actually Kallipyge was the name the Greeks had for it). Steatopygia (excessive enlargement of the buttocks) is a characteristic feature of the women of certain primitive communities in Africa, notably the Hottentots. (Another name for this grotesque protuberance is 'the Hottentot bustle').[1]

Among the efflorescence of flagellantist 'literature' that can only, in the main, be regarded as pornographic, the very names of the characters, as well as the titles of the works themselves, clearly suggest and confirm this almost demented glorification of the buttocks, especially, of course, the female behind. *The Callipyges*, for example, is a series of such things as 'A Lecture on Drawers' and hints on the vital importance of knowing just where and how to strike the "tempting globes" to obtain the best results, etc. The characters are women like Lady Richbuttock, Lady Fairbottom, Lady Finefleece, Lady Plentiful, Lady Spendidorb (note the snobbish incongruity of this compliment to aristocracy), Mrs Flog, Mrs Skintear, Lady Lovebirch, and so on.

Practically all the books produced last century on the whipping of females elaborately 'describe', not only the cheeks of the buttocks which, for variety's sake, may be of almost any size and configuration, but the entire gluteo-inguinal region, with sly references at times to "pearls" of moisture upon the "curtain of hair" hiding "love's secret grotto", etc., to suggest with somewhat grotesque subtlety that the victim is responding erotically to the castigation. Every bound and twitch is noted.

[1] Females of this tribe also have the famous 'Hottentot-apron' or over-developed vaginal lips, as described in detail in my companion book, *Lesbian Love Old and New*, Luxor Press, 9/6.

The Appeal of Flagellation to the Puerile Masochist

Although it may be assumed that many masochists experience the aphrodisiacal effects of a whipping, the stimulation of their *libido sexualis* is not their primary objective. Their principal aim is to be humiliated.

One of my patients, a confirmed masochist, was a man named Karl P. Although he did not come to me to be treated for his masochistic tendencies, he once confided to me a favourite day-dream of his that to many people must sound strange indeed.

He likes to imagine his firm is sending him to Paris. As he does not speak French he has to take lessons. He goes to a private instructress, a Mme Dupont, who is a very severe teacher and uses a cane to punish him for his mistakes. The more nervous he becomes the more mistakes he makes. So as not to interrupt the lesson Mme Dupont simply keeps count, aloud, of the 'points' as they mount up against him, and the 'payment' is to be exacted in full at the end of the lesson. Usually there are about thirty strokes to come—on his bare behind. He has to take down his trousers and his underpants and suffer the humiliation in full. He concluded his account: "My poor bottom raises itself in pain for the very last time ... Then it's all over. Now I feel a loving hand stroking the burning skin tenderly ..."

Karl P. is 47 years old, yet he dreams of being caned by his teacher for making too many mistakes during the lesson. He knows that he, an adult, kneeling in front of a couch with his trousers down, presents a most ridiculous sight. And yet in his phantasy he accepts the situation in all seriousness. This day-dream illustrates very clearly the irrational images of the masochistic world of make-believe.

The True Flagellant

There are flagellants of quite another nature. They like the act of flagellation for the state of ecstatic frenzy they can attain to through it. Their moments of ecstasy give them a feeling of purpose, of being fully alive. The sensation of elation, of being carried away beyond the purposeless dulness of everyday life, is what they pursue.

In my opinion these persons are the true flagellants. They must be differentiated from sadists and masochists with flagel-

163

lantist inclinations. In their nature and attitude there is nothing of the dark fatalistic atmosphere that marks the true sadomasochist relationship. The true flagellants are to sadists and masochists what a Gilbert and Sullivan operetta is to an opera by Wagner. There is room for amusement; they are capable of making light of their own folly. Although they are absolutely alone in their moments of ecstasy, they are by no means solitary freaks. They are not deprived of the ability to feel affection; on the contrary, they are truly affectionate towards their 'playmates'.

I do not mean to say that these people are always cheerful and happy. My only intention is to point out that they are not subject to the constant feeling of despair, so evident in sadistic and masochistic relationships. These true flagellants, like anybody else, have their fits of depression, but they have found a way to re-establish their happiness.

This piece of knowledge came to me during my student-days. I had been reading a work by Havelock Ellis that puzzled me. I offer here a quotation from that work:

"The fact that we are here primarily concerned with exercises in the field of emotion, only incidentally liable to reach the threshold of pain, is shown in the child's equal or greater liking to suffer its infliction. Games of 'punishment' with much reciprocal smacking have always been privately popular among children of both sexes, perhaps especially girls, the hairbrush often being used for this purpose. Self-flagellation is also sometimes practised, and even after puberty, when the genital centres are fully active, it may be adopted by either sex to heighten the solitary pleasure of the sexual impulse in the absence of a person of the opposite sex. Day-dreams of torture are a not uncommon source of pleasure even among young children, and at a rather later age one has heard of Foxe's *Book of Martyrs* proving a source of thrilling delight. Sometimes the child experiences an irresistible impulse to inflict pain on himself and often on his penis, which indicates that, even if not a source of sexual excitement in the adult sense, the penis is already a centre of emotional interest. Such facts recall the castration-complex to which some psychoanalysts attach enormous importance. A string may be strongly tied round the penis; or it may even be violently struck; and the case has been recorded of a girl of nine who tied a thread round her clitoris and was unable to remove it,

164

so that surgical intervention became necessary. Sensation and emotion are still in a comparatively diffused and, as it were, uncrystallised form. As the realisation of pain is necessary so early in life for self-preservation it is inevitable that painful emotions should be those in which the still vague pleasure impulses tend to take shape. Hamilton found among his subjects, who may all be said to be of high character and culture, only 49 per cent of men and 68 per cent of women who never experience pleasure in inflicting pain; while nearly 30 per cent of both men and women had had pleasure in experiencing pain." (*Adapted*.)

I did not remember ever having had these experiences myself and I had not witnessed them in others. As this urge was perfectly alien to me, I suspected Havelock Ellis of making a generalisation of an exceptional case. While discussing this with a fellow-student it came out that he was what I now call a 'true flagellant'.

I am still grateful for the unique opportunity I was thus afforded to obtain a glimpse of the truth behind one of the intricate phenomena we are dealing with in this book. As this man was very intelligent and quite capable of analysing his own feelings, and as we were furthermore equals, he was an ideal informant. In the physician-patient relationship the innermost significance of certain psychic phenomena is generally not so readily yielded.

He and his friends (girls as well as boys) liked to 'socialise' their mutual floggings. It seems that visualising and observing the floggings are sure expedients for heightening ecstatic frenzy. Though direct sex acts such as coition and masturbation might follow, this was not necessarily so. The main point, as he described it, was "mental orgasm". Afterwards he had a feeling of extreme well-being, clearness and cleanness. When every participant had had his or her share, the atmosphere was one of fondness and friendliness. He assured me that there were many more people devoted to this kind of recreation than I suspected, and during my subsequent practice this has proved to be true. Once one is fairly familiar with certain aspects and symptoms one may develop a sort of 'sixth sense' about a patient's hidden inclinations.

AUTO-FLAGELLATION

The abstract given above from a work by Havelock Ellis

indicates that self-infliction of pain is not infrequent among youngsters.

As a matter of course these motives arose also in the religious flagellation practised during the Middle Ages, when the flagellants who chastised themselves with religious zeal acted out of perfectly honest motives and never suspected what were the real mainsprings of their actions. If they felt themselves tormented by the 'worldly flesh', more and more severe flagellation was indulged in to cast out lustful emotions: Hence the beginning of a cycle that could grow into such awe-inspiring dimensions that the person concerned was considered a saint by his contemporaries.

A very obvious case dating from the Middle Ages is related by Joachim Pauly:

"One of the most famous flagellants of her age was Magdalena of Pazzi, a Carmelite nun of Florence, born into a very wealthy family. Her passion was to have her hands tied behind her back by her Mother Superior and to have her nude body flogged by the inmates of the nunnery.

"This delighted her so much and the flagellation she had endured since her early youth got so out of hand that the nervous system of the nun was seriously upset. During her ecstasy she thought mainly of 'love', crying: 'Let this flame that consumes me not burn higher. I don't want to die in this way. Too much lust and bliss would be found in such an end...' She admitted sometimes having lustful phantasies and complained of running the risk of losing her virginity. By regular and severe flagellation she hoped to cast out those phantasies and she did not suspect that by such behaviour she was only pouring oil on the fire that consumed her."

It is understandable that medieval flagellants did not recognise the true motivation of their behaviour. They lived in a benighted age, in utterly different circumstances from ours, and under the influence of different moral taboos from those we are familiar with today. They never suspected there was a connexion between pain and passion.

166

CHAPTER EIGHT

The Step-child of Psychiatry

THE STAND-BY OF PORNOGRAPHY

The sado-masochistic complex is the step-child of psychiatry. And no wonder. The number of patients affected by this anomaly who visit a psychiatrist is small in comparison with the number of patients who go there for other psychic ailments. Whereas a psychiatrist should have no more than four patients a day, if he is to do justice to them, he may frequently be called upon to attend twenty or more, day in, day out. Since sado-masochistic cases are generally 'difficult' ones, which seldom yield notable successes, it is conceivable that the average psycho-analyst or psychiatrist, over-burdened with work already, is not eager to spend too much time on them. This may also help to account for the fact that the scientific literature on the subject is vague and circumlocutory and of little help if one wants to get a clear insight into these difficult and complicated matters.

I had to find out for myself. I started at the bottom, never fearing to betray my ignorance. I was rewarded with the subjects' complete confidence and earnestness and eagerness to help me, which enabled me later to help many of them. One of the things I always asked them was which novels they had read dealing with their particular anomaly and which they liked best. For the novels that are accepted by them contain the language of the perversion and can thus be of great help to an outsider.

There can be no doubt that many, perhaps most, people who have strongly developed sexual appetites enjoy reading erotic, and even pornographic, literature. And the great stand-by of pornography is flagellation. Even those who 'wouldn't hurt a fly', as well as those who in ordinary circumstances are repelled by the very prospect of pain, usually find some powerful vicarious enjoyment in reading flagellantist novels. They seem subconsciously to identify themselves with either the dominant one inflicting the imaginary strokes or the submissive one who receives them. The mere fact that the action of the story *is* imaginary absolves them, as it were, from any responsibility: they can always dismiss participation as absurd and dissociate themselves completely by affecting revulsion. The same attitude is often adopted by individuals comprising audiences in cinemas where erotic films are being shown dealing, for example, with some anomaly, say homosexuality or rape. People who see such a film may be 'carried away' by it and even experience sexual stimulation, alone and in the dark, and then come outside and condemn the film they have just seen and enjoyed as obscene.

Besides, as we have seen, flagellation covers 'a multitude of sins': it is sauce for the goose and for the gander. It may provide a prelude to normal sexual indulgence. It delights the sadistic and the masochistic, and it even enables them, at will, to reverse their rôles. It may be a concomitant, an accompaniment, or a substitute, for almost any other sexual anomaly or perversion on occasion. Flagellation is the 'whipping-boy' for prude and puritan, for boor and bully. Even the 'honest citizen' who would be highly indignant at the merest hint that he had just the faintest sadistic streak in his nature may feel justified in demanding the retention or re-introduction of corporal punishment as a deterrent to crimes of violence. He cannot agree that he who is not against it is for it. The purveyors of pornography have always been well aware of the universal appeal of the wielded whip and the bare bottom, and they glibly exploit the old stand-by perennially throughout the centuries.

Many people are of the opinion that these pornographic novels cannot be regarded as solely pernicious. They may serve as safety-valves for many deviates and quasi-perverts who without them might possibly turn, in order to assuage their cravings, to other modes of conduct more likely to endanger society. To a certain extent I can agree with that view. I can understand why these generally badly-written, tedious novels are read. It is also clear to me why they are written.

Throughout the ages they have been poorly put together, by untalented authors, who had but one aim—to make money quickly. One of the few exceptions is the anonymously written

168

Die Memoiren einer russische Tänzerin, in which the story fascinates precisely because it is not merely a series of flagellation scenes. The truth is that flagellation, in itself, and when it leads to nothing more, is simply a bore. There is only so much that can be said, and when it is repeated and repeated at sickening length, however much the protagonists are varied, even the most ardent reader is inclined to lose interest. Of course, to a certain extent, the same may be said of all pornographic literature, but the theme of flagellation alone, more than any other perhaps, is soon inclined to seem cripplingly restrictive. When, to ring the changes, the writer concentrates his descriptive powers, such as they are, on the posterior of his victim, the thing is so likely to develop into sheer nates fetishism that the flagellantist element becomes subordinated or distorted.

If flagellation, in a mild form at least, can be conceived as having any usefulness in the way of an erotic stimulus, it should, can, and indeed often does, lead to more satisfying *coitus.* But in so many books on the subject, as in the series issued by the mid-Victorian publisher John Camden Hotten, the floggings and 'bum-ticklings' lead to nothing at all, or at the jolliest to an orgy of *cunnilinctus* all round. Generally speaking, the flagellation is an end in itself, the only focus of sexual lust. Besides, it is nearly always women who handle the birch, rod or whip, and generally girls or other women who are the objects of their attentions. This gives a rather one-sided, lesbianistic view of the subject.

PRUDERY AND PORNOGRAPHY

From the beginning of the nineteenth century, both prudery and pornography began to play important parts in English public life. As a matter of fact the gulf between the two extremes is not so vast as may at first be imagined, for in the last analysis they are, equally, expressions of an unhealthy exaggeration of the *libido sexualis,* the one taking refuge in repression, the other in defiance.

It was in the Victorian era, when many people were so prudish that they would refer to the 'limbs' of a piano or table rather than use the word 'legs', and offer a lady some 'white meat' at table so as to avoid asking her if she would like some of the breast of the chicken, that the flagellation mania reached a new peak. From the beginning of the eighteenth century, in

London brothels men could have themselves flogged if they wanted to, but by the middle of the nineteenth this had become such a popular pastime that on the Continent it was referred to as 'the English vice' (which, however, should not be taken to mean that it was a vice thriving on English soil only!) David Loth writes:

"As the mania spread in England, clubs were founded where members might whip each other. One connoisseur invented a machine which lashed forty addicts at a time. By the early nineteenth century these institutions were such a part of London life that George IV visited at least one, although it is not recorded that he took part in the ceremonies. Some flagellant brothels were famous enough to live in history—Mrs Collet's, Mrs Berkley's, Mrs Jenkins'—known to their patrons as parlours for massage. The success of these places has been attributed to a belief that many gallants, worn out by dissipation, needed the extra stimulation to go on dissipating".[1]

This was the age of William Dugdale, one of the most celebrated publishers of pornography. Together with his rivals in business he lived in Holywell Street, a short shopping thoroughfare full of tobacconists' shops and booksellers, where nearly all the windows had the most obscene books and pictures on display. The street itself disappeared about the turn of the century when the Kingsway area of London was redeveloped. William Dugdale's output was amazing. In the forty years that he busied himself with the publication of pornography he went to jail nine times. The profits he made from his business were so satisfactory that he gladly tolerated these interruptions in his soaring career.

At this time London had six thousand brothels and some eighty thousand prostitutes among a population of little more than a million souls.[2]

Not for nothing was flagellation called 'the English vice'. Many books on flagellation or with flagellantist tendencies are of English origin. Highly-placed persons in the British Government and in the Armed Forces, well-known representatives of the world of art and science, patronised, as Pisanus Fraxi states, the brothels which specially catered for flagel-

[1] David Loth: *The Erotic in Literature*, London 1962.
[2] A most illuminating first-hand description of the shadier side of London life in Victorian times is to be found in *Walter, The English Casanova*, Luxor Press.

170

lants. It was at this time that the notorious Mrs Theresa Berkley was flourishing in her establishment at 28 Charlotte Street, Portland Place. She invented her extremely popular 'Berkley Horse' in 1828, which at her death in 1836 was solemnly presented by her executors to that august body the Royal Society of Arts! There was Mrs Emma Lee (properly Richardson) at 50 Margaret Street, off Regent Street; there was Mrs Phillips at 11 Upper Belgrave Place, Pimlico; there was Mrs Sarah Potter (*alias* Stewart), at a number of different addresses; there were a host of other ladies all devotedly catering for the bizarre needs of gentlemen continually in search of erotic pleasure, and their name was legion. When Mrs Potter was arrested for whipping a girl (an affair that could only have been in the nature of a test case for it was a common enough occurrence), a certain amount of unwelcome publicity was given to the widespread mania—unwelcome for, as I have said, it was an age of prudishness and the very essence of prudery is to keep your sins private. A pamphlet appeared in 1863 called *Mysteries of Flagellation*, which blew the gaff somewhat by drawing attention to a lot of strange goings-on which no doubt even some of the roués themselves were glad to learn about. Details were given concerning "the den of Mother Commins" called "The White House", and about "the Elysium in Brydges Street".

It is generally supposed that British gentlemen have developed their amazing *penchant* for flagellation because of their early experience of corporal punishment at school. And in this respect it must be admitted that the penal system in vogue in British so-called public schools provided a training-ground *par excellence*. In a seventeenth-century comedy by Shadwell (*The Virtuoso*) an old libertine named Snarl goes to a brothel to be flagellated. When the prostitute asks him why he has such strange tastes he answers: "I became so used to it at Westminster School that I can't give it up". And indeed Westminster School was for long outstanding in notoriety for this kind of treatment and at one time a satirical magazine used to be issued at the school called *The Flagellant*. That the zeal of headmasters for flogging was not unmingled with sadistic tendencies is well illustrated by Cowper who relates that Westminster's Dr Parr was supplied with rods by a man who had been cut down from a gallows and revived: whenever

171

he took the rods from this man, says Cowper, he did so "with a pleased smile".

Many famous headmasters, like Dr Drury and Dr Vaughan (Harrow); Busby, Keate and Edgeworth (Eton); Dr Gill (St Paul's), and Dr Keate (Rugby), seem all to have shared the view which Edgar Allan Poe was to express at a later date, that "Children are never too soft for chastisement. Like tough steaks, the more they are beaten the softer do they become". Of Dr Keate it was said that "he knew the behinds of his pupils better than their faces". Lord Byron gave voice in verse to his acclaim for the merits of a good thrashing:

> "Oh ye who teach the ingenuous youth of nations,
> Holland, France, England, Germany, and Spain,
> I pray ye flog them upon all occasions,
> It mends their morals, never mind the pain."

If the gentler sex seem not to have been so commonly beaten as their masculine contemporaries, this was only so in appearance. What they missed by not going to boarding-schools (which so few of them did, relatively) they made up for in private. Girls of all ages, even up to the time of marrying, were constantly being thrashed by mothers, fathers, tutors or governesses. And even after marriage the practice was often carried on by the zealous husband. It was permissible for masters and mistresses to beat their servants. In women's penal institutions it was the practice to whip the girls on admission and again when they were released, and as a disciplinary measure at any time in between.[1] Prostitutes picked up in the streets by officers of the law were taken to these places and given a flogging. These whippings were nearly always carried out in public or before a select audience. For many people, particularly ladies and gentlemen of leisure, it was an exciting form of entertainment (and one that cost nothing) "to see the strumpets whipped at the Old Bailey".

In such an atmosphere, when almost nobody thought of flagellation as a plague to be stamped out (for even if one did not approve of it one merely accepted it with a shrug of the shoulders as a necessary evil), it is not to be wondered at that a spate of printed material on the theme proliferated. The very abundance of it, and the constant demand to be fulfilled

[1] See p. 34 *et seq.*

in an attempt to satisfy a greedy but, after all, depraved taste, made inevitable a lowering of literary standards, and indifference as to quality and content, and concentrated the acumen of publishers, as of brothel 'madams', upon the simple expedient of cashing in.

PART FOUR
CHRONOLOGICAL SURVEY

CHAPTER NINE

Sado-Masochism Through the Ages

FROM THE PRIMITIVE TRIBE TO THE MODERN FAMILY

It has universally been taken for granted that sadism and masochism are as old as mankind. At first glance this seems evident. In the animal world the male pursues the female; she is overtaken and possessed by force. In the world of man this has also been the case (and sometimes still is); vestiges of this practice can still be found in our marriage customs and our language, which give ample proof of it as I have pointed out before. Once again I repeat that the sex act is basically an act of violence. According to Krafft-Ebing, Freud and others, sadism and masochism are components of the sex play, having become exaggerated and independent.

Nevertheless we find no evidence of the existence of sadism and masochism as independent perversions among primitive tribes of today and we can safely assume that the same goes for primitive societies of old, including our own past. This can be easily understood if we take into account that for the member of a tribe no life is possible outside the tribe. The individual is dependent upon the tribe for his survival and the tribe is dependent on the individual for its continuance. Everybody eats or nobody eats; everybody lives or everybody perishes. One has to curb passions and desires that are contrary to the interest of the tribe. The aggression, created by this necessary continence, is directed towards strangers, non-members of the tribe. (An inevitable result of this is the custom of adopting a stranger as a member of the tribe, when continued friendly relations are appreciated). We find the same attitude in isolated rural communities where bloody fights often take place when, for instance, one of their girls is courted by an unwelcome male from a neighbouring village. Family ties within the tribe are very often rather loose, which is not a drawback for the individual because the whole tribe is one family. One has to, and accordingly one can, trust one's own kin (all the members of the tribe being akin) from sheer necessity. Evidence of this sense of kinship can be found in nomination customs, no distinction being made between brothers and cousins and fathers and uncles. The Chinese still have these customs of nomenclature: the father and all the other males of his generation are addressed with the same titles. Only the bond between mother and child makes an exception to this rule. Motherhood is undeniable, fatherhood putative. All this explains why transgressing the tribal customs was seen as a grave crime and very often was visited with capital punishment. The survival of the tribe was at stake.

When a community grows intricate and complex, the individual no longer feels and experiences it as a reality: it has become abstracted. He stands alone in a hostile world. It is the feeling of alienation I spoke of at the end of the first part of this book. His existence is not important to the continuance of the community. With or without him it will go on: he has become insignificant, expendable.

In our society, the family has to take over the task of the tribe of old. The family in our society is not only the place where its members find food and shelter: it must also be something the child (in the first place, but the same goes for the husband-wife relationship) can trust, where no ill-will is present. This is the *sine qua non* that determines the possibility of the social adjustment of the individual. When the individual has grown up in a family where there is an absence of mutual understanding and trust and of the conviction that ill-will does not exist, he will later trust nobody and consequently may come to hate everybody. This is the condition in which sadism and masochism may take root. In our disintegrating society the family is the last stand. If Western man wants to ensure the continuance of his society he will have to direct all his power towards the rehabilitation and preservation of family life. No social provision, however perfect it may be, can replace it. Social security increases the individual's leisure. Leisure creates boredom. And sex crimes (as Colin Wilson has pointed out in the brilliant introduction to his *Encyclopaedia of Murder*) are crimes of boredom.

Summing up, we may conclude that family conditions in a

complex society determine the individual's attitude towards society and the value he attaches to human life.

If we therefore care to look for notorious cases of sadism and masochism in historical times we shall find them in abundance in complex societies and especially among the leisured classes. In the Arabian book *The Thousand and One Nights,* the Sultan Shahriyar put to death by (strangling) every one of his brides after the first nuptial night. But Scheherazade, an amateur psychiatrist *avant la lettre,* succeeded in breaking through the Sultan's psychic stricture by telling him stories, night after night, thus escaping the fate of her predecessors. It may seem a bit irrational to start a historical review with a legendary figure, but one must bear in mind that legends nearly always have a factual background. We may therefore reasonably assume that some such sadistic ruler may have existed. It goes without saying that we have no data about the personal background of this man, but from the general knowledge we have of court life in ancient times, we can draw fairly accurate deductions.

For obvious reasons, the seraglio of a Sultan was forbidden territory to men; trespassing in defiance of this prohibition was a capital crime. Accordingly, male children were taken away from the seraglio and their mother at an early age, long before they grew sexually mature. They were cared for by servants and tutors. Incidentally these servants and tutors may have been truly devoted to the child in their care, but this could never replace the mother-child bond. These Eastern potentates lived in constant fear of betrayal and murder. Intrigues blossomed luxuriantly. In this atmosphere of alienation, stifling mistrust, envy and enmity, the princely child grew up. Unless he had inherited extraordinary mental faculties, such as great intelligence, clear judgment and strong willpower, he was apt to become an inconstant, capricious despot with the unlimited power of life and death over his subjects. He had ample leisure and he could have any woman to whom he took a fancy. What is too easily accessible has little value and becomes a bore. In such circumstances even sex loses its savour, resulting in a restless quest for other emotion-stimulating media, to resuscitate the waning appetite. The factors that contribute to the creation of an aberration were present in abundance.

What Scheherazade did was distract the mind of her Sultan

179

from his fixation and give his quest for new stimulation another direction. She gave him a purpose, and life a new value, even though this only consisted in looking forward to the next night's bed-time story. As far as I know, this simple explanation of the Sultan's cruel habits has escaped most researchers; they were no doubt absorbed by linguistic problems and questions concerning the origin of the book.

GREECE OF ANTIQUITY

The Greeks of old seem to have been a harmoniously-living, beauty-loving people. This may account for the fact that very little evidence of sadism can be found in their history

Theopompus of Chios, a Greek historian, who lived in the fourth century B.C. wrote a book called *Philippica*. It is a pity that only fragments of this book have been found. One of these fragments, however, contains a story that is worth noting: Cotis, King of Thrace, in a fit of rage cut up his wife with his own hands, beginning with the *pudenda*.

This act is almost characteristic of criminal sadism. It is to be found in the trial records of many sex-murderers. Krafft-Ebing explains it as due to the impotence of the murderer. The knife symbolises and replaces the non-coöperative *membrum virile*. It should, incidentally, be pointed out that Thrace was not a part of classical Greece, though distantly related to it. It may be that the mystic and fateful earnestness of the Dionysian cult had something to do with it. This cult at one time was imported from Thrace into Greece and is known to have been of great influence in the development of Greek tragedy.

We can find—curiously enough—more evidence of masochism than of sadism. It seems not too bold to claim that there is an indication of personal predilection on the part of certain clients of the hetæræ in the votive offerings of these women, unless the whip had no other function than as an aphrodisiac. I think we must give them the benefit of the doubt.

More clear is the story of Phyllis and Aristotle in this respect. The erstwhile respectable philosopher very much enjoyed acting as a mount to Phyllis and being urged on like a horse with the riding-crop. Hans Baldung von Grien in the year 1513 made an elaborate woodcut representing the reckless Phyllis riding on the back of Aristotle.

The decline of the Roman Empire was marked by the freakishness of its rulers. What I said about the court life of Eastern potentates applies also to Rome. Adultery, fornication, incest, abduction, poison, murder, torture, treason, were common features of daily life.

Tiberius, according to Tacitus and Suetonius, indulged in the most objectionable debaucheries on the isle of Capri, many of them sadistic. Maranon, one of the few writers who tried to prove that the records of Tacitus and Suetonius were mere gossip, tells us that Tiberius was sexually timid and almost impotent. Krafft-Ebing states that the combination of hyperæsthesia and impotence is often found among criminal sadists. Not being able to gratify their desire, they resort to acts of extreme violence in their impotent, over-sexed rage, continuing to mutilate their victims even after they are dead. So instead of reprieving Tiberius by clearing him of the accusations, Maranon by this statement merely seems to confirm them.

Caligula was even worse. Examinations under torture were performed during his banquets. The fact that epilepsy was hereditary among the Julians made them (and especially Caligula), as it were, predisposed to sadism in circumstances favourable to the development of this aberration. And that the circumstances were amply favourable we know already.

There is reason to believe that his successor, Claudius, was actually a masochist who had little opportunity to yield to his innermost longings because of his high position, though there are strong indications in that direction. For a time he was married to the notorious Messalina, whose conception of marital fidelity is well known. Messalina indeed not only put her husband to shame, but moreover made the Roman Emperor ridiculous in the eyes of all his people and the world. She committed her degenerate and depraved sexual activities quite openly. Some have compared Claudius to Sacher-Masoch who induced Aurora, his wife, as well as his various mistresses, to be unfaithful to him. But there is no evidence that Claudius in any way actively condoned Messalina's promiscuity. (Incidentally, it is said of Claudius that at one time he contemplated issuing a law allowing the guests at his banquets to fart and belch in his presence).

181

Nero seemed to combine sadism and masochism. He went through a kind of marriage ceremony with a slave by the name of Sporus, whom he had castrated with his own hands, and treated him as his wife; later he did the same with the freed man Doryphorus, but this time Nero was the 'wife'. He even went so far as to imitate the cries and lamentations of a woman being deflowered. He invented a game in which he was covered with the skin of some wild animal; Doryphorus then let him loose from a cage, after which he attacked the private parts of men and women tied to poles. After having sated his crazy desires, he was 'despatched' by his 'master' Doryphorus. Nero was unquestionably directly influenced in his extreme youth by his diabolically arrogant and managing mother Agrippina the younger. Although she had got rid of every possible rival in favour of her son, even he found her unbearable and finally murdered her. He also had his first wife killed. He kicked his second wife to death when she was pregnant. He then sought to marry Antonia, a daughter of Claudius, and when she refused him, had her put to death. He next married Statilia Messalina, but in order to do so had to get rid of her husband first, who of course was promptly assassinated. The legend of his 'fiddling' while Rome burnt arises from the highly suspicious manner in which the conflagration occurred; it seems certain, too, that he derived some bizarre enjoyment from watching the flames from an elevation at a safe distance, while reciting aloud verses commemorating the destruction of Troy. Afterwards he used the calamity as a pretext for ordering a liquidation campaign, involving the most hideous cruelties, against the unpopular new movement of Christianity. He died by his own hand in his thirty-second year.

As the last in our catalogue of demented Roman emperors we will name Heliogabalus, who obviously was a homosexual masochist. He sometimes used to wear a blond wig and stand in the doorway of a cheap brothel to attract passers-by. Dio Cassius said of him that he liked to imagine he was an adulteress caught in the act by her husband and then severely punished. He was murdered during an insurrection and thrown into the Tiber.

Flagellation was a common punishment among the Romans. Roman society was based on the slave system and the slaves were severely flagellated for the least offence. The Roman women, especially, were notoriously cruel in this way. This preference for the whip was not a one-sided affair as one might think ; some of the masters themselves liked an occasional whipping as could be seen from the custom of adorning the walls of lupanars with all kinds of whips, and the habit of prostitutes of offering whips to Venus. Rosenbaum, in his *Geschichte der Lustseuche* (*Plague of Lust*), writes that many prostitutes assembled near the *Circus Maximus* to intercept men returning from the games, these men generally being very excited sexually by the sight of the bloody performances.

THE TORTURE OF SAINTS AND MARTYRS

Torturing Christians in public was a great diversion, in Rome and elsewhere. Spectators were never lacking on such occasions. They witnessed for hours the sufferings and agonised cries of the victims. The methods of torture were often examples of refined devilish cunning. Galloni in his book *Traité sur les Instruments de Martyr* gives a complete description of them with many illustrations. The reader will excuse me for not reviewing this *in extenso*. The book contains no comments on the feelings of the spectators, but we can hazard a guess at them.

I still vividly remember a picture I once saw in the famous Münchener Pinakothek. It was called *Le Martyr de St Sébastien*. The saint was fastened to a wooden structure on the ground, while two men were turning a sort of roasting spit. A small incision had been made in the belly of the saint, his bowels drawn through this opening by the revolving spit. What gripped my attention in this gruesome picture was the benign look on the martyr's face. Since then I have often wondered whether some latent masochists may not have been attracted to the new creed by the perhaps dimly apprehended prospect of being tortured to death.

THE MIDDLE AGES

We have seen that the Romans used the whip for punishment and—on the side—for lust. In the Middle Ages we find a widespread submission to the whip by penitents. The regulations laid down by the founders of monasteries are excellent sources of information on this subject. To quote the Rev. Wm M. Cooper:

"In point of fact, the founders of monasteries had such faith in the Rod, that flagellation was the punishment appointed

183

for every imaginable offence, and for several offences the statutes enjoined the Superior to continue the flagellation *ad libitum*. It is scarcely to be wondered at that this arbitrary power should sometimes be abused, so that it was necessary for their bishop occasionally to remind them that they were guilty of homicide if they lashed offenders so severely that they died. The statutes did not neglect the novices, or those who were candidates for ecclesiastical life, but ordered flagellations for the improvement of their morals." And further: "Opinions differed in those days with respect to the manner of inflicting flagellation. In 817, at an assembly of ecclesiastics held at Aix-la-Chapelle, it was forbidden to lash monks naked in the presence of their brethren. The ordinance was obeyed in a few of the monasteries; but in many of these establishments the Superiors preferred to inflict the correction on the naked penitent, and further were of opinion that the merit of the performance was thereby enhanced."

In view of the attitude of Christianity from the earliest times towards nakedness (no doubt originating from the wish to differ from the pagan world) we cannot refrain from thinking that this gave the cat a chance to be let out of the bag. It is quite imaginable that both the penitent and the observers were apt to be excited by the public performance. If we recall the aphrodisiac influence whipping may cause, and take into account that monks lived (or were supposed to live) in complete sexual abstinence, we may have our doubts about the spiritual outcome of such a happening.

The founder of the Abbey of Cluny enacted in the statutes of his monastery that culprits should be stripped naked in the middle of the nearest street or public place, and be there tied up and lashed, so that every person who chose could see them. One cannot help thinking that exhibitionists and scopophils must have had a great time in those days.

To quote Cooper again: "Long before self-flagellation was adopted in a systematic manner by the Church, we find instances of it among saints. Peter the Hermit used it on one memorable occasion at least. Having rescued a young woman from the hands of a military officer, who wished to seduce her, his own inclinations became so strong that he was obliged to lock himself up and subdue them by means of a severe flagellation—the mother of the young woman being present at the infliction.

184

"The Order of Fontevrault may be here noticed; it was founded by Robert of Aubrissel, who, interpreting after his own fashion the passage (John xx, 26–27)[1] 'When Jesus therefore saw his mother and the disciple standing by, whom he loved, he saith unto his mother, (Woman), Behold thy son. Then saith he to the disciple, Behold thy mother. And from that hour that disciple took her (un)to his own home', held that Christ had enjoined community between the sexes, and the superiority of the female over the male. An abbess ruled both monks and nuns, the latter having privileges which they took special care to preserve. Good Saint Robert ordained that the two sexes should live together, and the result of such licence may more easily be imagined than described. At any rate, a separation speedily became necessary, as well as supervision of the founder's rules.

"This order existed as early as the year 1100, and at one time numbered as many as fifty establishments. Although the nuns flagellated each other, they greatly preferred, as we read, to apply the birch to the monks and novices. If a nun took a fancy to castigate a novice, he had forthwith to receive his birching with humility and gratitude. If he complained, very probably the abbess, instead of giving him consolation, gave him another whipping! Promiscuous flagellation was also allowed, and in such administrations both the Father Confessor and the Lady (Mother) Superior performed. To monks who complained of the zeal of the nuns, and felt shame at being flagellated by them, it was hinted that it was more agreeable to be birched by the soft hand of a woman than by the hard hand of a man."

Throughout the Middle Ages flagellation was practised in all the monasteries, and it is even said that some of them keep up the custom today. So popular did flagellation become that laymen were contaminated by the infectious urge too. During the thirteenth century sects of Flagellants sprang into life. St Justin of Padua wrote:

"When crimes of every kind were committed in all Italy, a superstition, until then unknown to the world, seized the inhabitants of Perusa, next the Romans, and then all the nations of Italy. Noble and common people, young and old. men and women, and even children five years of age, walked naked in

[1] In the King James (Authorised) Version the correct reference is Joh xix. 26–27.

185

the streets without any sense of shame, carrying with them scourges. They lashed themselves till the blood ran, weeping as if they were really witnessing the Passion of our Lord."

It is said that their number amounted to ten thousand. Soon the rage spread over Germany, Poland and Alsatia. In the year 1349, when Germany was swept by the plague, the movement reached a new peak of frenzy. Crowds of people stripped themselves in public and performed ritual penitences under the supervision of fanatics. At first the Church approved. But when the sects went off into the meadows and woods to perform their rites, and the rumour got around that after the flagellations many of the participants felt the urge to continue the casting out of evil spirits by more conventional means, this was something the Church could not so readily sanction. So a Papal Bull was promulgated, forbidding the sects and condemning their practices.

In the fifteenth century there was a revival of the sects of Flagellants, but this time the Inquisition took summary action and caused about ninety persons to be burned alive at Sangerhusen and large numbers in other places.

In the sixteenth century flagellation groups came into existence in France. The King himself patronised the movement, and the Jesuits did much to encourage the women to follow the example of the male sex without shame. To overcome occasional reluctance to go naked or semi-naked in the streets, they were permitted to wear masks. In the year 1601 the Parliament of Paris passed an Act of Abolishment against all sects of Flagellants, and the example was followed by other cities. Thereafter the brotherhood declined and disappeared from France. Occasional recrudescences of such movements have been reported in subsequent ages in other countries, the last known being in Lisbon as recently as 1847.

Bavaria is sometimes named the classic land of the scourge. Scenes of the most outrageous and scandalous nature took place there after the abolition of the sects—in private social gatherings. Cooper gives an example of this in his *A History of the Rod*:

"A capuchin in the convent of Düren, Father Achazius by name, through his sermons and confessional talk, exercised a great influence on the minds of the people. Forbidding in appearance, but gifted with eloquence of the most persuasive kind, his power over the female portion of his flock was unbounded. Widows and women of mature years were in particular devoted to him. Beginning with these, he soon inoculated others of younger years, for it was part of his instructions that they were to try and win over the young ladies of their acquaintance to elect him their spiritual adviser. His creed was: 'Man, considered in and for himself, is incapable fully to tame the desires of the heart; but the spirit can continue virtuous, whilst the body, according to its usual desires, sins. The spirit belongs to God, the body to the world; yet the last itself represents both in its two parts: God speaks from the body to the superior part, the world to the inferior part: that which belongs to each must fall to it; therefore to keep the soul pure, one must allow the body to continue to sin'. It is easy to see where such a doctrine leads to. The father organised a regular Adamite Whipping Club, wherein many strange things were enacted: it is said that he performed the discipline himself, with rods steeped in vinegar and salt. After some years the proceedings of the society came to light, in consequence of the confession which a young nun—carried out of her convent—felt herself compelled to make, upon her marriage to a French officer. An examination was instituted, which continued for a long time, when it was found that the members of many respectable families were involved. One woman who was examined told an acquaintance, who expressed astonishment for her strange taste for such a hateful man as Achazius, that he had so entirely bewitched her that she was bound to him with infinite inclination, and submitted to everything like a child without will. With the consecrated rods he had beaten her so much that she was sometimes compelled, under one pretext or another, to keep her bed for three weeks. There were so many of these details, and others of an unmentionable nature, that the procurator-general was ordered to quash the whole proceedings. The only punishment that was inflicted on Father Achazius was close confinement in a convent. Afterwards the acts came before a court of justice at Liège, but the records have been destroyed or mutilated, through the influence of some families who wished to extirpate such memorials of their shame."

In Spain the ceremonies of the Flagellants were distinguished by scenes of gallantry as well as acts of devotion. An ancient writer thus describes the mania: "Lovers will often go at the head of a procession of friends, and discipline themselves under the windows of their mistresses; or when passing those windows in a procession to which they belong, they redouble the smartness of their flagellation. All disciplinists show attentions of the same kind to such ladies as they meet, especially if they are good-looking, and they try if possible to sprinkle them with a little blood in passing. The lady is expected to reward the devotee for this delicate and agreeable courtesy by raising her veil."

From flagellation as an act of gallantry to the 'service of ladies', also widespread at that time, is but a short step. This adoration of the suitor from afar, without even presuming to approach nearer to the beloved person, performing acts of heroism in her name, taking part in tournaments in the lists, at the risk of life and limb—with, if possible, a piece of lace from her veil on his lance, longing for the sake of longing, pining away from love-sickness—all this is as clear a masochistic trait as one can imagine, for all the flamboyant protestations of virility. I personally think the origin must in some way be related to extravagant veneration of the Virgin Mary.

It would be irrational to apply the epithets 'active' and 'passive' to true flagellants. The mere fact that there is one party that wields the flagellating instrument and another at the receiving end is not in itself a justification of such a distinction; the fact is that the whipper and the whipped can, and often do, change places. What then are the feelings of the person who whips? I must again resort to the observations of that fellow-student of my youthful days ...

The person who administers the flogging is not giving way to his aggressiveness. His act is an act of servitude, of benevolence; he is not unlike the Boy Scout dutifully performing his good deed. He (or she) takes delight in the stirring of emotional feelings in the whipped person. The element of identification also plays an important part. The strokes are measured with preciseness and applied with skill so as to obtain exactly the right effect.

The terms 'active flagellant' and 'passive flagellant' are only applicable to sadists and masochists who have a distinct preference for the whip one way or the other. The sadist's act is an act of revenge, or of self-defence against the charms of the fetish. The masochist's willingness to undergo the whipping is an act of atonement for the sinful desires he fosters. But the chastisement does not purge away the desire. On the

188

contrary he sees it as a vindication of his intention to preserve his cherished desire. There is no hope of deliverance: the only practicable alternative is total exhaustion. The masochist tells himself that that is the real thing.

The sadist is denied even this consolation. He is puffed up to overpowering rage; then despair over the impossibility and aimlessness of it supervenes. And this is the point at which he is in danger of committing a capital crime.

THE RENAISSANCE

Literally the word 'renaissance' means 'rebirth': in the first place rebirth of man as an individual, for man was definitely emerging from the Dark Ages as an individual being claiming his right to human dignity and personal interpretation of the phenomena of life in its fullest sense. The time of Michelangelo Buonarotti, Dante, Petrarca, Boccaccio, Leonardo da Vinci, Galileo, Copernicus, Grotius, Kepler, Erasmus and Thomas More to name but a few. But it was also the time of the Borgias. The Borgias were men of their epoch, no less individualistic, but in a negative sense. They did not recognise any value, least of all the value of human life, their own lives included. Everything they did was aimed at their purely egotistical inclinations. It is tragic to note that—in an age that opened unlimited vistas for the development of the human mind—they earned their place in history by their fiendish acts of contempt for man, born of defeatism and rejection of any faith in the future of mankind.

Their status was based on securities which derived from values they no longer believed in. They lacked the imagination to see the possibility of new values and purposes. This intellectual cowardice led to a sullen unwillingness to give up things they had no faith in, desperately clinging to the power and the profits that devolved from them.

Their family had its origin in Spain. At the beginning of the fifteenth century members of it settled in Italy, where they became in a short time the mightiest power through their unscrupulousness. Rodrigo Borgia, better known as Pope Alexander VI, and his son Cesare were notorious sadists. In his graphic but horrifying book *La Rome des Borgia* Guillaume Apollinaire gives many examples in illustration of this. Here for the edification of the reader I offer some excerpts from this work:

189

"Their attention was suddenly attracted by an ironical and joyous clamour. Alexander asked the reason for this unlooked-for manifestation: a dancing-girl, quite confused and trembling, declared that three monks had been caught in the act of pederasty in the vineyard. The Pope, who did not at once understand what it was all about, ordered the three monks to be brought inside. Soon the monks were humbling themselves before the Pope, prostrate on their knees, their foreheads at the feet of Alexander. The Pope ordered them to repeat the scandalous act in the banquet hall. Filled with shame, they declined, acquiescing in the acceptance of whatever severe form of expiation they might have to endure. Alexander used soft words and threats, but to no avail.

"Cesare approached him and whispered something in his ear. Alexander ordered the lights to be put out, and in the almost complete darkness commanded the monks to obey. In the night, he said, only God could see them, or his Surrogate on earth. In order to be able to forgive their sin it was necessary for His Holiness to know exactly in what position they had been found: otherwise he could not judge them. He promised them absolution immediately afterwards. Slowly the monks seemed to regain their self-assurance and they accepted the sanction which His Holiness imposed upon them.

"All this time the guests were silent. There was no reason to be impatient. Bodies intertwined, connexions were made. No sound was heard except the creaking of the high chairs of the excited guests and occasional subdued laughter. They knew that Cesare was going to light the lamps again. Masses of sweet-scented flowers seemed to charge the hall with a voluptuous atmosphere. The hall was adorned like an ancient temple.

"La Vanezza rose and, climbing on a chair, closed the curtains of a niche containing a statue of the Madonna and an ever-burning lamp, so as to hide the coming spectacle from the Virgin's sight. Alexander ordered the monks to close their eyes. While they did so, Cesare entered suddenly with the lights, revealing to the eyes of the guests the 'shame of the flesh', to quote the Book of Ecclesiastes. Suddenly a clamour mounted amid the joyous cries of the spectators. It came from the mouths of the desperate monks who, contorted with agony, were bathed in their own blood. Their elbows, their knees, their hands, slithered on the red, slippery floor.

"With two strokes of his dagger Cesare had severed them asunder with the same ease as he would have cut the Gordian knot. Cesare announced cynically, dagger in hand: 'They shall perish—there where they have sinned!'

"He was applauded.

"An orgy took possession of the guests around the table. Only the Pope was silent and pensive. Cardinal Orsini asked him laughingly what he was dreaming about. For answer he smiled weakly.

"They pressed him to speak. Julie Farnèse, seated on his lap, cajoled him but he refused quietly. But when Julie pressed him further, the Pope thought aloud in a high, ringing voice, tinged with a vague ecstasy and an amorous nostalgia:

" 'I was thinking about the men in between ...' "

Excited by the bloody scene, the guests now play *Qui trouve, prend* (Finders keepers). The adjoining rooms are darkened. The guests grope about and find each other as best they can. They are supposed to discover each other's identity without speaking—with the help of their hands only ...

"Women detest men, but some men know how to requite them very effectively. Cesare Borgia, who had determined to revenge himself on Cardinal Ascanio, had his mistress abducted and brought to San Pietro ad Vincula. There he laid her stretched out on boards covered with nails, disposing her shamelessly for the use he desired to make of her. He remarked later that he had never experienced greater voluptuousness. The unfortunate creature, her body penetrated by the sharp spikes, had lost consciousness. Cesare then invited all the males of his household to follow his example. It was what one calls a 'thirty-one'. They violated her in turn, giving full play to their most whimsical fancies. After that, the dogs were brought in, and the sated servants allowed the beasts free rein."

Cardinal Ascanio's mistress had merely remarked of Lucrezia that she was nothing but a bitch. It had thereupon become Cesare's wish that she should forthwith find out what it was like to be a bitch. Hence the bestial punishment Apollinaire describes. She succumbed to her wounds, but as it happened the Cardinal did not mind very much. This fact was revealed some time afterwards by a drunken servant. For his indiscretion, which plainly robbed the Cardinal's protest of effectiveness, the servant was impaled.

191

"They called Cesare 'the Justifier', and more than once he showed that he knew how to live up to this title.

"At one time he was very much infatuated with a girl from Ponte Sisto who had just started in the profession she exercised for a living. He made love to her but was unable to fecundate her.

"He got wind of the fact that the girl had a young lover. He waited long for his vengeance.

"One morning he invited the young woman to go for a stroll in San Pietro ad Vincula, and she went with him. Furthermore, he arranged for the young man to be offered a large sum of money if he would be the lover for one night of the wife of an old baron, who wanted a child.

"The young man believed the tale they told him and agreed to do what was asked of him. He was blindfolded because he was not to be allowed to see the face of the lady in question. He arrived at San Pietro ad Vincula at the same time as his sweetheart.

"On his part, Cesare had told his mistress that he wanted to find out whether her barrenness was caused by the vehemence of their embraces, and requested her to give herself to a young gallant, whom he would select, and in his presence. But she would be required to wear a blindfold during the act of *coitus*. A physician would be present to ensure the act was properly consummated.

"When the moment came, the well-perfumed lovers met in each other's arms. After the preliminaries, the physician, acting as *metteur-en-scène*, united them as the ox-drover brings the bull to the cow.

"Cesare had a crucible of molten lead in his hands. The physician arranged their limbs in such a way that Cesare had easy access. The lovers, believing implicitly in the skill of the practitioner, lent themselves to the task with ingenuous complaisance . . . Suddenly . . . the sizzling of burning flesh, two agonised cries . . .

"Stuck fast upon each other, the prostitute and her gallant were united for ever.

"The servants, farmers, labourers were called in and while Cesare smiled happily at the dying creatures, the physician explained in well-chosen words the meaning and the moral of the whole procedure."

192

It is true that the time was ripe for man to break the chains he had been kept in by theocracy, but the conduct of those who held exalted positions in the Church hierarchy did much to hasten the process. The Church, recognising the desperate situation it was in, took to violent means to regain its absolute power. The task of tracking down and examining heresies and heretics had been granted to Dominican monks by a Papal Bull, issued by Gregory IX. Pope Sixtus IV, in 1480, allowed the kings of Castile to appoint inquisitors, and from then on the Inquisition became a political instrument also. Their sinister power was so great that everybody lived in fear of them, from the king himself to the serf. In the fifteenth century the Inquisition was very active, providing incidentally an excellent playground for sadists. Most notorious of them all was Tomás de Torquemada (1420–1498), first Inquisitor-General of Spain, who, having persuaded Ferdinand and Isabella to induce the Pope to sanction the institution of the 'Holy Office' of the Inquisition, proceeded to organise and personally to supervise the infliction of the most fiendish cruelties.

As an interesting example of how even the most repulsive historical circumstances can be presented in fascinating fictional form, I should like to present a few excerpts from Prof. Roland Gagey's *L'Inquisition et ses Tortures*, in particular from the tale called *Torquemada's Last Amorous Passion*:

"Virgin though she was, she was no fool; besides, in those times, too many girls, in the heat of a scuffle, fell victims to the excited soldiery; on the other hand, the lustful reputation of the inquisitors and their satellites was too clearly established for the daughter of de Saavedra and close friend of the executed Moresques to be unaware of the danger she was in now that she had fallen into the hands of the Holy Office.

"A courageous virgin knows how to resign herself to death; it is more difficult to face up to the frightful vision of the violent obscenities which, she knows, threaten her ...

"Were they trying, by causing her to fast, to deplete her resources of physical and mental strength? Whatever the reason, during the whole of that day they brought her nothing at all to eat ...

"During the night Concepción had not the strength to fight off sleep, the need for which overwhelmed her. And so, unable

193

to prevent herself, drowsily on the edge of the bed she fell asleep upon one of the cushions. But it was a restless sleep, troubled by nightmares.

"One hour, two, three perhaps, went by, and suddenly the girl felt in her sleep something soft caressing her lips. The sensation awakened her; she did not open her eyes at once, surprised as she was by the gentle odour of an exquisite perfume.

" 'Am I dreaming?' she said to herself.

"For a moment she remained uncertain; then, realising she was quite awake and feeling the renewed sensation of a kiss upon her lips, she trembled, sighed, opened her eyes and, uttering a cry, she sat up with a start.

"All white in the bright illumination from the candles of several candelabra placed at various points in the room, a man was standing.

" 'Torquemada!' she exclaimed. For all at once she recognised the Inquisitor-General ...

"... she glided from the bed, recoiled a little, then curtseyed with one knee on the carpet.

" 'Rise, my dear child!' said Torquemada in a soft voice; 'won't you please rise? but how can it be that we find you at this late hour, fully clothed, asleep outside the bed, and your cheeks wet with tears?'

"The daughter of de Saavedra was a courageous soul. Seeing before her the Inquisitor-General, about whom whispered accounts of abominable stories went from ear to ear .., she had grave doubts about this formidable monk's intentions. But she resolved to feign confidence in him as long as possible, and, rallying her strength, she said in a voice tremulous with emotion:

" 'Monseigneur, what is it Your Eminence wants of me? I beg you to save me from the anguish I am in...' And no longer having the strength to continue the rôle she was playing, the poor girl fell on her knees, burst into tears, and stammered, her hands clasped together: 'I beg you, oh I beg you—please, do not harm me!'

"Torquemada looked at his victim with a satisfied smile. She was just as he wanted her: terrified, in tears, a supplicant ..

" 'Conchita! Conchita!'[1] he murmured, his voice hoarse, and

---

[1] 'Conchita' is the familiar form of Concepción in Spanish. (It also happens to be, in some Spanish-speaking countries, a popular term for the female sex organ. Literally, it is a diminutive of *concha*, a shell).

he grasped and held tightly in his own hands hot with the fever of passion the ice-cold hands of the young girl. 'Conchita, stand up, come! Seat yourself at my side! Let me look closer at your eyes, at your throbbing chest!'

"He drew her towards him, lifted her with such force that she was incapable of resisting.

"He made her sit down very close to him, and with his right arm encircled her waist and held her, while with his left hand he tore open her bodice and violently thrust in his hand and seized one of her breasts.

"At this first encroachment upon her virginal flesh, this trespass so abrupt and so adroit that she had never even dreamt that it might happen, nor had the time to evade it by any reflex action of her whole being, Concepción let out a piercing cry, tore herself away from the Grand Inquisitor's hands, and fled distraught to the other end of the room.

"Frowning, harshly staring now, his teeth clenched, his eyes sombre, his whole frame taut with the violence of desire, he rose and strode towards her. Just as he was about to reach her and clutch at her, she slipped under his arm, lithe and agile, and for some seconds he had to search to find where she had gone.

"The girl had taken refuge in the next room..."

The chase continues and at last Torquemada and Concepción are face to face in the brightly-lit room with the heavy table between them.

" 'Enough of this game, Conchita!' he said, his eyes flashing. 'Ever since I first saw you, almost a year ago, I have loved you. I should have liked to save your father in order to acquire the right to become acquainted with you, but my men arrived too late.

" 'Nevertheless, the wrong that has been done you I with my supreme power can put right. You shall have a high position at Court, Conchita! You shall be rich, flattered, feared even, if that pleases you! But I love you, and my love is capable of doing you just as much harm as good! I will be your lover, Conchita, if you are willing... But do not forget that I am the Inquisitor-General and I will take by force what you refuse me; and in that case my love will become, for you, the blackest and cruellest of hatred! ...' "

Conchita rejects him again. He pleads and threatens in vain.

" 'No! No!' she cried. 'No! You shall never have me with

195

my consent, and if, as I know all too well you could, you use my body against my will, my soul will never cease to curse you!'

"There was such a note of revulsion in her words that the Grand Inquisitor stood as if his face had been slapped! Slowly he seemed to recover from the outrage, pulled himself together, recollected the quasi-divine dignity of his station, stopped short, gritted his teeth, so tremendous was the excess of emotion he was experiencing; then he said hoarsely:

" 'Very well! I do not insist, Conchita. But, for you, for your fiancé, for the chaplain your accomplice, it means every kind of torture! And in the midst of your howls and groans of agony I will rejoice to satiety at all the charms and all the palpitations of your flesh! We shall meet again soon'."

The infamous Inquisitor is as good as his word. Concepción's fiancé, Pérez de Herrera, is tortured mercilessly before the girl's very eyes, and all three are held prisoner and, as Torquemada has threatened, are repeatedly subjected to hideous torments, which Roland Gagey describes with blood-curdling reality. No one among their influential friends has had the courage to intervene on their behalf. The young nobleman is held in a deep dungeon, the chaplain in a slightly more comfortable cell, and Concepción in a magnificent room furnished with all the comforts of the age. These high-born prisoners, accustomed to every luxury that wealth could provide, are now at the mercy of the 'Holy' Inquisition and submitted to the capricious whims of uncouth jailers and torturers, who take pleasure in humiliating and cruelly mistreating their victims.

Concepción, in a state of exhaustion and nervous prostration, is raped by Torquemada. When she realises what he has done to her she is more defiant than ever. After that she is stripped and flagellated nearly every day, often drugged and sexually assaulted. But never once does she give herself to the Inquisitor willingly—until one day . . .

" 'Stop! Stop!' shrieked Concepción. 'Do anything you like to me, but stop that!' "

Her spirit is broken. Her own life has long since ceased to have any value for her, but she still hopes by her self-sacrifice to save the shattered body of her wretched fiancé. He has been racked till his bones are broken, subjected to the water torture until he could barely be revived, branded, and his wounds covered with molten lead. Concepción has been flogged naked in front of him and subjected to every indignity, while he is powerless to intervene. And now when her lover's resistance has been completely crushed, she can no longer bear to watch his torments: she hopes to save him also from having to witness hers.

"He [Torquemada] made a sign and she followed him in silence. Once in the chamber, he began to undress her slowly, lovingly it seemed. Her beautiful body, all covered with weals from successive flagellations, was laid bare, and he smothered the marks with his kisses more and more ardently.

"Presently she was completely nude.

"He carried her and placed her on the bed, on which she lay without resistance. She was motionless, and were it not for a shudder that convulsed her breasts, upright and firm, which the whip had spared, one would have thought her dead.

"The torturer began to caress that beautiful, abandoned body: his hands wandered feverishly everywhere; then, suddenly, his fondling became more vague, less active, and ceased altogether.

"After a long pause, Concepción opened her eyes and looked up. She saw a spectacle that she was very far from expecting to see. Standing motionless beside her, his head in his hands, Torquemada was weeping. Tears were running silently down his emaciated cheeks, and his chest showed scarcely any movement... Concepción gazed at him bewildered. This silent scene continued for some time. 'What pain can it be', she wondered, 'that can make such a man weep, a man who is indifferent to the most hideous sufferings of others, who rejoices at them in fact?'

"She did not know the Torquemada who, after nights of debauchery and cruelty, plunged himself into the most rigorous devotional exercises and acts of penance, the Torquemada who was a powerful and violent being utterly unbalanced by his religious fanaticism and sexual aberration...

"What had given rise once more to this thirst for repentance before the consenting body of Concepción, offered to him at last, was that he found himself impotent now that he suddenly was made aware that he could possess this young woman whom for weeks he had been tormenting and defiling. The awareness of the failure of his virility submerged and overwhelmed him in a flood of remorse.

"Suddenly he felt disgust for this body that offered itself insensible to his caresses, this body that was offered it was true, but cold as a corpse. In a flash he reviewed all his turpitude of those last weeks, all his desires, his covetousness; and the realisation of his impotence became more violently, more painfully clear. He began speaking, softly, his voice sounding faint, far away:

" 'I have sinned! I have sinned! I have sinned! For your sake, Concepción! And you too have consented to that sin, to save your fiancé. God in his immeasurable goodness has shown me the abyss into which I was about to fall, the inferno gaping at my feet. I am an old man, and I was losing sight of that fact. You have revealed to me my decrepitude. Unwittingly you have been the instrument of my salvation ... I have loved your body in sin, I want to love your soul in God ; we shall follow the same road—of penitence, fasting and mortification of the flesh.

" 'Your fiancé, who is as guilty as yourself, shall accompany you on the way of repentance ; and I, from now on, following the path that God has revealed unto me, will be merciless towards others as I am, and will continue to be, towards myself.

" 'Concepción, you shall burn in this world so as not to have to burn in the next.' "

And that indeed is her fate. She and her fiancé are burnt alive at the next *auto-da-fé* in Seville. But not before Concepción has for several days before her execution been the plaything of her jailers.

SLAVERY

Any list of sadists who have stained the pages of history could be extended *ad infinitum*; but it is not my purpose to attempt a complete historical review. It does seem to me, though, that some mention should be made, however brief, of the vile practice of slavery that for so long allowed free rein to sadists to show how far man's inhumanity to man could go.

In the prosperous epoch of colonial exploitation of the Americas English, Spanish, Portuguese and Dutch vessels roamed the West African coast in pursuit of their trade in 'living ebony'. The Spanish Government regarded the importation of slaves into the southern half of the New World as their own monopoly; in the year 1517 an *Asiento* (agreement or convention) was issued, granting a licence to a Flemish nobleman to transport 4,000 slaves to the Antilles. Many other *Asientos* followed, with the Genoese, the Portuguese, the French, the English. In the second part of the seventeenth century the Dutch outstripped all their rivals: slaves were being transported to Curaçao to the tune of 200,000 a year. Incredible hardships and privations caused one-third of the poor wretches to die before they reached their provisional destination. The slaves were purchased from African tribal chieftains, mostly of the warlike Ashanti tribes who captured them in the interior, but ever-increasing demand soon induced them to sell their own subjects also. North American plantation owners paid the best prices and had first choice in the auctions at the slave depot of Curaçao. What was left over the Dutch West Indies Company distributed among their own settlements.

The treatment these human creatures suffered beggars all description. The only exceptions to this general pattern were the comparatively few who had been brought to the Dutch East Indies, where they served as soldiers, and generally became freed men after some time. They were then called *Mardijkers* (from the Malay word *mardeka*, free). Descendants of these *Mardijkers* still live in a village near Samarang on the island of Java.

The published findings of the Hakluyt Society in England and the Linschoten Society in Holland provide many shocking details of most sadistic treatment. The slave ships were always followed by shoals of sharks. Such slaves as had the bad luck to become ill were thrown overboard without ceremony, as fodder for the sharks. Sometimes they were hung at the stern of the ship so that the sharks had to leap up to reach the bait. The living victims were gradually lowered. This slow devouring of human beings by sharks was a favourite pastime aboard many ships to while away the tiresomeness of the long voyage, especially when there was no wind. Sometimes the poor wretches were brought on deck, tied to one of the masts and tortured for some offence, real or imaginary, for the entertainment of those on board.

A certain lady, known by the name of Miss Jans, owned a plantation about thirty miles up the Surinam river in Guiana. This sadistic woman has become a legend and the cruelties she committed are still the subject of stories told by the present-day population of that country. The site of her plantation became known as "Missi Jans-kondre" (Miss Jans' country [land]). Big male negroes she became displeased with, or who took her fancy, were tied to poles or trees and slowly tortured to death. Generally she undertook the treatment herself, which always ended with the cutting off or mutilation of the victim's *membrum virile*, the mere possession of which was most probably the man's only 'offence'.

As for the flagellations and miscellaneous inhumanities that were practised against slaves in the southern states of North America, enough has been written on this subject already. Suffice it to say that the Abolition acts did not put an end to slavery at once. A good deal of slave-trading was still carried out on the sly. Today, with the exception of a few remote and secluded parts of the world, slavery has disappeared. But we have by no means eradicated the aftermath of ages of savage discrimination. It will take a long time before we shall be able to say that the 'blues' as an expression of the sufferings of a dispossessed race have no longer any reason for existence. Nor has the inclination towards sadism vanished—as we shall see in the next chapter.

PART FIVE
SADO-MASOCHISM TODAY

CHAPTER TEN

The Sado-Masochistic Complex in our Time

DECLINE OF SOCIAL STANDARDS

In former times when man had to work fourteen hours a day to earn his living, a living that barely sufficed for subsistence, deprived as it was of anything that went beyond the barest necessities, he had little reason to become bored with sex. Five days of the week he was too tired for it, so the gratification of this need was confined to Saturdays and Sundays and performed in its most simple and primitive way. It was a mere physiological necessity, on the same level as eating. When a man has only now and then occasion to take a square meal he does not care about exquisite eating utensils or refined table-manners: his only all-important aim is to fill his belly as soon as possible.

The subsistence of man's family was wholly dependent on his health and capacity for working; his interest was the interest of the family too; he came first in everything, took the decisions, and nobody contested his authority. The behaviour and conduct of the members of the family were defined by strict rules based on, directed by, and subject to, the welfare of the family. Family ties were strong, out of sheer necessity. The form of the union and the pattern of family life were thus distinctly patriarchal.

I am firmly convinced that forms of marriage and patterns of family life are *exclusively* conditioned by economic and social circumstances; no eternal values or divine laws are involved. Perversions were almost exclusively the privilege of the leisured class, who had ample time to get bored, as can be confirmed from the historical cases noted in the foregoing chapter. To those who may wish to point to the fact that sadistic criminals like Vacher, Kürten, Haarmann, and others, were of the working class and lived in the days when hardships beset

203

the under-privileged, I would answer that these criminals were moronic tramps and outlaws who had put themselves outside the pale of society. In other respects, too, they were exceptional, which explains the profound commotion their crimes caused.

The age of prosperity we now live in has thoroughly transformed the pattern of family life and marriage. Working hours have been reduced to a reasonable number. A great part of man's responsibilities towards the welfare of his family has been taken over by the State. Risks to life have been reduced to a minimum by an extensive structure of social securities. Today many married women work outside the home. The youngsters do odd jobs in their spare time. They are no longer completely dependent on the income of the husband and father. Everybody pursues his own happiness, scarcely minding the interest of the family as a whole. If the father is still head of the family it is only by virtue of the lingering influence of outdated laws; whether he still has any authority at home depends on his own personality, not any longer on his natural position in the family. Family ties are loose. Conscious ties with the community are practically non-existent. Everybody has ample leisure. It is no longer a virtue to be a law-abiding citizen; the ideal is to be 'clever' or 'smart' and find the holes in the net of the law to wriggle through. The disintegration of family life results in more freedom for the individual but also in emotional poverty. Nobody really cares much about anybody else any more.

I do not preach a return to the hard times of old. What I think is needed is something to fill this void in man: a purpose, a possibility of adjustment to a society he must feel bound to. If we do not succeed in creating a relation between society and its members, man will quickly fall back to the stage of the savage of primeval days.

Nowadays, the James Bond type seems to be the ideal. His fans admire the way he steps, carelessly smiling, over the corpse of his adversary. Following his example, they supplant love and affection by seduction—the momentary conquest of a female with the right kind of face and figure being the aim, without second thoughts or inhibitions.

Political leaders are wandering in the mist. Some try vainly to turn the tide; others—more aware of the social changes that are taking place—are earnestly looking for a solution.

Decisions are taken at random. A steady increase of sadistic-ally-coloured crimes is one of the fruits of this random harvest. Typical of most violent crimes of today is the total absence of emotion on the part of the perpetrator. Our time seems to be an excellent matrix for cruelty and sadism. Most repulsive in this respect is the unscrupulous way in which the base, anti-social and egotistical inclinations of the masses are exploited through the important communication media—the news-papers, magazines, books, radio, television and films.

SADISM THROUGH MASS-COMMUNICATION MEDIA

As often as not the silver screen of our modern cinemas resembles a playground for sado-masochists. No movie about gangster life or historical or Biblical events can do without at least one big sado-masochistic scene. Whips, fire-brands, and more grisly instruments of torture, are employed, and one wonders whether these gory shows are part of a system. Is there a purpose behind it all? Is it all part of a method?

A whipping has become a traditional part of a movie about Roman times, the Middle Ages, or life on the high seas. No modern movie fan bats an eyelid when on the screen a man or a woman is whipped and blood flows freely. To scare people stronger stuff is needed and presented. No self-respecting hor-ror movie can do without scenes in which the infliction of most hideous torments is represented.

Sometimes the scenario writers of screen plays feel the urge to write novels. Ben Hecht for instance. This well-known Hollywood author dedicated his novel *The Sensualists* "to David O. Selznick of Hollywood and the Moon". In this novel a police sergeant commits two murders that surpass almost anything that writers of sadistic stories (including de Sade himself) have thought up on the subject until now. The first of his victims is a woman called Greta Getz. The policeman, who commits these hideous crimes under the influence of drugs, wrenches out Greta's false teeth and rams the denture down into her windpipe until she chokes to death.

The second murder is infinitely more horrible. The insane policeman, having stunned his mistress, Liza, with a savage blow from his truncheon, proceeds to perform unimaginable and unmentionable atrocities upon her naked body while she is still conscious, but gagged and bound, spread-eagled on a bed. Then showing her the knife and telling her calmly exactly

205

what he proposes to do to her, he rips up her abdomen with a surgeon's blade and dissects her anatomy with unhurried deliberation. Finally, as the police burst in, he places the barrel of his service automatic in his mouth and blows the top of his head off. Even so he is able to crack a little joke to his friends on the Force: "Hello, Mac. I closed the case", he quips as "his half-head" lolls to one side.

The revolting brutality of this sort of thing is enough to make one have serious reservations about the mentality of those who delight in it. But because no sexual action, as such, is specifically referred to and no sexual connexions are even hinted at, this kind of writing is not officially regarded as pornographic, and so the authorities do not intervene. It can be circulated quite freely. Opinions differ widely as to whether such books are really pernicious in their effects. One thing that can be affirmed with certainty is that they are in execrably bad taste. Some leading psycho-therapists, however, believe that "people who read salacious literature are less likely to become sexual offenders than those who do not, for the reason that such reading often neutralises what aberrant sexual interests they may have".[1] On the other hand, it may be seriously doubted whether it is wise to risk appealing to the sadistic tendencies of an unknown public. It seems to me not impossible that by such means some unsuspected subconscious urge may, through the striking of a sympathetic chord, be roused into an overt form of physical manifestation.

SADISM IN ADVERTISEMENTS

Sales promoting has become a science. Advertising agencies make use of the findings of depth-psychology research. The drift towards sadism that seems to be carrying with it a large sector of the public has not escaped their attention. Films, television and books, like the one referred to above, are obviously useful media for the dissemination of propaganda: books not only provide a valuable market themselves but also condition the public taste for a more thorough acceptance of current forms of direct commercial propaganda. I remember seeing, not long ago, an advertisement for men's shoes that left no doubt about the message of the designer. In the foreground stood a man of the ruggedly masculine outdoor type,

[1] This is the opinion expressed by Dr Benjamin Karpman, chief psychotherapist at St Elizabeth Hospital in Washington.

with one foot on a stool, displaying his shoe. In the background was a girl wearing a torn dress and tied to a ladder or something. Underneath this astonishing illustration was the caption: "Real men wear —— shoes".

Our society with all its weight of tensions, prohibitions and restrictions creates a great deal of frustration. Frustration gives rise to irritation and aggression; nowadays these cunning ad-men are steering this aggression definitely in the direction of sadism. Sadism is becoming a fashionable attitude among young people—the 'in' or 'with it' thing to be. To most it is still just a pose: they act hard-boiled' and indifferent (they believe it is considered old-fashioned to be tender or sentimental); but to many it is an outlet for something that otherwise most probably would have been kept in the shadows. Now that it is openly approved of by their generation, and is furthermore pandered to by all the big commercial media, it no longer need be concealed. The results, I believe, are already becoming clearly discernible.

As this book goes to press, a report to the Home Secretary in London by the Criminal Injuries Compensation Board indicates that a startling figure of 24 per cent. of assaults were made by strangers in the street. Many seemed to be "simply casual and unpremeditated acts of brutality."

The crime wave is more than a wave: it shows signs of swelling into an inundation. It has been estimated that in the United Kingdom, according to present-day statistics, during the next twelve months one in every eight men and one in every fourteen women will commit some indictable offence that can be described as a crime. And the chances of detection and punishment seem to be diminishing almost in inverse proportion to the incidence of criminal acts. Worst among these acts is, as always, murder. There are more murders, worse murders, and a larger proportion of unsolved murders, than ever before. The reader may open any newspaper at random and see for himself. I have before me in my files issues of newspapers from various countries. A casual glance through these newspapers for the period January to August, 1966, has revealed the following sadistic crimes (only a small proportion of the total, of course):

January 26: A student and his girl friend out for a walk on a wooded hill are met by a man who is carrying a 9-mm revolver. The stranger threatens them with the gun, and indecently assaults the girl. After two hours of this, the student in desperation attacks the man, who shoots and kills him. The murderer escapes.

January 27: A boy is tortured to death in a partly-demolished house in Stockholm, *just for fun,* by two boys with whom he shared a room. The boys say they were curious to know what it would be like to murder someone.

In the same edition: A man of 25 kills his fiancée with an axe because she broke off their engagement.

February 25: A young German breaks into the room of a girl student and kills her. He claims to have acted from "an inner urge".

"I do not feel sorry", he says coolly; "that would be a weakness, a retrograde step. It would automatically lead to the next conflict." He claims to have been working off his hatred against the world.

March 5: A mixed group in Antwerp (a French girl, some Belgians, one German, one American, two Dutchmen) kill a cat by hanging it and then crushing its head in a door. Afterwards the cat is skinned, cooked and eaten by them. This ritual killing of a cat is to be repeated, they say. It "gives a greater kick than marijuana, hashish, or LSD". One of them, named Billy, is a 40-year-old Belgian who speaks five languages fluently, is very intellectual, but addicted to drugs. He is an important figure in the Antwerp cultural *milieu.* He always carries about with him a book translated into French from the original English, a book about the Thugs.

March 8: A pyromaniac sets fire to houses in the centre of Amsterdam. Eleven people have been burnt to death.

April 15: A 32-year-old man confesses to having strangled eleven women in Boston. He had been arrested in 1964 for sexual offences.

April 22: Two inhuman monsters (a man and a young woman), in England, struck a boy with an axe. They also stripped and thrashed a little girl before killing her. They made a tape recording of her screams and pleadings.

May 21: A 29-year-old man attempts to strangle a boy of 12. The boy escapes with his life by managing to stab the man in the face with his penknife.

May 21: A 17-year-old girl is tied to a bed in a chalet in Switzerland, near Zürich, and flagellated and tortured by members of a crazy religious sect, of which her father is the leader. The participants are allowed to give free rein to their sadistic desires upon the naked body of the girl, and get drunk on champagne to give more zeal to their prayers. After being whipped, branded, and tormented with medieval instruments of torture, the girl dies.

July 18: A seaman, aged 25, is charged in Chicago with the murder of eight student nurses.

July 28: The nude body of a negress is found in Hampstead, London, her hands and feet tied together behind her back. She has been slashed twelve times on her back and arms with a razor and her head has been shaved.

In the same edition: A man has been charged with the murder of a woman whose body, with twenty stab wounds, was found in a train.

August 2: A former U.S. marine, having killed his wife and his mother, shoots from the 26th-floor observation room in the tower of the University of Texas at passers-by, thirteen of whom lose their lives in this way. Another thirty-one are seriously wounded.

August 6: An English girl, aged 15, has been found raped and murdered, almost naked, on a beach near San Francisco.

FETISHISM IN THE UNITED STATES OF AMERICA

Since the second World War a form of fetishism has made its appearance in the U.S.A. which by now has reached grotesque proportions. I refer to bust fetishism which, while many Europeans can sympathise with it to a certain extent, is in general regarded outside of North America as childishly overdone.

Some commentators[1] have suggested that it is because American babies are artificially fed and because their parents prefer to make use of bottles and patent formulas that the American adult male demands large breasts, as a sort of belated compensation. The American woman, being childlike at heart and anxious to retain her hold on her man, is only too willing to oblige.

Be that as it may, there is a new mania which seems to be spreading in the United States that other nations, despite their vulnerability to American influence, find less easy to go along with. This is the absurd 'tie-and-truss-up' mania that so appeals to the vast numbers of American sado-masochists. It is a

[1] John McPartland and Geoffrey Gorer for example.

209

mania that goes hand in hand with flagellation and embraces a whole gamut of fetishism of its own. Here the fetish is not the nates. Nakedness, indeed, is not only unnecessary but even undesirable in these manifestations of sado-masochism. Special leather garments, boots, gloves, shoes with unbelievably high heels, and articles of clothing made of rubber, play the most important part.

In America many magazines are published nowadays for people who share this particular sexual tendency. Recently these magazines have begun to circulate in Europe too, and their contents give a graphic insight into sado-masochism of this kind. Magazines like *Bizarre, Fantasia, Ultra, Exotique, Continental* and *Extatique* and various sado-masochistic comic-strips, as well as photographs in stills and movies, are regularly published and widely disseminated

Often the editor publishes letters from his readers in which they describe their experiences. The publications also run articles on how to improve techniques in relation to these fetishistic practices and suggest new ideas that can be tried out in private circles. Not long ago *Bizarre* put forward an extraordinary new idea: would it not be exciting to have a woman captured in her own skirts after they had been pulled over her head and tied together? Trapped like this, the victim would be defenceless, unable to use arms or hands or to see where she was going; at the same time she would be offering anyone who happened to be around an unobstructed view of her legs and underwear. *Bizarre* followed this up with a 1,500-word letter from a correspondent who stated that his home life, and that of the other members of his household (his sister and his wife), had been revolutionised by this marvellous idea. They had for long been fans of *Bizarre*, from which they had obtained many splendid hints, but this was really tops. He, his wife, his sister and her boy friend, and four other married couples, had previously been having fun in other ways: being in revolt "against all the meddlesome regulations ..." of the society in which they lived, they "did all that most people would like to do and don't do because of lack of courage and out of convention or habit". Now, when he came home in the evening, he always found one or other walking about with her skirts over her head and then he had to punish her ...

Elsewhere a reader tells how her husband chains her body so that she can hardly walk straight. Chained and bent, she is taken to parties by her husband.

Another discloses that at a party she had to walk round the outside of the house three times, dressed in a simple satin dress, while a blizzard was raging.

A designer's wife tells how her husband dresses her up in white chamois-leather so that not one bit of her skin can be seen. He covers her head with a napu-leather cap on which a face has been painted. It gives her the feeling of being a doll, which she is beginning to enjoy more and more.

The curious aspect of these fetishistic games is that the participants are attracted more by the clothing than by the wearers of it. The skirts tied above the head envelop the wearer in an absolute anonymity, just as in the other fetishistic manifestations the identity of the person is no longer of importance. And nobody even vaguely thinks of *coitus*. These games seem to be satisfying in themselves. Those who go in for such pastimes sometimes organise themselves into clubs complete with insigniæ, their own magazine and meetings. In a country that is perhaps the most puritanical in the world a sexual trend has arisen that can itself be characterised as puritanical. The woman who lets her husband dress her in leather specifically states that no part of her flesh is visible. Instead of being naked, she prefers to be dressed as completely as possible. This tendency is thoroughly fetishistic and perverted all through. All healthy sexual feeling is absent from such practices.

Some researchers are of the opinion that these bizarre goings-on originate in the extreme conformity of American society. The ordinary American longs to be different, to do great things and excel. This he can never do in public, for in American society one is expected to melt into the crowd and suppress originality. The only place where originality can be tolerated is in the sanctuary of one's own home or one's own bedroom ; there one is free to do as one wants.

But this newly-gained 'freedom' serves to enable them to tie and truss each other up. Could anything be more paradoxical? Sexuality is still curbed and frustrated, and the result is a kind of fetishism. Even this cannot have an honest life of its own: it is camouflaged as a family game, a *Spielerei* of a most infantile kind. Instead of realising one's own desires, one tries and works out ideas from a magazine: in doing so one can always be sure of being one of thousands of readers who do exactly the same and who form a society of their own with

211

its own norms and regulations. The American psychiatrists London and Caprio have made an investigation of this subject and have found that such games, very popular in the United States, are played very often in private homes, and scarcely ever lead to further sexual actions.

It is the women who reign in American society. Women's organisations bring pressure to bear on authorities to ban books and motion-pictures, ostracise as *personæ non gratæ* actors and actresses who do not conform to certain moral standards, and put their puritan stamp upon American public life. After ridding themselves of the domination they have endured so long, American men, by and large, from the first day of their wedded lives, fall under the mastery of their wives. In the United States this modern matriarchy is all-pervading. So all his life the American male has to combat the domination of the female. It is a measure of his frustration that women are generally the victims in these sexual games. But by nature woman is not the one to dominate. She is ready and willing to surrender to male mastery, and these pastimes give her the chance to do so without ceding her privileged position in society.

FETISHISM IN PHOTOGRAPHS

A photo-series in *Bizarre* clearly shows how amazing the phantasies of its readers are. One photograph shows a 'bat-woman' who is all dressed in black leather. Her face is covered with a black leather mask. Only the shape of her ample breasts reveals that under the leather covering a woman is hidden. In the second photograph there is an identically-attired 'bat-man'. The series ends with another photograph, in which the bat-woman sits, heavily bound, in a chair. In these 'comic'-strips, by the way, it is always a woman who tortures, binds and flagellates a man or another woman. This kind of thing not only pleases the very sizable lesbian element among the readership: it has a practical motivation of another kind. By not having men perform in these scenes it is possible to evade censorship problems. Besides, it has been proved that men of a sadistic or masochistic turn of mind can very easily identify themselves with the torturer or the victim.

TRANSVESTITISM IN THE UNITED STATES

As we have seen, transvestitism is not something that appeals to homosexuals only. Psychologists see in it an identification with, and a longing for, the mother; and in a society where the mother is such a dominant figure it is not an unexpected phenomenon. Time and time again one may read in American sado-masochistic magazines the confessions of men who are only happy when they are able to play the rôle of a woman in their own home without losing their heterosexuality. Trans-vestitism of this kind, with the entire approval of the wife, is a typical form of submission to the female. In all the cases I have known the males confess that their wives have taught them how to walk on high heels, how to cope with the intricacies of feminine underwear, and how to move gracefully. Wives who describe 'experiments' of this kind talk of husbands who have become "real sisters".

Transvestitism is not an indispensable indication of submission on the part of the male, as a letter from a reader in *Fantasia* shows:

"My husband and I can't do without your magazine any more. You must know that we are no ordinary couple and that we often feel very lonely and isolated.

"We believe that a man must really submit to his wife and that in a happy marriage the wife must play the part of house-tyrant as well as possible.

"It has always been like this in our marriage. I punish my husband for every error or for being unattentive. If he hasn't done anything wrong I still punish him to remind him of his marital status. All his wrong-doings are written down in a book which he has to carry chained around his neck.

"He likes to be humiliated in this and other ways, and as he loves me like a goddess I like it too. I force him to be my maid after he comes home from work. On winter nights, after he has done his chores, he enjoys more than anything to curl up on the floor, in front of the hearth at my feet, while I sit and read the evening papers."

It's a dawg's life, in fact, but some people enjoy it!

SADISM FOR THE MILLION

There is a great deal of emphasis on cruelty in the United States: it is reflected even in children's books and comics, and in cartoon films. It is not so strange as it may seem that this attitude should exist in a country where people do their utmost to be 'good neighbours'. The American finds in his society all that he can wish for—except a safety-valve for his aggression. It is in manifestations such as racial fights, or in practices like those described in the kinds of magazines we have been considering, that the American finds an outlet for that aggressiveness. He has to contend with sexual frustration arising from a puritanical sense of shame accompanied by a constant synthetic titillation of an appetite that cannot relieve itself in honest lust. Readers of sado-masochistic magazines are better off: they at least have a safety-valve for their disturbed sexuality. And every effort is made to convince them that they belong to a vast community.

In a catalogue that is sent from coast to coast I find advertised: a "leather strap gag" ($10), that "cannot be removed once applied", "providing the victim's wrists are secured . . ."; "leather pom-pom" ($25), which is a short whip that "stings, but that is all"; a "leather thong whip" ($25), a more formidable weapon that "should be used with great care". Discreetly but distinctly the firm points out that any "special demands" receive their very particular attention.

It is easy to say that no harm can come of all this, but it is no less pertinent to ask where the sheer sadism of concentration camps comes from. It is a proven fact that a terrifyingly large number of people turn into dangerous sadists when given half a chance. Even to this day prisoners are being tortured and manhandled, men and women submitted to vile indignities; and this can be happening around us, in our very midst, or in places we go to on holiday.

Amnesty International, an organisation concerned with safeguarding the interests of political prisoners by investigating allegations of ill-treatment, made such an enquiry in Aden in 1966. A report by the Swedish doctor who undertook the Amnesty enquiry alleged that brutal methods of interrogation were used by British military and police personnel and by Adenis under the control of British authorities. Included among the "tortures" alleged to have been used were the following:

Forcing suspects to stand naked during interrogation;

Detaining them in extremely cold cells;

Forcing them to stay awake for days;

Offering suspects food and then removing it before they could start eating;

Forcing them to sit in pools of water;

214

Hitting and twisting their genital organs;
Extinguishing cigarettes on their skin;
Forcing suspects to run in circles until they dropped from exhaustion;
Banning suspects from visiting the lavatory.

The charges, incidentally, were refuted in London. In November 1966 Amnesty International reported that their London offices had been burgled and papers relating to the investigation had been stolen. That such accusations of cruelties should have been made in the first place is probably an indication that all was not well.

Not long ago a respectable butcher, 'Papa' Kaduck, was arrested and charged with the murder of thousands of innocent people without cause. This man, a German with no criminal record, was one of the guards in the concentration camp at Auschwitz, Poland. In that capacity he excelled in beating, kicking and clubbing prisoners to death.

After the war this man went back to society, took his place behind the counter of his butcher's shop, and became a friendly, considerate man in the neighbourhood where he was liked and respected. If the authorities had not tracked him down and brought him to justice, he would have lived his respectable life out in peace to the very end, forgetting the insane sadism that possessed him in those palmy days of Nazism.

With the glowering menace of wars and rumours of wars hovering over us all once more, and now that fears are being revived of recrudescent political creeds that prate of a 'Master Race', who can say that the spectre of 1939–1945 will not walk again? Nothing has happened to give us any cause to believe that man is a chastened being or that, by and large, he has learned from his inglorious past to conduct himself at all times henceforward like a truly sentient creature.

EPILOGUE

I do not pretend that this book is a complete treatise, but the line has to be drawn somewhere. The possibilities that lie within the scope of one book are limited. The principal aim has been to give the interested reader an insight into phenomena that otherwise might have been largely incomprehensible to him. The situation today, however, demands that everybody should at least have some understanding of the increasing sadistic and masochistic tendencies in our society. Enormous evils are being perpetrated in our midst and the man in the street seems almost completely indifferent to them.

The perversions we have been dealing with in this book are illnesses that affect the individual's chances of happiness and equilibrium. No happiness is possible for the average individual without a complete and healthy sex-life. The individuals who are suffering from the aberrations we have mentioned are sexual cripples. Owing to the poverty of their emotional life, often arising from a faulty upbringing, they have to content themselves with substitutes that are never fully satisfying. So they tend to look for ever stronger stimulants, the stimulant becoming the substitute for satisfaction. At the same time this identification with the sex-replacing stimulant strengthens their lack of affection and increases their alienation from their fellow-men.

It is a wrong conception to think that these illnesses can be cured by the suppression of their outward manifestations. There is a tendency to demand the re-establishment of capital punishment, as if this could ever be a solution.

The changes in the economic structure and in the social welfare of society result in a sexual pattern to which the values of former times are no longer wholly applicable. It is like a grown-up man trying to clothe himself in children's garments.

They burst open all over the place and cannot cover his nakedness. This nakedness cannot be compensated by the social securities society offers. On the contrary, the love of ease man derives from this *purely materialistic security* lessens his sense of responsibility and strengthens his egocentricity. Consequently the necessity and desirability of inter-human relationships, based on mutual dependence, have generally lost much of their meaning for many people nowadays.

Taking away the risks of life also means doing away with excitement. This, and the governmental tutelage that inevitably accompanies such extensive social provisions, creates a great deal of aggression, irritation and resentment. These circumstances are a perfect hotbed for the breeding of sadism and masochism.

Many people cry for revenge whenever a sadistic crime has been committed. "They should be hanged, drawn and quartered" ; "Skin them alive" ; "Beat them to death" ; "Shooting is too good for them"—these are some of the thoughtless comments one hears people make, who do not realise that they are offering sadism for sadism. The fact that we ourselves do not actually commit such crimes does not eliminate the fact that we have accepted and encouraged the development of a social situation that provides the right conditions for enabling sadism to flourish. Alexander Woollcott once confessed to thinking, every time he read about a criminal being led to the gallows, "There, but for the grace of God, go I."

When a child grows up without having received love, he will be unable to give love. When he has never known the feeling of security at home, he will not feel secure in society. One can only reach a certain amount of social adjustment in this complicated society of ours when one has learned the rules of the game in one's youth. Conditions in the family decide conditions in society. There can be no doubt that most of the aberrations discussed here could have been avoided if the socio-moral atmosphere in which these sexually-disturbed people lived and moved, and the parents, teachers and others responsible for their upbringing and development, had imparted to them the feeling of safety and security of which man stands in need in order to satisfy his natural tendencies in a harmonious and ordered manner.

My own view, as I have stated at the appropriate point in this book, is that we must look upon the decline of family life

217

as the major single cause of these abnormalities we have been examining—and indeed of many others too. No amount of social security, governmental tutelage, or State intervention, can successfully supersede congenial and well-equilibrated family life in which the child and the parent have their rightful places. Nor will the rigid re-application of outworn patriarchal taboos or the synthetic revival of ancient inhibitions solve our problem: as a matter of fact, this would merely aggravate it and inevitably turn many another individual into a pervert, and often into a criminal.

Both sadism and masochism are almost invariably acquired, not hereditary or congenital conditions. They cause endless harm to the subject himself and not infrequently to one or more of his fellow-men. But because they are acquired they can, and must, be prevented. I hope that such books as this will serve to awaken in men and women of goodwill a keen desire to seek an intelligent and satisfactory solution.

INDEX

('n' indicates 'Footnote')

219